Directions in Staff Development

SRHE and Open University Press Imprint
General Editor: Heather Eggins

Current titles include:

Ronald Barnett: *The Idea of Higher Education*
Ronald Barnett: *Improving Higher Education*
Ronald Barnett: *Learning to Effect*
Ronald Barnett: *The Limits of Competence*
Tony Becher: *Governments and Professional Education*
Robert Bell and Malcolm Tight: *Open Universities: A British Tradition?*
Hazel Bines and David Watson: *Developing Professional Education*
Jean Bocock and David Watson: *Managing the University Curriculum*
David Boud *et al.*: *Using Experience for Learning*
Angela Brew: *Directions in Staff Development*
John Earwaker: *Helping and Supporting Students*
Roger Ellis: *Quality Assurance for University Teaching*
Gavin J. Fairbairn and Christopher Winch: *Reading, Writing and Reasoning:*
  A Guide for Students
Shirley Fisher: *Stress in Academic Life*
Diana Green: *What is Quality in Higher Education?*
Jill Johnes and Jim Taylor: *Performance Indicators in Higher Education*
Ian McNay: *Visions of Post-compulsory Education*
Robin Middlehurst: *Leading Academics*
Henry Miller: *Managing Change in Universities*
Jennifer Nias: *The Human Nature of Learning: Selections from the Work of M.L.J. Abercrombie*
Keith Noble: *Changing Doctoral Degrees*
Gillian Pascall and Roger Cox: *Women Returning to Higher Education*
Graham Peeke: *Mission and Change*
Moira Peelo: *Helping Students with Study Problems*
Kjell Raaheim *et al.*: *Helping Students to Learn*
Tom Schuller: *The Future of Higher Education*
Michael Shattock: *The UGC and the Management of British Universities*
Geoffrey Squires: *First Degree*
Ted Tapper and Brian Salter: *Oxford, Cambridge and the Changing Idea of the University*
Kim Thomas: *Gender and Subject in Higher Education*
Malcolm Tight: *Higher Education: A Part-time Perspective*
David Warner and Gordon Kelly: *Managing Educational Property*
David Warner and Charles Leonard: *The Income Generation Handbook*
Sue Wheeler and Jan Birtle: *A Handbook for Personal Tutors*
Thomas G. Whiston and Roger L. Geiger: *Research and Higher Education*
Gareth Williams: *Changing Patterns of Finance in Higher Education*
John Wyatt: *Commitment to Higher Education*

Directions in Staff Development

Edited by
Angela Brew

The Society for Research into Higher Education
& Open University Press

Published by SRHE and
Open University Press
Celtic Court
22 Ballmoor
Buckingham MK18 1XW

and 1900 Frost Road, Suite 101
Bristol, PA 19007, USA

First published 1995

A catalogue record of this book is available from the British Library

ISBN 0 335 19270 X (pb)   0 335 19271 8 (hb)

Library of Congress Cataloging-in-Publication Data

Directions in staff development / edited by Angela Brew.
    p.   cm.
Includes bibliographical references and index.
ISBN 0–335–19271–8.   ISBN 0–335–19270–X (pbk.)
1. College teachers—In-service training.   2. College personnel
management.   I. Brew, Angela, 1943–   . II. Society for Research
into Higher Education.
LB1738.D57   1995
378.1'25—dc20   94–28837
                                                                 CIP

Typeset by Graphicraft Typesetters Limited, Hong Kong
Printed in Great Britain by St Edmundsbury Press,
Bury St Edmunds, Suffolk

Contents

List of Contributors

Lee Andresen, Professional Development Centre, University of New South Wales, Sydney.

Liz Beaty, Department of Management Development, University of Brighton.

Joyce Barlow, Department of Learning Resources, University of Brighton.

Carole Baume, Educational Methods Unit and Centre for Staff Development, Oxford Brookes University.

David Baume, Staff and Educational Development Service, London Guildhall University.

David Boud, School of Adult and Language Education, University of Technology, Sydney.

Angela Brew, Academic Development Centre, University of Portsmouth.

John L. Davies, Anglia Business School, Anglia Polytechnic University.

John Doidge, Staff Development Service, Nottingham Trent University.

Lewis Elton, University of Surrey.

Graham Gibbs, Oxford Centre for Staff Development, Oxford Brookes University.

George Gordon, Centre for Academic Practice, University of Strathclyde, Scotland.

Robin Middlehurst, Higher Education Quality Council, London.

Jennifer Pittman, Student Assistance, Learning and Information Centre, Southern Cross University, Australia.

Bob Ross, formerly at Open Learning and Educational Technology Information Services, Griffith University, Australia, now Pro-Vice-Chancellor at the University of Newcastle, New South Wales, Australia.

James Wisdom, Staff and Educational Development Service, London Guildhall University.

Acknowledgement

I am grateful to all my colleagues in the Academic Development Centre at the University of Portsmouth. They have provided valuable assistance, in a variety of ways, during the preparation of this book.

1

Trends and Influences

Angela Brew

This book is concerned with all those activities which extend the knowledge, skills and attitudes of the staff of universities or colleges of higher education. At a time of unprecedented changes in our higher education institutions, it is appropriate that we should take stock of the ways in which we encourage individuals and groups of staff to develop, how we organize ourselves to do this, the qualifications and experience of the kind of professionals entrusted with the staff development task and indeed what the best approaches are. When we have intervened in some way to bring about individual and institutional changes we need to know how effective were our interventions.

Our focus, then, is on the process of learning and growing as individuals, as groups, as organizations and as higher education communities. The book has been written at a time of rapid growth and change in staff development. Staff developers and their managers are presented with a confusing array of models of staff development organization and practice. How are they to distinguish the good practice from the mediocre? It is hoped that the book will be a source of information for managers responsible for the organizational arrangements for staff development and for policy and strategy within their institutions. It is hoped too that it will be an encouragement to new staff developers, and that it will provide a source book for established ones as they increasingly assert their professional identity.

I wanted to put together this book because I had become aware that there were a number of excellent practitioners and a wealth of expertise and experience about the theory and practice of staff development in higher education. Yet with the exception of specialist and ephemeral publications very little of this has been written about. Staff developers are essentially pragmatists, concentrating on the next meeting or the next course or consultation. The best of this work is informed by theories about the nature of human learning and curriculum, and by values about what a university is. More often than not these ideas are not articulated. In this book, I have endeavoured to bring together examples and discussion of good practice which illustrate some underlying messages about the nature of staff development. This book draws together contributions representing a number of different facets of staff development practice, and attempts to tease out some common underlying principles and values. These provide directions and challenges for the future. It would be a bold assertion to say that they provide a theory of staff development, yet I do believe that they go some way towards building a theory of practice.

Setting the scene

There is increasing recognition that in a large and complex organization such as a university, the staff development and training needs are vast and multifaceted. Staff development is a growing area of university activity across the globe. This trend is intimately related to changes which have taken place in higher education in recent years. It is therefore pertinent to begin by examining these changes and to explore the challenges they present for the organization and practice of staff development.

Traditionally, higher education has been allowed, indeed expected, to get on with its work irrespective of the world in which it is situated. It was left to academics to decide on the nature of the educational experience of their students. Higher education was viewed as broadly separate from the economic activity of the nation. This is no longer so. In recent years, universities have been forced to take greater account of a number of outside influences. For many reasons, universities are no longer as free to go their own way.

An influential factor in this concerns the anxiety of governments in relation to how public funds are being spent. The publication in Britain of the Jarrett Report (1985) on the management of universities and the introduction of appraisal systems, as well as the quality assurance mechanisms which are being put in place, manifest a greater demand from governments and outside agencies for greater accountability. In these developments we see an uneasy tension between the institutional autonomy universities have traditionally enjoyed and social control. Fleming (1992) suggests that accountability may lead to a minimalist approach, with institutions trying to see how little they can get away with. Yet even doing this involves, as we shall see, considerable staff development investment.

In talking of universities and of institutions of higher education we are not talking about a homogeneous set of establishments. Many institutions, including Polytechnics in Britain and Colleges of Advanced Education in Australia, now enjoy the title University. In some cases this has been brought about by the amalgamation of smaller institutions of higher education – in some cases, as a consequence of allowing institutions to confer their own degrees, for example, those formerly under the aegis of the CNAA in the UK. This points, however, not to a mono-culture, but rather to a diversification of the concept of a university which now embraces a wider range of activities and types of study patterns, part-time and full-time study, degree and sub-degree level work, and continuing education than ever before. Thus it is not immediately obvious from the title of an institution what the full range of its activities is nor who the students are likely to be. Assumptions about the nature and range of expertise of the staff have therefore had to be re-examined.

Concern in society about higher education has been fuelled by the views of industrialists and manufacturers who, when asked what they need of university graduates, stressed not a narrow set of subject specific skills and competencies at degree level, but placed an emphasis on personal skills and qualities (Ball 1990). They said they needed people who knew how to learn, who were capable of taking decisions, who were self-aware and who could communicate. Industry recognizes that it is extremely unlikely that the students of today will do the same job for the whole of their working lives. They will need to train and re-train. They will need to be flexible and adaptable. They will need to know how to learn so that when their tutors are not there to help them, they will go on learning. Education is now no longer seen as something you just have a dose of when you are young. The expectation has become that education carries on throughout life.

Once this is recognized, a range of aspects of personal and professional development necessarily become part of the staff development agenda. This includes developments which inform the teaching of students and the management of the organization as well as those which enhance the skills, adaptability and flexibility of staff themselves. The expectation that learning carries on throughout life affects staff as much as their students. The need for continuing development of all staff, as the higher education scene and their role changes, is clear.

There is, too, the increasing influence of links between education and employers. Again this is not unique to any one country. It may take the form of industrialists taking part in course teams, and carrying out an advisory role in curricular developments. It may take the form of industrial secondments, consultancy or the provision of specialist professorships. It may take the form of increased opportunities for student industrial and commercial placements. In some cases it may take the form of one or more companies working jointly with university staff to design degree curricula for their employees. All of these arrangements serve to remind university staff that they do not work in isolation from their industrial and commercial neighbours. It is naive to assume that they have all the skills they need for this. There are staff development implications in all of these practices.

Further changes in higher education include the trends towards mass higher education and an increased heterogeneity of the student population combined with a reduced unit of resource. These have now given staff development work a pressing urgency and more focused remit. The more heterogeneous student population brought about by changes in school education, access courses and alternative entry routes including overseas recruitment, pose new challenges for higher education teachers and also

for the staff working alongside them. All of the changes in student population contribute to academic, administrative and technical staff having to
face unfamiliar situations and new demands (Candy 1991). Students with
their different backgrounds have different levels of understanding of the
subject discipline and different expectations of the teaching and learning
process. They may be non-native speakers of the language in use and have
different cultural norms and expectations. Mass higher education has meant
larger classes. There is much scope for developing creative ways of teaching
larger numbers of students at once.

But traditionally there has been a disregard of training for teaching in
higher education. This has left many academic staff ill-equipped for these
changes. Staff development to assist with individual, departmental, faculty
and university-wide developments has now become urgent. This may include extending understanding of a wide range of educational processes:
methods of teaching effectively, student learning, assessment, resource-based,
open and distance learning. The increasingly widespread use of information technology both in teaching and in administration and management
also presents a whole range of training challenges for the modern university. Training in word processing, desktop publishing, use of databases and
spreadsheets and computer networking as well as keyboard skills and telephone techniques are all relevant to a wide range of staff at all levels.

Understanding and dealing with students is an area of staff development
traditionally seen to be in the province of academic staff. However, many
more staff are now affected by this. Allied staff are having to take on a wider
range of roles and responsibilities. Understanding the differing needs of
first-year students, mature and overseas students, dealing with student queries including student finance, responding to student problems, counselling skills, personal tutoring skills and referring students for professional
help are all areas for development of a wide range of staff.

A further trend in higher education which is having an effect on the skills
and competencies of the staff of our universities is the increasing trend
towards internationalization. This manifests itself, for example, in Australia
in its relationships with its Asian and Pacific neighbours and in the UK in
its links with Europe. The future employment prospects of undergraduates
are increasingly being seen in an international context. The marketing of
courses, as well as responding to students' queries and problems, increasingly require staff to have cultural awareness and expertise in other lan-
guages. This again has implications for training and development.

The worsening financial position of universities has had a number of
significant effects on both staff and students in higher education. In the
first place there is the decrease in relative salaries of academic staff and a
worsening of working conditions (Candy 1991). Universities are tending to
recruit teaching staff without traditional academic backgrounds. This is
justified on the grounds of the need to have staff with relevant industrial
experience. However, such staff present institutions of higher education
with a further set of staff development challenges. These include induction

into the higher education system as well as basic training in teaching and learning techniques.

There is, in addition, a range of research and consultancy skills for which staff development may be needed. Some of these derive from the new financial climate with its emphasis on entrepreneurialism and devolved budgeting. They include the skills needed to obtain money for research as well as the skills of project management. Presenting papers at learned conferences has traditionally been seen as an important part of the training of an academic. However, the earlier tendency to confuse staff development with research is not defensible (Billing 1982). In Britain the research assessment exercise means that training in how to supervise research students, writing theses and academic papers, supervising laboratory research, and presenting papers at conferences, may now have direct financial consequences.

The emphasis on student loans and the worsening financial position of students also has repercussions in teaching. If it is not possible for students to buy the books they need, teaching needs to take account of this; the provision of library and other resources is also affected. Again, there are significant staff development implications.

A further movement in higher education which significantly impacts upon staff development is the increased trend towards corporate management practices. Many would link this trend with the desire for universities to become more like industry, some would attribute it to the greater demands for accountability. Whatever the cause, however, the effect is widespread.

The development of management-related skills: leadership, negotiation, team building, training related to the handling of disciplinary matters, assistance to new heads of academic and administrative units through training courses and consultancy, staff appraisal training, equal opportunity training, training for recruitment and selection of staff including interviewing skills, and so on, are all important for institutional effectiveness. There is, too, the increasing professionalization of university administration. Traditionally, a somewhat *ad hoc* approach has been adopted; management skills being assumed to simply emerge as the individual takes on such roles and responsibilities. Institutional managers require a greater range of administrative and managerial skills than ever before. Administrative skills training is also relevant to a wide range of staff.

All of these developments are leading managers to consider more systematically the training needs of their staff and to bring staff development activities much more into the centre of the organization. In many cases they are leading to more systematic and often targeted development activities for all staff.

Changing knowledge

In addition to these changes in the broad context of higher education, staff are facing changes which lie at the heart of our ideas about knowledge, about the nature of facts and the disciplines which bound them. The enormous expansion in knowledge and the speed at which new knowledge is replacing old means that being able to access data, to organize and to critically evaluate it, while being flexible enough to leave behind ideas as they are replaced, become increasingly important. There is a growing recognition that we need to prepare students not to solve the problems to which we already know the answers, but to solve problems we cannot at the moment even conceive. The skills of being able to adapt to the facts which are relevant at the moment, including taking on new knowledge, has become more pressing than the acquisition of traditional factual knowledge. This requirement of itself places a strain on undergraduate teaching. New structures are needed, but staff often lack the basic tools of the educationalist's trade which would enable them to critically evaluate the options. The staff development implications are profound.

Theoretical and experimental findings during this century have challenged the philosophical basis of our traditional subject disciplines (Bateson 1972; Capra 1983) which now appear to be on the decline. What is replacing them is an emphasis on interrelationship and interrelatedness. This is manifested in the growth of cross-discipline studies, including an increasing ecological awareness. Single subject scientific disciplines are finding it increasingly difficult to attract students, despite in the UK at least, the government's efforts to stimulate interest in them. There is a rise in subject disciplines which are about human processes, such as marketing and strategic management, and human resources management. Inter-disciplinarity and multi-disciplinarity are on the increase. This will increase with the growing trend towards modularity which gives more student choice. The trend is towards different ways of organizing knowledge.

In addition, knowledge is increasingly being seen not as something 'out there' to be discovered or transmitted, but as the creation of meaning within each person. The individual makes sense of the world through interacting with it. Hence the growth of student-centred, problem/situation-based approaches to teaching and learning, the emphasis on developing the student as a whole person and the integration of theory with practice.

Staff development arrangements, in that we are concerned with preparation for the future, have to take account, explicitly or implicitly, of all of these issues. In the chapters which follow, we see an emphasis on taking account of the needs of all staff, an emphasis on the development of personal skills and competencies and an emphasis on bringing theory and practice of teaching and learning together. We see, too, an emphasis on the individual creating meaning and critically examining past experience in the light of research findings to develop new understandings.

Dilemmas

Recent developments suggest, then, that the traditional lack of interest in staff development in higher education is ill-founded. Indeed, staff development is now becoming more organized, applied to a wider range of staff and addressed to a wider range of issues than ever before. All staff in institutions of higher education are now directly or indirectly affected. However, we are faced with a number of problems in the organization, resourcing and practice of staff development. Embedded in current practice are a number of dilemmas. These become all the more significant with the increase in demands upon staff development services. In presenting some directions for the future, this book suggests ways out of these difficulties; not in terms of simple recipes for action, but in terms of guiding principles by which we may see our way. In the remainder of this chapter the dilemmas are outlined. Subsequent chapters draw out underlying values and assumptions to underpin future directions and show how these can be put into practice.

Who are the staff?

Arrangements for staff development currently existing in many institutions reflect the two cultures of staff which co-exist in higher education. The academic work-force are highly skilled professionals with a tradition of autonomous working. Professional up-dating and renewal for them has traditionally been viewed as an academic activity.

It is significant that we lack an all encompassing term to describe staff other than academic staff in higher education institutions. They are referred to variously as allied staff, general staff, support staff, or even non-academic staff. These staff range from highly skilled professionals and technical workers to clerical and unskilled manual workers. They have the common characteristic of being viewed as a somewhat lower class than academics. In North America, academics are referred to as faculty and the rest are referred to as staff. In Australia, the term general staff is becoming widely accepted. Unfortunately all of the existing terminology symbolizes an inappropriate class distinction between two groups. In this book we refer to staff other than academics as allied staff. This overcomes to some degree the idea of a group of people being defined by reference to what they are not. It avoids the implication that they merely provide assistance, and it has the sense of allied or partners with.

The term staff in a higher education context is linked, as Tipton (1981) points out, to the process of hierarchy and the provision of different amenities and different working conditions for different categories. This derives from a situation where the work of the two groups was seen as being sharply distinguished. However, in recent years, as we have seen, there has been a trend towards increasing professionalization of higher education administration. This, together with the move to active management which was also noted above, means there is now a wider range of administrative and managerial roles falling to academic staff, administrative staff are becoming increasingly involved in course management and student guidance, and overall expectations of management performance are becoming higher than ever before. Traditional boundaries between academic and non-academic work are therefore becoming blurred.

> While there are clearly differences between the central concerns of mainstream academic staff and staff with purely technical or general administrative and clerical duties, there are also major points of convergence. For instance, word processing, time management, interviewing skills, stress management, interpersonal effectiveness, writing skills, and many aspects of supervision or management are relevant to employees across the institution. Furthermore, academic and allied staff, for instance, lecturers and librarians, researchers and secretarial staff, or tutors and laboratory technicians frequently find themselves working in combined teams or other work settings where their needs for staff development arise at least in part from the nature of their joint work. Accordingly there is an argument for the integration of staff development for academic and allied staff based on their integrated work settings.
>
> (Candy 1991: 6)

The organization and practice of staff development is influenced by history. That history is characterized by separate staff development arrangements for different groups of staff. Cultural change must inevitably question tradition. As we shall see later, there are difficult organizational issues posed for managers in deciding where to locate staff development services within the organization if inappropriate distinctions between staff are to be broken down and staff development needs are to be addressed on a more equitable basis.

Freedom and constraint

One facet of university practice which has had a significant influence on the way many academic staff view staff development arrangements is academic freedom and autonomy. The principle of academic freedom has often been used as an excuse for a *laissez-faire* attitude. In developmental terms this is translated into the idea that academics can decide in an *ad hoc* manner what is best for their own, their students' and their institutions' development. At its worst, academic freedom is translated into the freedom not to undergo any form of training and development should an individual feel so inclined. Such attitudes are less common nowadays but current practice is still influenced by them.

Allied staff are more constrained in contractual terms than academic staff and this affects training requirements. An effect of the two cultures is that where there are moves to bring academic and allied staff together for training and development, they often attend on different terms, for example, the former making their own decision to participate, the latter requiring the nomination of a supervisor.

Balancing priorities

Where there is a tradition of autonomous working, conflicts arise through the need to balance both institutional and individual needs. Where staff development is geared to institutional imperatives, individuals are invited to abdicate responsibility for their own development. Where there is a tendency to compel individuals to undergo training in particular areas, professional autonomy is called into question. Encouraging individuals to take responsibility for their own development may be problematic if the needs of the institution are considered primary and individual development only necessary to achieve the institution's mission. Responsiveness to institutional/management imperatives may be at the expense of the individual's conception of what is in their own best interests and their perceptions of the interests of their work unit or department. Heads of academic departments have to perform a delicate balancing act between different needs and priorities. A developmental model of appraisal, if carefully designed and negotiated, may assist in aligning individual and institutional needs. It can encourage a climate where individuals are willing to voluntarily undergo training, or where training is an intrinsic, embedded part of their work, where staff can feel confident to expose their weaknesses and find solutions to problems without fear of penalty, and which recognizes the integrity and professionalism of the individual and the importance of development. These aspects, Lonsdale (1990) argues, are vital to effective staff development. A judgmental model of appraisal can, on the other hand, neglect these aspects, relying instead on extrinsic motivation.

The relationship between an individual's development and institutional strategy and planning is a complex one requiring a great deal of sensitivity on the part of managers. Sending individual staff on time management courses, for example, will not solve structural problems of inefficiency in the workplace. Setting up observation of classes will not move the institution forward in creating new structures for teaching and learning. Staff development needs are intimately related to institutional structures. A change of structure such as course unitization may identify a new staff development need, but equally a staff development need may be eliminated with a change of structure, for example, a centralized admission system. But caution needs to be exercised. The addition of a unit or department with responsibility for a particular development, for example, open and distance learning materials, does little to fill the staff development need for institution-wide expertise. But the very existence of such a unit may serve to divert attention away from the problem it was set up to address.

A good deal of work in academic institutions is done in groups – hopefully in a spirit of collegiality. Groups need to develop the skills of working collectively on work-related problems. This may involve, for example, training in team-building, learning how to utilize all of the team members effectively and developing problem-solving skills. Where staff development needs are identified on an individual basis and perhaps where staff development functions run alongside the personnel functions of recruitment, discipline matters and pay tensions may occur. Maintaining a balance between staff development for individuals and for groups is problematic in such circumstances. Individual appraisal systems tend to focus staff development attention on individuals. Yet often team development is more important. This applies, as we shall see, throughout the institution. Team development at all levels contributes to the development of a learning community.

Whose responsibility?

A further dilemma with implications for the theory, practice and organization of staff development is where the locus of responsibility lies. Clearly, institutional managers have a responsibility to decide on broad areas of policy and to provide appropriate resources for staff development. Decisions about priorities depend in the first place on the establishment of a staff development policy. Staff developers often work without such a policy in their institutions, or one not suited to the institution's needs as they perceive them. The establishment of an appropriate policy and framework for staff development is affected by the level of understanding of the managers responsible for it. There is, as we shall see, a need for this to be continually enhanced in order to ensure that the range, scope and potential of staff development is fully understood, that activities reflect best practice and that the consequences of their decisions are adequately explored.

The responsibility for deciding on particular needs is not clear-cut. A traditional approach is for anyone in the institution, at whatever level, to identify a need and to set out to address it, calling on available resources to assist. In higher education at present, however, the speed of change is simply too great to wait for individuals and small groups of staff to decide on the priorities for themselves. Moreover, owing to serious deficiencies in the levels of basic training, for example, in teaching, many staff do not know where their deficiencies lie. A further problem, and one which has dogged staff development in higher education for many years is, as Yorke (1977: 166) points out, the act of faith required by managers to provide funds for this approach.

There is evidence of a move towards decisions on staff development matters being taken by managers and away from committees or staff development units (Guildford 1990). There is, too, increasing recognition that it is the responsibility of each function unit to carry out staff development with regard to teaching users about its functions. For example, computer specialists, library and financial staff need to train users in their own specialist functions.

New forms of financial management mean that it is the responsibility of the devolved budget holder to make decisions about staff development expenditure. There are problems, however, in deciding on the appropriate balance of resources for a central staff or educational development unit on the one hand and for academic departments and support units on the other. Institutional managers may lack appropriate criteria for such decisions. Political expediency may be at the expense of staff development effectiveness. Concentrating too many resources for staff development at departmental level may neglect the need for staff development specialist expertise, make institution-wide developments difficult to implement and lead to a wastage of resources due to duplication across departments. Effectiveness of staff development depends on having the appropriate staff available to carry out the training and to make the necessary arrangements. There is often a mismatch between what staff development units are asked to provide and the resources to provide it. However, concentrating too many resources in central staff development units may lead to staff development being viewed as remote from the needs of the staff designed to benefit from it and may concentrate attention on general training rather than being designed to meet the specific needs of departments, individuals and groups.

The staff development profession

As we have seen, many people in the institution are engaged in development activities for staff, but there are some people whose primary responsibility is staff development. Many of the shifts in higher education discussed in this chapter present dilemmas for people calling themselves staff and educational developers. As a profession, staff developers are called upon to take on many roles. Lee Andresen (1991) summarizes the main ones:

- Teachers (of academic and allied staff as students)
- Researchers of curriculum development, teaching and learning in higher education
- Academics – scholars who show their scholarship in the way they do everything
- Administrators – of institutional policies and practices relating to a range of staff development activities
- Organizers – of courses, workshops, etc.
- Brokers – finding the best deal and most appropriate resources to meet a staff development need
- Managers – of resources (finances and personnel)
- Change agents – innovators and stimulators of change
- Advisers – giving advice to staff and to managers
- Counsellors – to help staff cope with problems and difficulties
- Consultants – working with teams of staff on particular issues
- Evaluators – judges of quality of academic practices
- Appraisers – helping staff appraise their performance and plan for the future
- Subversives – helping to foment revolutionary changes

- Publishers – producing printed materials to help with teaching and learning changes
- Disseminators – spreading good ideas and useful materials
- Tokens – simply being there, living proof that the institution takes staff development seriously
- Leaders – blazing a path of good practice that others may follow.

Finding their way through these, staff developers emphasize different aspects. In his review of staff development in the United States, Canada and the UK, Fleming (1992: 4) identified four styles:

Thinkers: Researching, writing papers, pushing forward the boundaries of teaching and learning
Brokers: Coordinating development away from the centre in which they work, using external or other providers
Doers: The 'sleeves-rolled-up presenters'
Strategists: The 'control tower operators' who use distance education and set up cells of development independent of their own office. They are similar to brokers but also negotiate support of those in high places.

The wide variety of approaches to their task, together with the competing demands and dilemmas outlined in this chapter, have contributed to the failure of staff and educational developers to organize professionally. Many of the pitfalls to professional identity to which Becker alludes are familiar to those working in this field:

> the failure to monopolize their area of knowledge, the lack of homogeneity within the profession, the failure of clients to accept professional judgement, the chronic presence of unethical practitioners as an integrated segment of the professional structure and the organisational constraints on professional autonomy.
>
> (Becker 1970: 103)

One of the problems is that there is not a unified view of staff development. Some practitioners are academics with academic backgrounds and aspirations. They may talk in terms of educational development and pursue educational research and development projects. Some staff developers in institutions of higher education are administrative staff. They work on different kinds of contracts, and may see themselves more as trainers or human resource developers than academics. Indeed, higher education personnel managers, following an industrial notion of training, increasingly perceive that they have a responsibility and a role in staff development. Staff development is often viewed by the senior management as a service, not as a scholarly activity. It is often viewed quite separately from and having no links with educational development with its emphasis on teaching and learning.

Yet if staff development is about the process of assisting staff in the performance of their institutional roles and in their lives, the narrow notion of training held by many managers is not, by itself adequate. One of the problems is that it tends to focus on activity-based staff development unrelated to solving problems in the work-place with often no follow-up transfer of training into the working environment. Staff development needs to take account of the particular professional quirks of academic life. While we wish to see a breaking down of the two cultures through effective staff development, we have to take account of their existence.

Moses suggests that where staff developers do not identify with educational development it is 'partly due to the staff developer's non-academic status, partly to the absence of a discipline called "higher education" or the equivalent to "Hochschuldidaktic"' (Moses 1987: 472). Problems arise for staff developers if and when they are asked to perform tasks which they do not see as being within their remit. Problems also arise if staff developers are located in an area of the institution where it is not possible to perform their roles in a way which is consistent with their beliefs and values. In addition, staff developers need to be at one and the same time in touch with staff needs and priorities, and to be seen as colleagues, friends and counsellors, while at the same time commanding respect and trust from their senior managers. There is a tension between working for the managers, for example, to achieve institutional objectives, on the one hand; for the individual development of the staff, on another hand; or in order to pursue their own educational research and philosophical interests on yet another (Moses 1987: 457).

There are also difficulties with short-term funding arrangements, and part-time seconded appointments where the relevant expertise is not developed. There is no career structure. In trying to respond to everybody's demands there is, though, a danger of fatigue and burn out of the staff developer. Yet as Candy (1991: 2) points out there is always the need for the staff developer to be able to respond to unexpected demands. The problem is usually that there are many clients who expect different things. Indeed, many decisions about staff development in higher education are made without reference to or consultation with professional staff developers and this also leads to difficulties.

Value tensions

The issue of professional identity is now being addressed in the UK by the introduction of a scheme for the professional recognition of staff developers in higher education. This is being established, like the scheme for the accreditation of higher education teachers which is discussed below, by the Staff and Educational Development Association. The scheme provides a quality standard by ensuring that professionally qualified staff developers have demonstrated they have met a range of objectives and subscribe to a set of clearly defined values. It is an important first step on the road to professionalization.

Yet there is another dilemma. The values are based on deep-rooted philosophical commitments which give staff development work coherence, consistency and integrity. Assumptions and the implicit theories and models which are guiding current practice provide a beacon by which staff and educational developers can see their way in the future. However, these are often compromised because they conflict with or fail to be understood in their institution.

Managers' views of staff development will influence their approaches to strategy, policy and organization. But their decisions are not value-neutral and have important consequences for those whose primary job is to assist staff and the organization in its development. Deriving perhaps from the failure of staff and educational developers to organize themselves professionally, the nature of their expertise is often misunderstood. Staff and educational developers are faced with questions of loyalty – whether to the institution as a whole, to their managers, to their faculty, department or to their unit or home discipline, to individual clients, to the staff as a whole, or to students. The professional staff developer has a responsibility to balance these different interests. Their values determine how they do this but they may also be the very factors which alienate them from their managers.

The plan for the book

In discussing the wider context of developments in higher education and in outlining dilemmas in the practice and organization of staff development, this chapter has now set the scene for the rest of the book. Tensions and pressures in the field of staff development in higher education and the existence of different traditions with their different approaches and discourses provide a rich experience on which to build. They suggest, however, that the time has come to look for some clear directions for the future. It is important to recognize that what we have at the moment is the product of circumstances and *ad hoc* decisions. It is not the rational outcome of considered judgement. This book captures developments at a particular moment and suggests some themes which will inform the challenges ahead.

The aim of the book, then, is to draw together some of the best practice in staff development in higher education, to provide a source book and state of the art statement and to inform staff and educational developers and institutional managers. It also aims to raise important issues relating to the scope of staff development activities and to its organization and effectiveness. This book brings together contributions by people working across the university community and raises issues in staff development for all staff. It is, therefore, a step in the direction of working towards overcoming the academic apartheid mentioned earlier.

It is not the intention to present a comprehensive coverage of issues or approaches; impossible in a book of this length. Nor is this a book containing a series of recipes for action. There is, for example, no discussion of the *ad hoc* workshop or seminar, no discussion of staff development through mentoring, or through networking. Neither is there any discussion of what makes a good staff development policy. What is intended is that in reflecting on the examples and issues discussed, the reader will be facilitated in making informed decisions about directions to take.

The book is organized in three parts: Part 1 presents the educational development tradition which has largely been concerned with the development of staff as teachers, but which, as we shall see, has important lessons for the practice of staff development more widely. Part 2 considers issues relating to the professional development of a range of staff in managerial, administrative, clerical, technical and manual tasks. It is noticeable that there are many threads in common with the educational development tradition. In Part 3, we explore a number of questions which are crucial to the organization and practice of staff development, which have an impact on its effectiveness and which affect its relationship to institutional plans.

Staff development is concerned with helping people to grow within the organizations in which they are employed. This process must begin with a recognition that each person has learning needs, and brings knowledge and resources to the learning process. All of the chapters in this book, in their different ways, embody this principle. It is an idea which reflects findings in research on learning which emphasises the need to take account of different perceptions of the learning process. It is also rooted in and informed by developments in the field of adult learning and experiential learning. This idea very obviously applies to staff development for teaching and learning. But it also applies just as much to staff development for allied staff including managers. Indeed, as we shall see, it applies no matter what is being learnt, or who is learning it.

Particular emphasis is laid here on a belief in the importance of critical reflective practice. The book contains numerous examples of ways in which staff developers can and do encourage this. There is an emphasis throughout the book on enhancing the professionalism of staff. This includes approaches to staff development which encourage continuing and in-depth study and gaining additional qualifications. The increasing emphasis in higher education on the development of skills for life-long learning and personal growth and fulfilment alluded to earlier, underlines the importance of sustained development rather than short term patching-up operations. Staff and educational development are concerned with empowerment. This means assisting in the development of individuals, groups and institutions, so that they can achieve more and are enabled to develop greater capability and competence. Good practice in staff development in higher education increasingly lays stress on the development of the whole person. This work is again influenced by developments in the field of adult learning, experiential learning, recurrent education and associated collaborative and participatory research methodologies.

The book acknowledges that staff development should be informed by a sense of community. This is an important aspect of our universities which we are perhaps in danger of losing. Taking problems out of the workplace in the hope of solving them in a course for an individual rather than assisting a department, unit or team to tackle it together does little for the community. Staff development should be a community activity. The staff development arrangements we make need to assist us to develop into the kind of community we would like to be. They must be capable of being responsive to the special nature of the academic culture and to its changing demands. They must sensitively balance individual and institutional imperatives and be responsive to the needs of individuals and groups at all levels.

Staff development, in its broadest sense, is about change. As universities change, so staff development grows and develops. Staff development is about helping individuals to learn. It is about helping groups to learn and it is about helping institutions to learn. This book captures the state of the art at a particular moment in history. It indicates that developments have been hitherto somewhat patchy and it suggests how we might go forward. In doing so, we change both the nature of the institution and the role of staff development. The form of organization for staff development, as well as the issues addressed and the way in which they are addressed, is a function and perhaps a measure of the organization's level of development which grows and changes over time. It is, by its very nature, a dynamic process. If institutions succeed in developing into learning organizations, their forms of organization and their staff development needs will change. In the short term, we have a need for courses which raise awareness of a broad range of issues. In the long term, if the habit of learning is cultivated, we may see more examples of reflection in action and less emphasis on traditional notions of training.

As light is reflected from a many-faceted glass prism, so themes are reflected in the pages of this book. These themes are, I suspect, more enduring than the vehicles in which they currently have their expression. In this sense, the book reflects current trends but it also moves beyond them to provide a vision of where staff development and indeed higher education may be going. We need to take up the challenges that are offered, for fresh vision and new ideas are essential ingredients for the university of the future.

Part 1

Approaches and Methods in Educational Development

A major part of staff development in institutions of higher education has traditionally been to do with developing academic staff in their role as teachers. More specifically, staff development has often been equated with developing pedagogical skills in the subject discipline. While it is now widely recognized that academic staff need to develop a broader range of skills and competencies including management and interpersonal skills and that academic staff are only one segment of a complex and diverse academic community, educational development still occupies a central and important role.

Educational development has been much influenced by research in learning and teaching in higher education over the past twenty years. This includes the encouragement of meaningful learning and study including systematic reflection in relation to learning tasks and learning content, the provision of a variety of learning challenges, the recognition of the desirability of requiring students to take responsibility for their learning and of the need to design courses where students exercise autonomy over the mode and pace of their study and its assessment, and the recognition of individual differences in learning and of the importance of the context in which learning takes place.

In Part 1, we present a range of approaches to educational development which show ways in which it can both embody the principles of good teaching and learning, and also move staff forward in their practice. The aim is to reflect a number of important trends in educational and staff development. Each chapter includes a section in which the author reflects back on the example presented and asks how effective it has been in achieving what it set out to do.

Changes in higher education are not confined to one country. The examples in Part 1 show similar trends in staff and educational development within different countries. This serves to highlight that these developments too are transnational and applicable across a spectrum of political contexts.

Research on how individuals learn in an academic context has been enormously helpful in understanding ways in which teachers in higher education can enhance the learning experiences of their students. In Chapter 2 some of the more important aspects of this research tradition are outlined. Graham Gibbs describes the way in which action research projects throughout a range of institutions in Britain were used as a vehicle for staff to consider how to use the findings of research on student learning in their own courses. He shows how engaging in such projects leads lecturers not only to change what they do but to change their underlying conceptions of the teaching and learning task; a change essential for sustained pedagogical development.

One of the trends exhibited in this book is that towards more systematic organization of development activities. This is demonstrated in the existence of programmes offering academic credit for learning achieved. On the one hand this may indicate a more instrumental approach to staff development on the part of those undertaking it. On the other hand, it suggests that staff development is being taken more seriously by institutional managers and governmental agencies and that staff see that teaching is of more significance in the development of their careers. At the very least, it makes it more difficult for those providing funds to reject programmes for being *ad hoc.*

The desire for credit is linked, of course, to wider trends in credit accumulation and transfer and reminds us that staff development in higher education is part of the wider process of education for lifelong learning. It is also linked to the growing demand for professionalism in teaching in higher education. Professionalism in teaching in higher education implies a more public exposure and discussion of teaching performance, course design and teaching materials. It also means that higher scholarly status is given within a discipline to the design and delivery of good teaching in that discipline. In 1992 the establishment, by the Staff and Educational Development Association (SEDA) in Britain, of a national scheme for the recognition of courses and programmes leading to the accreditation of teachers in higher education, is an indication of this trend. There are now many examples of universities which have validated courses offering specific higher education teacher training to their academic staff.

In Chapter 3, Lee Andresen discusses one such programme offering academic credit and involving sustained study over a period of time. It enables staff to work towards post-graduate qualifications in the theory and practice of teaching in higher education. This chapter also continues the discussion of action research as a model for staff development which embodies a process of action and reflection to change existing practice and therefore has the capacity to bring about lasting changes.

· The potential for using open learning and distance education for staff development is considerable. Yet if, as Graham Gibbs suggests, ideas and suggestions for changing teaching have little impact at a fundamental level and do little to change teachers' underlying conceptions of the nature of teaching and learning, then the design of materials for staff development at a distance becomes problematic. In Chapter 4, Bob Ross and Jennifer Pittman take up the themes of action research and courses offering credit and look at how critical reflective practice can be encouraged through distance learning methods. They discuss an example of a collaborative project between Griffith University and Southern Cross University which has been used to address these issues.

Action research involves professionals carrying out work-based research projects with the intention of improving practice. The strategy of releasing staff from some of their normal teaching duties in order to carry out projects of this kind has been used extensively and in many different ways through the UK Department of Employment's Enterprise in Higher Education (EHE) Initiative. The scale of this work with some 60 institutions participating and over 2,000 projects completed or under way (The University of Portsmouth 1994), many of which involve releasing staff time, has resulted in widespread innovation in Britain. Yet this is not confined to EHE. We see the effects of a similar development in releasing staff which has taken place in one institution in Chapter 5. This focuses on a set of six linked projects at the University of Brighton. The purpose of these was to make a significant institutional move forward in the area of managing independent study. Joyce Barlow shows how the process of reflecting on their students' learning through an action research project fosters the habit of critical reflective practice; essential, according to Schön (1983), for professional development.

In Chapter 6, James Wisdom presents an agenda for staff development which arises from consultations with students about their learning. In his discussion of the practice of course consultation developed at Kingston University, he reminds us that even staff development for teaching and learning involves academics in a wider staff development agenda than simply the development of pedagogical skills. Management and communication skills are also involved as are skills of personal effectiveness. When a course has been affected by a number of piecemeal changes brought about by such things as changes in personnel and increases in student numbers, students notice. Engaging them in a dialogue draws attention to inadequacies in teaching methods, course design and management and suggests areas where action is needed. In presenting the issues and topics most frequently discussed by students and in his discussion of the staff development implications of both the process and the outcomes, James Wisdom shows too just how intimately the practice of teaching and learning in higher education is tied up with administrative, management and technical support functions and suggests that allied staff are also involved in aspects of the teaching and learning process and play an important part in the quality of students' learning experiences. The chapter highlights how often opportunities for dialogue are missed. In pointing to the importance of including administrative, technical, clerical and manual staff in course teams, the chapter challenges the distinction between staff and educational development. Moreover, it draws attention to the fact that a university is a community and that we need to learn from each other.

Part 1 draws attention to the fact that developing the learning experiences of students is not just a matter of developing technical competence at teaching. It is something which engages the whole person. This is a theme which echoes throughout the book. The trends in educational development which are illustrated have important messages for staff development in all its aspects. We are concerned in Part 1 with staff development designed to assist academic staff to develop their students' learning in the traditional sense. But all staff development is about developing learners in a different sense. For whether the participants on a staff development programme are teachers, managers, administrators, technicians, manual or clerical workers, they become learners in the staff development process. The use of work-based learning and action research projects, the design of staff development which offers credit, and the use of resource based, open and distance education are all potential vehicles for the delivery of staff development right across the institution. The task of embedding the principles illustrated here in programmes for all staff is an important challenge for the future.

2

Changing Lecturers' Conceptions of Teaching and Learning Through Action Research

Graham Gibbs

Much educational development is conceived of in terms of changing lecturers' practice – their techniques and skills – and the methods employed commonly involve training and practice. This chapter explores staff development as a process of changing lecturers' conceptions of teaching and learning through action research. It examines alternative frameworks for understanding conceptions of learning and conceptions of teaching, the theory and practice of action research, and the use of action research to change lecturers' conceptions. It proposes a closer link between theory and practice and more integration between research and development in the way staff development operates, not through staff developers making the links, explaining educational concepts or using research evidence, but through lecturers researching their teaching.

Background

In the late 1970s I was a Research Fellow involved in research into student learning. My colleagues and I wrote for education journals and our work was read by a very small group of fellow researchers in the UK, Sweden and Australia. At conferences researchers talked to researchers. Lecturers did not read this work and little or no practical use was made of it. Practical research tools with considerable potential, such as the Approaches to Studying Inventory (Entwistle and Ramsden 1983) were not taken up by lecturers despite extensive supportive studies. The gap between theory and practice and research and development was very wide indeed.

Throughout the 1980s I worked as a staff developer. Most of the evaluation work I undertook on behalf of lecturers or alongside them was relentlessly pragmatic. It wasn't all trivial and it didn't focus only on teaching. As well as feedback questionnaires on teachers and teaching I helped lecturers to find out more about what their students did with their study time and undertook a good deal of informal hypothesis testing about why courses didn't work as well as they might. But nearly all this work had no theoretical underpinning. While it helped lecturers to make decisions about what to do and how much to do, it was not oriented primarily towards developing their understanding of how students learnt on their courses and provided little in the way of a robust rationale for future action. In particular, it seldom challenged lecturers' conceptions of the teaching and learning process. My work may have improved the efficiency of courses and changed their outcomes quantitatively, but only from time-to-time did it reorient them and change their outcomes qualitatively.

I was aware that those to whom I was acting as a consultant frequently had a very different conception of what was going on in their courses than I did. They were working with different implicit models of learning. Sometimes these differences have been almost farcically wide. On one occasion while running a staff development workshop on large seminar classes in politics, I had been demonstrating a series of techniques which involved dividing the seminar group up in various ways so that students were, in effect, discussing in small tutor-less groups within a much larger class. Throughout the demonstrations the professor had been looking increasingly perplexed and disengaged and he eventually brought proceedings to a halt with the statement, 'I can't see what students could possibly gain from talking with each other.' With gulfs in understanding of this depth there was little to be gained by further demonstrations. What was needed was an exploration of his beliefs and perceptions of the use of discussion and his underlying assumptions about how learning takes place and hence the purpose of teaching.

A number of writers have explored these implicit conceptions of teaching and learning which so pervade lecturers' thinking and decision-making. The following two sections will examine studies of students' conceptions of learning and teachers' conceptions of teaching.

Students' conceptions of learning

Säljö (1979) found that when he was interviewing students about whether they were taking a deep approach (attempting to make sense of material) or a surface approach (trying to reproduce material) they used the word *learning* to mean different things. He interviewed many people about what they meant by learning and was able to distinguish five categories of answers, listed here, with examples of the kinds of things students who have these conceptions say.

1. *Learning as an increase in knowledge*
   The student will often see learning as something done to them by teachers rather than as something they do to, or for, themselves. Learning is

simply a quantitative accretion of information. 'To gain some knowledge is learning . . . We obviously want to learn more. I want to know as much as possible.'

2. *Learning as memorizing*
   The student has an active role in memorizing, but the information being memorized is not transformed in any way. 'Learning is about getting it into your head. You've just got to keep writing it out and eventually it will go in.'

3. *Learning as acquiring facts or procedures which are to be used*
   What you learn is seen to include skills, algorithms, formulae which you apply, etc., which you will need in order to do things at a later date, but there is still no transformation of what is learnt by the learner. 'Well, it's about learning the thing so you can do it again when you are asked to, like in an exam.'

4. *Learning as making sense*
   The student makes active attempts to abstract meaning in the process of learning. This may involve only academic tasks. 'Learning is about trying to understand things so you can see what is going on. You've got to be able to explain things, not just remember them.'

5. *Learning as understanding reality*
   Learning enables you to perceive the world differently. This has also been termed 'personally meaningful learning'. 'When you have really learnt something you kind of see things you couldn't see before. Everything changes. You have become a different person.'

Subsequent longitudinal research has confirmed these categories and elaborated on category 5, distinguishing between 'seeing things in a different way' and 'changing as a person' (Beaty *et al.* 1992). There are other developmental schemes, describing how students change in the sophistication of their perception of the learning tasks they face, which embody very similar descriptions. Perry (1970: 9) outlines a nine-stage scheme of development in which the first stage is described in almost identical terms to those of Säljö ('the quantitative accretion of discrete rightness to be acquired through hard work and obedience').

In Säljö's scheme, categories 4 and 5 are clearly qualitatively different from categories 1–3. Students who understand what learning is at Levels 1, 2 or 3 may have trouble comprehending what a deep approach consists of and are very unlikely to take a deep approach to learning tasks. Students who are at levels 4 or 5 can take either a deep or a surface approach, depending on the task and their perception of its demands. The connection between these underlying conceptions of learning and the approach students take to specific learning tasks is so strong that it is possible to predict the quality of learning outcomes directly from students' conceptions of learning. All you need to know about students is that they have a conception of learning at Level 1, 2 or 3 and you can be fairly certain that they will only derive a superficial and fragmentary understanding from activities such as reading a chapter (Van Rossum and Schenk 1984). For some students, then, their limited understanding of what learning consists of prevents them from approaching learning tasks in a deep way and therefore from learning effectively. Could the same be true for lecturers – that their unsophisticated conception of teaching and learning prevents them from teaching more effectively? While Säljö's categories were derived from interviews with students, they provide insights into why some lecturers justify the teaching methods they use. I once heard a Harvard professor say that 'students need to be able to drink from a fire hose if they are to succeed on my course.' I don't think he realized that his boast about the rate and volume of his lecturing simply revealed an unsophisticated conception of learning in which students' ability was seen in terms of their capacity to absorb information.

As well as exploring students' conceptions of learning, research has also explored students' conceptions of good teaching. Not surprisingly students have widely varying ideas of what constitutes good teaching. This is very important because theory-free standard student feedback questionnaires are being responded to by students who believe completely different things about what teachers ought to be doing. It is common for some students, and particularly some overseas students, to prefer straight lecture programmes and predictable exam questions and react strongly against student-centred methods and open-ended tasks where students share responsibility. There is evidence from questionnaire studies that students who take a surface approach have a different view of what good teaching consists of from that of students who take a deep approach (Entwistle and Tait 1990). In one case study in Gibbs (1992) an innovation designed to move students from a surface to a deep approach had to be abandoned due to the strength of student opposition to any change in the superficial demands their courses made. We tend to respond to student feedback as if all students believe the same things about what constitutes good teaching and that these beliefs are the same as ours. This is clearly not the case and interpreting student feedback is fraught with difficulties. Chapter 6 will explore this problem further in the context of using student feedback in staff development.

Van Rossum and Taylor (1987) found that some students think that the teacher should do all the work and make all the decisions. The teacher should select the subject matter, present it in teacher-controlled classes, devise tests and mark students on how well they have learnt the material which has been presented. What is to be learnt and what learning outcomes should look like should be completely defined by the teacher (a *closed* conception of teaching). They found that other students think that while the teacher has responsibility for setting the learning climate, for making learning resources available, and for supporting students, all the responsibility lies with the student: responsibility for selecting learning goals, devising appropriate learning activities and for judging when learning outcomes are satisfactory (an *open* conception of teaching). The closed conception of teaching is held almost exclusively by students with Säljö's conceptions of

Table 2.1 The relationship between students' conception of learning and their conception of teaching

CONCEPTION OF LEARNING (Säljö)	CONCEPTION OF TEACHING (Van Rossum and Taylor)
Reproducing (Levels 1, 2 and 3)	*Closed* Teacher selects content, presents it and tests whether it has 'stuck'
Meaning (Levels 4 and 5)	*Open* Learner functions independently with the facilitation of the teacher

learning at levels 1, 2 or 3, while the latter, open, conception of teaching is held by students with conceptions of learning at levels 4 or 5. This relationship is summarized in Table 2.1.

The key issue here is whether students see good teaching as closed teaching because they have a reproductive conception of learning, or whether they have a reproductive conception of learning because they have been experiencing closed teaching. I believe the latter explanation, for three reasons. First, it is easy to see even young children taking a deep approach to learning. They are able to tell you when they don't understand and they can sometimes surprise you by announcing when they have really understood something which previously they had only learnt by rote (Rogers 1969). It seems as though an implicit understanding of different levels of learning is somehow lost through schooling. Second, high school pupils have been found to progressively abandon a deep approach over the four years of their studies, implying an effect on their studying of the type of teaching commonly used to prepare pupils for that level of exams (Tobin and Fraser 1988). Third, longitudinal studies of students in higher education have plotted rapid developments in the sophistication of students' conceptions of learning, attributed directly to the nature of learning tasks and assessment the students have experienced (cf. Gibbs *et al.* 1984). It seems that students can become more sophisticated as learners as a consequence of their experience of more open-ended learning environments. This is a well documented and commonplace experience of students undertaking third year undergraduate project and dissertation work after two years of lecture-based and examined courses.

So here we have a picture in which the quality of student learning outcomes is affected by students' approach, their approach is affected by their conception of learning, and their conception of learning is affected by the type of teaching they experience – not the teaching and learning methods themselves so much as the underlying model of teaching and learning these methods embody. So next we need to explore these underlying models and lecturers' conceptions of teaching and learning.

Teachers' conceptions of teaching

There have been a number of accounts of fundamental differences in what lecturers believe themselves to be trying to do in teaching in higher education. Some relate to discipline differences while others have been based on teasing out underlying conceptions of teaching. Northedge (1976) explored what he called 'our implicit analogies for learning process'. He contrasted *building* and *gardening* analogies, illustrating the way these powerful analogies imbued the decision-making logic of lecturers even where they had no conscious knowledge of a theory of learning (and would probably deny the value of such theories). He showed how apparently rational decisions about how to design courses could be traced back to these implicit analogies.

Fox (1983) described four conceptions of teaching and learning based on interviews with new lecturers. He proposed a 2 × 2 model in which he distinguished between who initiates the learning (the teacher or the student) and the focus of learning (content or change in students' understanding and skills). So, for example, some lecturers believe they have the responsibility to initiate learning and they see their goal as knowledge acquisition while others believe that students have responsibility to initiate learning and the goal is changes in students' understanding and skills.

Trigwell *et al.* (1993) used phenomenological methods to explore lecturers' approaches to first-year teaching on science courses. They describe five categories of approach to teaching evident in lecturers' explanations of what they do and why.

1. *A teacher-focused strategy with the intention of transmitting information*
   The focus is on facts and skills but not the relationship between them. Prior knowledge is not seen as important and it is assumed that students do not need to be active in their learning.
2. *A teacher-focused strategy with the intention that students acquire the concepts of the discipline*
   It is assumed that concepts can be transmitted by telling them to students and that students do not need to be active.
3. *A teacher/student interaction strategy with the intention that students acquire the concepts of the discipline*
   Students are not seen to construct knowledge but to gain it through active interaction in the teaching–learning process.
4. *A student-focused strategy aimed at students developing their conceptions*
   It is assumed that students need help to develop their world view or the conceptions they already hold through the active construction of knowledge.
5. *A student-focused strategy aimed at students changing their conceptions*
   It is assumed that conceptions cannot be transmitted but that students have to reconstruct a new world view or conceptions.

Table 2.2 Approaches to teaching

| | STRATEGY | | |
INTENTION	*Teacher-focused*	*Student-Teacher interaction*	*Student-focused*
Information transmission	A		
Concept acquisition	B	C	
Conceptual development			D
Conceptual change			E

This category system embodies two key variables: intention and strategy. The four intentions involved are information transmission, concept acquisition, conceptual development and conceptual change. The three strategies are teacher-focused, teacher-student interaction and student-focused. The relationship between these two variables is summarized in Table 2.2.

It is a common experience of staff developers to, from time to time, encounter almost total intransigence from some individuals in the middle of workshops. After a period of apparent open-mindedness and interest, participants suddenly dig their heels in and stop you dead in your tracks. No matter how many practical objections you manage to respond to with practical solutions, no matter how many examples you are able to provide of the use of the methods under discussion or even hard evidence of their success, a complete impasse has been reached. Participants start every sentence with 'yes but . . .' and engage in all kinds of extraordinary defensive mechanisms. A clue to what is going on can sometimes be found when they appeal to some vague sense of 'what university education is all about' or your 'not understanding the nature of the discipline'. I have gradually learnt to recognize that what has usually happened is that I have tripped over a fundamental underlying conception of teaching and learning which is challenged by the conception implicit in the methods being discussed. These fundamentals may involve the notion of a fixed corpus of knowledge which must be covered, the belief that students require some kind of mastery of a body of knowledge before anything else can be tackled, or the conviction that students are incapable of making any appropriate decisions about what or how to study because they are not yet subject experts. Brew and Wright (1990) encountered a range of conceptions underlying different Open University tutors' resistance to using methods in a staff development resource pack. For example, one technology tutor explained why he didn't adopt any of the suggestions for group discussion in tutorials: 'with the limited amount of time with the students, being an engineer, I tend to think that I have to get the facts across . . . and I think that is the important thing, to try and summarize the important points.' Staff development runs up against these notions, and the conceptions of teaching and learning which underlie them, all the time, and cannot make much headway without tackling them. The problem is *how.*

The *53 Interesting Ways To Teach* series of books (cf. Gibbs *et al.* 1984) were written in an attempt to avoid this problem. Because lecturers were so uninterested in theory or reluctant to reconsider their goals, indeed resistant to any frontal assault which involved thinking rather than action, we attempted to change lecturers' conceptions by subterfuge. The teaching methods we described nearly always shared an underlying implicit model of teaching and learning. However, we seldom mentioned this underlying model. Methods were presented in a brief and attractive way which made them look possible to try and were clearly targeted at teaching and learning problems lecturers could recognize and frequently experienced. We hoped that by trying out simple methods, without being asked to think about theory or abandon cherished belief, lecturers would learn experientially. The methods would inevitably work because they were so brilliant. Lecturers would see how student learning changed qualitatively and their eyes would be opened. To an extent this strategy actually worked and we have had many conversations with and letters from lecturers who picked up methods simply by reading and who subsequently realized all sorts of interesting things about teaching and learning as a consequence of trying methods on a purely pragmatic basis.

However, the way these lecturers articulated their understanding left a lot to be desired and would seldom have provided a sound basis for decision-making beyond the immediate vicinity of the particular methods with which they had experimented. Even those who took the trouble to write or phone us had not often reflected to any great extent on why methods worked; as well as signs of evidence of dawning understanding, we saw signs of mechanical and thoughtless repetition of techniques. I once had an early morning call from an anxious lecturer from Trondheim about to start a class, asking if, as his class was 55 minutes and not an hour long, would the carefully timed sequence of activities on page 54 still work?

Methods and models

I have argued in the past (Gibbs 1981) that study skills on their own are of limited value and that students are perfectly capable of taking any particular study technique and corrupting it to achieve their own, often inappropriate, ends. Ramsden *et al.* (1986) showed how a perfectly well conceived study skills course succeeded only in orienting students to take a surface approach and failed either to change students' skills or orient them towards attempting to make sense of the material they were studying. Without some understanding of the type of learning they are supposed to be engaging in, study skills on their own are unlikely to help students to learn appropriately or effectively. The most important aspect of students' studying is their sense of purpose rather than their technique (Gibbs 1983). They need to have a clear sense of what they are trying to do and what they want out of their studying efforts. I believe the same arguments apply to lecturers and teaching techniques as to students and study techniques.

It is not enough to select new teaching methods or course designs on purely pragmatic grounds without an understanding of the way students are likely to respond to these methods or any engagement of lecturers with the conceptions, values and purposes underlying methods. Blackmore and Harries-Jenkins (1994) reported how a lecture-based accountancy course with large student numbers was replaced by a course involving less teaching and more, supposedly independent, learning from learning packages. This is the kind of change in methods which staff developers (and management) often encourage. However, the course succeeded only in moving the students from a deep to a surface approach and reducing their motivation. Students gave up trying to make sense of the material and only attempted to reproduce it, and some students gave up altogether. It is not enough simply to innovate. Without a more sophisticated conception of teaching and learning, lecturers will often be in no position to make appropriate decisions about what directions to innovate in or how to implement innovations effectively. I have often heard lecturers say 'Oh, we've tried group projects [or any other method they can think of] and they don't work.' Without a more sophisticated conception of good teaching or good learning, lecturers will often be in no position to understand why things have gone wrong or even to notice that things have gone wrong. In Blackmore and Harries-Jenkins' study (1994), the best clues about why the quality of student learning had declined so much came from the use of the Approaches to Studying Inventory.

Just as I have argued that students need to experiment with study techniques and try to understand why some methods work in some situations but not in others, so lecturers must experiment and try to understand what is going on and why some teaching methods and course designs work in some contexts but not in others. Just as I used to tell students that I didn't care what study methods they used as long as they were in a better position to make principled decisions about how to tackle any particular learning task in the future, so it is more important that lecturers understand better what is going on in their courses than that they have mastered a new technique. The main feature of the programme for new lecturers at Oxford Brookes University is not the list of teaching topics which are covered – the programme is not competence based – but that lecturers leave the programme in a better position to make appropriate decisions about how to teach.

Action research

The Council for National Academic Awards (CNAA) funded project, Improving Student Learning (Gibbs 1992) employed action research as a vehicle

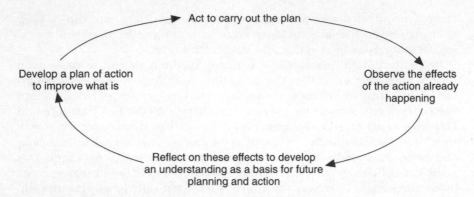

Figure 2.1   The four stages of action research

for getting lecturers in ten institutions to develop their understanding of the way their courses were operating at the same time as developing their practice and their courses. The project was designed to apply student learning research to the improvement of courses and student learning. Action research brings practice and theory, action and research together. It involves lecturers researching their own practice in a cyclical sequence in four stages (as shown in Figure 2.1). Originally developed by Lewin in the USA in the 1940s and applied by Stenhouse to curriculum development in schools in the UK in the 1970s, action research has become widely adopted as a model for change in courses and teaching. A number of useful guides to action research practice in higher education are now available (cf. Kemmis and McTaggart 1988; McKernan 1991; Kember and Gow 1992; Zuber-Skerritt 1992; Kember and Kelly 1993) and I will not attempt to provide an instant guide here. From the point of view of the Improving Student Learning project, action research had the following advantages.

- Those studying the innovations would be very close to what was happening; the project was not concerned with neutral objectivity.
- What was learnt would be able to be applied immediately, even though that would change the nature of the innovation. The project was not concerned with tightly controlled experimental comparisons of fixed alternatives.
- Those involved would learn and develop as teachers; the project was concerned with staff development as well as with innovation.
- Through the cyclical process of action research, more progress would be made in developing teaching and assessment methods and in developing ways of monitoring the quality of student learning.

Action research differed in important respects from what could have been mere case studies of innovations, as summarized in Table 2.3. The Improving Student Learning project used the notions of deep and surface approaches

Table 2.3 Comparison of case studies, undertaken by external researchers, and action research undertaken by lecturers

Issue	Case study	Action research
When does the research take place?	After the innovation is in place usually as a 'one shot' picture.	Throughout the process of innovation
Who does it?	A neutral person, usually an outsider.	Those involved in the innovation
Do the researchers implement the innovation?	No	Yes. Those studying the innovation are those who implement it.
When does learning take place for the innovators?	Afterwards	Throughout
Who does the learning?	The researcher	The innovators
Is the innovation fixed in advance?	Yes	No, it is modified by what is learnt through studying it, as it develops
Whose perspective does the research take?	That of the researcher	That of those involved

to learning as the theoretical context for action research and the Approaches to Studying Inventory and in-depth interviews as the main research tools. It supported a team of lecturers in researching their own innovations. The project demonstrated that it was possible to shift students from a surface to a deep approach and to improve the quality of learning outcomes in a variety of contexts and through a variety of innovations, and to identify under what circumstances and through what mechanisms these beneficial changes were possible. The outcomes of the project have been disseminated through two conferences in the UK, 30,000 leaflets and a book (Gibbs 1992), and have been publicized widely in the USA and in Australasia through conferences and workshops in a number of institutions. One heartening outcome of this dissemination was evident at the 1993 Improving Student Learning Symposium at Warwick (Gibbs 1994). Although the keynote papers were presented by researchers, most of the papers were by lecturers who were researching their own practice and most of the participants were lecturers, not researchers. This was a marked contrast to the kinds of event described in the second paragraph in this chapter which took place in the 1970s. The research basis, concepts and research tools were very much the same, but the use to which they were being put was very different.

Action research as a staff development process

In this section I will give brief accounts of a variety of staff development initiatives as a way of distinguishing between different kinds of action research which are driven by theory or institutional processes to a greater or lesser extent.

Pure action research and grounded theory

In Australia, Zuber-Skerritt (cf. Zuber-Skerritt 1992) has led an action research movement underpinned by the notion of *grounded theory* (Glaser and Strauss 1967). It emphasizes the importance of the understanding lecturers develop from their action research emerging out of the specific teaching and learning contexts they are working in, rather than being derived from existing research and theory. This contrasts with the use of existing theory and research tools applied by lecturers to their own situation, as used in the CNAA Improving Student Learning project described above. At the University of Queensland in Australia, the Departmental Excellence in University Education Project (Zuber-Skerritt 1993) used Australian Federal Government funding to support nine major action research projects. I was involved in presentations, workshops and consultancy with those who were about to bid for these funds. Those involved had already been to a workshop on action research and some of their reactions were not positive. It was seen by some as 'organized common sense', 'process without any content' or 'a time-consuming way to re-invent the wheel'. I found those involved eager to be given practical research tools and a strong research framework within which to work (such as that provided by student learning research), rather than having to start from scratch. The rationale for grounded theory is that participant observers should not be constrained in what they see by preconceptions from theory derived from different contexts. However, as we have seen, lecturers already have implicit theories of learning and teaching and these will greatly influence their perceptions. There is a real danger of action research operating only within existing implicit models and not being challenged, of lecturers collecting only the kinds of data which fit their implicit models (for example, only quantitative measures of learning outcome) and of any grounded theory being developed simply being an externalizing of implicit models. As we have seen, what students say about teaching is also rooted in their conceptions of learning and it takes more than a commitment to action research to interpret students' responses. It takes a familiarity with the kind of research literature referred to earlier in this chapter. Lecturers need to collect the kinds of data which could challenge their unsophisticated conceptions and models of learning which can help in interpreting this data.

Innovation and evaluation

In the UK there have for some years been institutions which have funded educational development projects (Jaques 1987) and such schemes are becoming commonplace. At Oxford Polytechnic a Staff Release Scheme was modelled on Brighton Polytechnic's similar scheme and has supported 20 or so projects a year since the early 1980s. Most of these projects involved introducing new teaching and learning methods into courses, and it has always been a requirement to plan and undertake evaluation of the innovation's effectiveness. However, most of this evaluation has been pragmatic and theory-free and has led to little reconceptualization of the immediate practical problems, let alone a reconceptualization of the nature of teaching and learning. Such schemes are usually described as staff development programmes, but it is not the case that development of courses or teaching materials inevitably leads to staff development.

In contrast, the TRAC (Teaching, Reflection and Collaboration) project at Queensland University of Technology (QUT), supported by the same Federal funds which supported their rival's DEUE project described above, involved extensive reflection and write-ups of projects, peer collaboration and clinical supervision in an action research approach to innovation (cf. Carr and Kemmis 1986). The reports from the projects involved in this initiative (Weeks and Scott 1992) involved references to published literature on teaching methods and research methods. This differed from the Oxford Brookes model in being more reflective and from the University of Queensland model in being less pure about grounded theory. At QUT the lecturers were making use of available theory and being encouraged to reflect upon it, supported by educational development staff. Here course development and staff development went hand-in-hand, driven by reflection and supported by research.

Beyond evaluation

In my experience it is not enough to sell to lecturers the advantages of action research or to simply explain the action research cycle. They want to know exactly how to find out what is going on in their courses. They may well have undertaken evaluations of teaching or courses in the past but usually this has been for the purpose of checking that a course or a teacher is not rated much worse than other courses or teachers or checking that enough students are reasonably satisfied. Even where evaluation has been fairly high profile there has seldom been a genuine desire to understand what is going on. As a result, few lecturers know how to do action research: they simply don't have the research tools.

In the USA, where enormous quantities of student feedback are collected, the American Association of Higher Education (AAHE) have found

it necessary to publish a collection of techniques for what they call classroom assessment (Angelo and Cross 1993). They use the term assessment
to include what we would term evaluation and also ways of ascertaining
what students have learnt and understood. The AAHE have run conferences based on this theme as part of an initiative to encourage faculty to
research their own practice. This initiative was triggered in part by a Carnegie
Foundation Report (Boyer 1990) which was concerned with the notion of
the 'scholarship of teaching' – an attempt to bring to the improvement of
teaching some of the individualistic creativity and rigour which academics
bring to the scholarship involved in their research.

There are also a number of accessible publications from the UK and
Australia designed to give lecturers good ideas about how to collect useful
information to follow up hunches about what might be going on in courses
(cf. Gibbs *et al.* 1989; McKernan 1991). The importance of going beyond
routine evaluation to the committed exploration of practice has been
emphasized repeatedly by Ramsden (cf. Ramsden 1992) who has done more
than most to explain and demonstrate the relevance of student learning
research to the improvement of student learning. In the CNAA Improving
Student Learning project those involved did not simply evaluate their teaching. They had all undertaken evaluations in the past. Instead they researched
it, using research tools and research concepts.

Action research and initial training

At the University of Brighton the programme for new lecturers has involved
the use of *action learning sets* (cf. McGill and Beaty 1992) in which, at
regular meetings between lecturers (*learning sets*), participants took turns to
gain the support of the set in tackling teaching problems. They undertook
action learning between meetings, learning through personal experimentation and reporting on progress at subsequent meetings. However, these
were not *theory-free* discussions and neither was the theory *grounded.* The
programme also contained workshops which familiarized lecturers with student learning research; it is this research base which informed their action
learning. At Oxford Brookes University the programme for new lecturers
involves negotiated learning contracts in which lecturers engage in small
scale innovation and reflection on their practice. However, there is little
theoretical or research basis for this innovation and the only preceding
workshops are concerned with teaching and assessment techniques rather
than with the kind of theory or research tools which could enable reflection
to go beyond past experience. Much initial training is evolving from skill
development models towards *reflective practitioner* models (cf. Schön 1983),
but there needs to be careful attention paid to the tools, both practical and
conceptual, with which lecturers are equipped if their reflection is to lead
to worthwhile development.

Conclusion

Traditional research into student learning has had little impact on practice in higher education. Part of this research helps to explain why, by showing how lecturers have different conceptions of teaching and learning and defend their conceptions from alternatives. Action research has offered a way of engaging lecturers directly in researching their own practice and this has held out the promise of lecturers developing their own conceptions. However, such changes, it is argued, are unlikely to come about through lecturers' development of grounded theory, which may simply reinforce preconceptions. Instead, action research should take advantage of developments in research and research tools and build directly on more sophisticated conceptions of teaching and learning and challenge preconceptions. Whether institutional funding for educational development projects and initial training bring about conceptual change as well as practical innovation may depend on the extent to which those involved are assisted in reflecting on their practice from a theoretical standpoint.

3

Accredited Courses in Teaching and Learning

Lee Andresen

This chapter describes an innovative approach to academic staff development in which academic credit is gained for formally assessed study of university teaching and learning over a sustained period. It is a form of action research where participants undertake semester long projects to study, through action interventions, their teaching and their students' learning.

The primary goals are two: for participants, to establish habits and skills for lifelong critically reflective professional practice; for the institution, to enliven and invigorate departments with a cadre of committed, well-informed, thoughtfully critical teachers, conversant with student learning research and adult learning principles, able to give intelligent reasons for action.

A Schönian view is taken of the theory practice relationship; theories of practice are understood to develop out of the study of effective practice. Participants exercise a high degree of autonomy and learning independence. Designed for academics, the programme focuses solely on teaching and learning. The approach, with slight modification, could be focused on administration, leadership and institutional renewal and hence be applicable to academic and non-academic university managers.

Unlikely hypothesis

Since early 1991, generous funding from the Australian Federal Government has enabled us, at the University of New South Wales (UNSW), to test an hypothesis challenging the central assumptions of three decades of staff development. Academics across all disciplines and levels of appointment will, it is believed, willingly engage in the intellectually rigorous study of university teaching and learning, but only if this leads to academic credit. Our novel, articulated programme demands sustained, within-service study while participants continue regular academic duties. After one to three years of successful study they receive a Graduate Certificate, Graduate Diploma or Masters Degree in Higher Education. Evaluative studies now undertaken lend strong support to our hypothesis. The discipline and profession of higher education has become regarded, by the majority of participants, as intrinsically worthy of study as their own disciplines – an acceptance presumably heightened by the strategic value they place on the resultant accreditation for career development.

In the last two years, similar developments nation-wide across Australia indicate a rising level of interest in graduate programmes. Ours remains the only one offering a full range of subjects to Masters level. The United Kingdom's SEDA scheme for Initial Accreditation of Teachers in Higher Education (Baume 1992) has substantial similarity to the UNSW approach, despite important formal and procedural differences between the two schemes. The eight SEDA objectives match almost precisely the content of the UNSW subject descriptions. The SEDA values statements which encompass student learning and individual differences, education as development, academic scholarship and teamwork, equal opportunity and reflective practice capture very accurately the ethos of our programme. Thousands of miles apart, these strikingly similar developments suggest independently conceived but parallel solutions to a common problem. For the first time in recent years academic staff development credit programmes are sensed to be feasible and acceptable. We think they are also superior.

Surprising outcomes

Five full semester cohorts, about 25 academics in each, have participated. Almost 150 are currently enrolled and over 100 study a subject each semester. Four graduation ceremonies have seen the first small proud groups of Certificands and Diplomates taking out credits – some, insatiably, returning to study more. The first Masters cohort completed their major projects in 1993.

How might one measure an institution's level of application to professional development? Using as index the number of person-hours spent (private study, programme attendance, and on-the-job application) our participant group amasses an impressive total. For a Graduate Certificate one invests two semesters, around 28 contact hours, and three to four times that in project-based action research – all without forsaking normal teaching, research, administration and community service. The most addicted workshop junkies might attend six half-day workshops a year – some 15–20 hours – but median attendance would be around three hours a year for the clientele of short-course programmes. But we would conservatively estimate our participants' commitment at 120 person-hours per semester, representing a convincing quantum leap in institution-wide commitment to professional development.

The sceptic argues that under conventional programmes the sheer number of staff able to be contacted and influenced is obviously larger. We believe, on a growing body of evidence, that the total institutional and personal impact of credit programmes, albeit undertaken by fewer staff, is likely to be much greater. Indeed it may prove to be the investment having highest impact, hence most strategic, among all current approaches to academic staff development.

Roles

In a credit programme the traditional staff developer role of colleague and peer-consultant needs to be modified. While firmly remaining academic colleagues and peer-consultants to participants, we must also present ourselves as, and work to be accepted in, the new, difficult role of academic supervisor and ultimately judge and assessor. Participants become our students in a full academic sense, a status unlikely to be experienced in conventional non-credit programmes. Yet, in becoming academic supervisors, we never cease to be fellow academics and colleagues. It would be futile to hide this conspicuous role-ambiguity. Our difficult but achievable task is to avoid even the appearance of role confusion by, among other strategies, identifying and acknowledging the two roles and encouraging participants to understand their corresponding dual roles of student and colleague to us.

Participants

Academic and professional pursuits of our group cover the entire spectrum of university life. On the one side participants come from design, fine arts and humanities; on the other from surgery, law, engineering and physics and everything between. Appointment levels range from quasi-academic (instructional designers, professional officers, part-time tutors) through tutors and lecturers (the majority) to senior lecturers. We even have a sprinkling of associate and full professors. Most are in their first few years of university teaching but we discourage (without forbidding) enrolment in the first teaching year. The distribution is changing, however, and each successive intake shows a growing 'hump' around 6–12 years experience. Women are represented at least in proportion to their relative numbers on staff, sometimes in excess of that.

Persistence

In each cohort a couple may drop out early, frequently with enormous regret plus strong assurances to return soon. Drop-out is almost always because of lack of departmental support. Some cannot find time for giving study the justice it deserves, largely through the unreasonable demands of senior administrators. Even fewer leave displeased or disillusioned, saying 'not for me'. Our late-1993 evaluative study found that only one out of 20 interviewees found study unsatisfying, and even that respondent admitted receiving considerable benefit from the programme.

However heartening this evaluation might seem, the most convincing evidence lies beyond the statistics in participants' astonishing level of enthusiastic commitment. When polled as to how many study hours they spent on a subject, many describe without any regret a time outlay far beyond what we had asked or hoped for, and explain that they gave this time purely because they wanted to – not because we demanded it. Some of our earlier jaundiced views on academics' potential for ever being 'turned on' by education studies have been radically challenged. Though the experiment is not yet over, in the motivation stakes at least the evidence is convincing.

Distinctive programme features

Subjects

Except for Masters Projects each subject comprises a one semester one-credit individualized programme of project-based study:

Foundation subject:

• Introduction to University Teaching	Basics of reflective practice and action-learning plus findings of student learning research

Certificate-level subjects:

• Communication and Knowledge	Language, reading and writing: the construction of knowledge between teachers and learners
• Facilitating Student Learning	How students learn: current research and theorizing, and their implications for practice.

Diploma/Masters level subjects:

• Designing and Developing Curricula	Design and evaluation of subjects and programmes
• The Context of Teaching and Learning	The academic profession in social/political context
• Assessment and Feedback	Assessing students; its relation to the quality of student learning and development
• Information Technology for Teaching and Learning	Computer, communications and information technologies as efficiency tools
• Varieties of Teaching and Learning Process	Origins and justifications, and ways of challenging, dominant ways of constructing educational experiences

• Professional Expertise	Theory and implementation of reflective practice: critical study of Schön's work
• Researching Educational Practice	Strategies for teachers to set up small-scale investigations into their own practice
• Supervised Masters Projects – major (4-credit) and minor (2-credit)	Substantial action research investigations into selected aspects of participants' own practice or that of their departments

Flexibility

Within a closely articulated programme structure, this range of subjects appears to be diverse and comprehensive enough for most if not all participants to have their individual needs and interests met. They are encouraged to be opportunistic in their choices. Some who decide to study Designing and Developing Curricula, for instance, have done so because they were already engaged in, or expected to have to undertake, substantial course development or evaluative work in their departments. They thus constructed their action research project around that very task.

Participants find it particularly congenial to be able to:

• enter, if they choose, with advanced standing for subjects of similar kind studied elsewhere;
• enter with a waiver of the requirement to study the foundation subject first, if they can establish their experience and practical familiarity with action research and reflective practice;
• suspend studies for one or two semesters while they catch up on research or cover particularly heavy periods of teaching, then return without loss;
• negotiate, at will, alternative project specifications within any subject, to suit unusual or unexpected teaching circumstances and career needs;
• should they feel they have studied enough, take out credits appropriate to whatever level of achievement has been reached, regardless of which programme they were enrolled in;
• return to study at any subsequent time, cashing in credits previously taken, in order to continue towards a higher level.

Ethos, directions, values

Lynch-pin to the whole structure is the constant challenge to learn to engage in critically reflective practice. Our use of this notion, from *The Reflective Practitioner* (Schön 1987) is strongly coloured by Brookfield's (1990) and Mezirow *et al*'s (1990) interpretations of criticality in adult learning, and also by influences from Habermasian critical theory and its action-learning applications developed by Altrichter, Kemmis, Bawden and others (Zuber-Skerritt 1991). There are three levels at which this challenge is explicitly encountered in the programme. By explicitly I mean engaged in, named, discussed, observed, becoming itself a subject of curriculum discourse.

1. Every subject is project-based. There are no examinations and little or no ordinary academic essay writing of the kind intended to prove that one knows something. Assessable, small-scale investigative or reflective projects are conducted within the context of either self-selected or directed reading programmes and reported in ways appropriate to the subject matter. Each investigates and develops an aspect of the teacher's work or of student learning in a subject being taught. A condition of enrolment is to be currently employed in tertiary teaching.
2. The teaching method, whether interactive class process or independent study materials, is the subject of ongoing critical reflection by each responsible teacher on our team. Our instruction of our participants is itself promoted to become an item of critical discourse and part of the overt curriculum. Staff strive to set a model of critical self-reflective practice. The fortnightly foundation subject newsletter regularly challenges participants to ask why we have chosen particular ways rather than others for engaging them with the content. We offer reasons for our choice of method but freely admit to the same dilemmas and uncertainties our students face in their teaching. We challenge them to ask what factors are influencing their own learning, and how this might relate to the approaches their own students take.
3. While the experience of becoming a student again is a crucial factor, this must take place within a critical and supportive community. In attending conventional short-term activities, academics typically remain teachers – their status is never challenged. In our credit programme design they become students-who-are-also-teachers. This can have startling, immediate impact on their conceptions of what teaching and learning mean. The foundation subject, for instance, introduces the group to self- and peer-assessment through debating and voting for criteria by which their project work will be assessed. They test the criteria by exchanging and appraising one another's efforts at the first piece of project work. In a typical outburst one may say (as did occur) 'This is the first time I have ever actually thought about what assessment means, and I've been assessing my students for five years! Why hasn't anyone told me before?'
4. Everything that transpires can be taken as material having potential to reflect (in Schön's metaphor of the 'hall of mirrors') the teaching/learning relationship between participants and their own students. Some typically have trouble producing work on time and ask for extensions – an ideal opportunity for critically reflective action-learning. We may ask,

'How would you respond if your student came to ask you for an extension and offered a reason like the one you are giving me?' No deserved extension will be denied, but the learning value is that they should understand how every transaction between them and us mirrors an identical potential transaction between them and their students. Participating means studying teaching and learning as present transactions between us and them, as well as through their own teaching. There seems to be something inherently attractive, educationally relevant and mutually motivating in this process.

Research basis

Within the under-arching theoretical platform a further plank is the notion of changing conceptions of teaching and learning. Introduced mainly through the work of Ramsden (1992) and Bowden (1988) this perspective enables us to understand our work with participants as consistently analogous to their work with their own students, particularly in regard to the Gothenburg/Lancaster (Marton *et al.* 1984) notions of deep/meaningful versus surface/reproductive learning which were spelled out in the previous chapter, and of how the essence of the teaching/learning transaction involves changes in ways of viewing the world. That body of research is given high profile with two goals in mind.

First, that participants will permit it to profoundly influence their own approaches to teaching – and the evidence is that they do. The foundation subject's first task, based on one devised at the Oxford Centre for Staff Development (1989) requires them to interview three students and make conclusions about approaches those students take to study and conceptions they hold of learning. The experience of doing the exercise is typically profoundly illuminating. They write, some passionately, how this is the first time they have listened to students' own stories of the experience of learning. 'I never expected that X would think about learning in that way.' 'Y's study motivations are the very opposite of what I had always assumed!'

The second goal is for participants to understand themselves (as our students) to be capable of developing a richer conception of what teaching itself might mean. This is not an easy task, much more difficult for some than others. End-of-session course appraisals reveal how some aspect of the course or of their outside circumstances has inclined them to adopt a more superficial approach than they wished, or that some experience plunged them into adopting a deep approach, spending more time exploring the subject than they had ever intended. For those able to take this step into critical reflection on their own learning, the programme can evidently become a springboard from which they sometimes take off into full flight. The congenial and supportive community enables them to develop and refine their own embryonic sense of what good teaching and learning mean, in order to go back into their departments and begin making changes.

But we are beginning to understand how changing conceptions of teaching and learning is most difficult for those whose obsolete view of good learning (as 100 per cent recall of information transmitted) and of good teaching (as ability to transmit a body of knowledge faultlessly) has been sustained without challenge from their own student days and nurtured by working in a department where a similar ethos prevails. They are shocked to encounter a programme having no syllabus to be learned, where teachers are didactic only reluctantly and by special arrangement, and where the criterion for success is not how much can be remembered. The most we may achieve is to have generated the awareness of an alternative conception, that things are not as cut and dried as they previously thought. The experience probably also engenders a heightened sense of confusion and uncertainty. They will have to resolve this themselves in the future.

Skills

The programme does not focus primarily on the development of skills or discretely defined teaching competencies, nor is it behaviourally-based. We generally eschew micro-teaching approaches and may never actually observe our own participants teaching. We do not, on the other hand, ignore the place of skills in good teaching. Modelling, demonstrating and practising a range of effective techniques occupies a substantial place in the foundation subject and in some others. But the clear message is that no amount of clever teaching can make much difference unless participants develop a robust understanding of how intimately their work as teachers is related to their experience of having been, and now being again, learners; of how their conception of good teaching is a corollary of their own conceptions of what good learning means; and of how that is likely to profoundly influence their students' conceptions of and approaches to learning.

Credit

The fabric of university culture is deeply invested with a currency intimately bound up with the value of academic credit. The baccalaureate, diploma, Masters degree, PhD, all signify not merely the achievement of a level of intellectual and/or professional competency, but that the thing that has been studied is itself a worthy object of study. Pursuing this value is readily distinguishable from the mere 'paper chase'. We have become strongly confirmed in our initial belief that the challenge of rigorously studying the profession of teaching, following the best traditions of scholarship, is not only far more motivating than the mere lure of a degree or diploma, but actually operates to heighten the value and regard in which participants and the rest of the academic community hold that profession.

It would be naive to deny that the promised qualification is one important factor helping people remain on task over a difficult one, two or three years of study. Anecdotal evidence suggests, however, that an even more powerful factor may be the shame of being seen to have given up on a worthwhile academic task to which they have publicly committed themselves. This factor is unlikely to be present in short-term programmes. In sum, it seems that if a thing is worth working hard at, it is worth getting credit for, and, in the absence of credit, people are unlikely to work hard enough to make significant changes in themselves or the culture of their academic environment, nor will their colleagues seriously respect the work they have done.

Other than when teaching, much of a programme coordinator's time is spent consulting with participants about their progress, goals, satisfactions and – inevitably – their motivations. I cannot conceive of this programme being as motivating as it is without the reasonable, indeed necessary, prize of substantial academic credit at the end of the road. Studying, rigorously and painstakingly, one's own teaching and one's students' learning, is – and is seen publicly to be – a task in which success is worthy to be crowned with honours in the same way as any other kind of scholarly enterprise.

Communication and support

Years of exhaustive evaluation of short courses, seminars and workshops consistently demonstrated to us the importance of one particular impact factor which has become recognized in programme design. That factor embraces all aspects of teachers' relationships to one another. It encompasses communication and support, teachers sharing and being with other teachers, disclosing their fears, joys and hopes, and viewing one another as non-competitive colleagues with much to teach and learn from one another. Recent work on teachers helping teachers is in this mould (Willerman *et al.* 1991). Some particularly facilitative strategies include the following:

- Peer-observation and peer-support are placed within mandatory project work so that, for instance, participants are expected to observe and comment upon one another's classes and record those experiences in journals and final reports. This leads, we believe, to appreciating how each teacher's problems are unique in the sense that no technical fixes are ever sufficient to solve them; yet at the same time no teacher's problems are so unusual that observing another and discussing common experiences cannot illuminate the path towards finding solutions.
- Peer support, communication and group problem-solving are used in face-to-face class work. That means, for instance, starting a three-hour workshop with forty minutes of 'I have a problem' groups, or with twenty minutes of silent listening activities in pairs or triads. Most people, with practice, learn to value the opportunity to recount events of their past weeks, their achievements and their failures. 'Others have problems just like mine – I'm not alone after all! And I'm neither stupid nor incompetent

just because I have problems!' 'Some of the most unlikely others occasionally have brilliant ideas that I can use.'

- In various ways we either prescribe or encourage writing and sharing
autobiographical reflections on ourselves as learners and as teachers. Journal writing on day-to-day hopes, trials and experiences of learning-by-
doing are, to some extent or other, part of every subject and obligatory
in some. Autobiography, as recommended by Brookfield (1990) can relate our own experience of having been learners to our present role of
teacher and facilitator of other people's learning. A major autobiographical essay with which one subject begins is described by participants as
being at once the hardest and the most rewarding piece of academic
writing they have ever done. Reading Logs are also used in subjects where
appreciation of a literature base is important and critical reflection upon
set or personally selected texts is required.

- We encourage electronic mail networks among those staff able to communicate via their computers, and – in open learning subjects – telephone conferencing gives people a sense of being members of a learning
community. They exchange telephone numbers, arrange local meetings,
pair off to support one another, or whatever they may wish. These strategies provide pointers to how participants' own departments and institutions can be moved in the direction of learning organizations using
networking for critical sharing of views not only in teaching but also
in wider spheres of management and academic work. Regrettably,
technophobia continues to rule in some participants' lives and it can be
difficult to get them motivated and willing to use the powerful but sometimes intimidating networking technologies now available. There is a case,
though we have not yet followed it through, for making electronic networking mandatory within a programme of this kind (Davies *et al.* 1993).

Institutional change

We always encourage, and in some subjects explicitly demand that participants share with colleagues in their school or department whatever they are
learning and discovering out of our programme. Some report their projects
to school meetings, others choose to circulate their every project report to
departmental colleagues or table them at staff meetings. We hold that it is
vital for academics to understand that they do not and cannot teach in
isolation of their whole departmental and institutional community. We know
that one single graduate is unlikely to have much influence on a department's culture, but we also know that success breeds success and satisfied
participants regularly recommend the programme to their colleagues. From
some departments we have enrolled a number of participants through
personal recommendation. A critical mass may yet form that will challenge
and transform that department's culture somewhere down the track.

We are becoming more adventurous in trying to crack one or two of the really hard 'nuts' of traditional university practice – such as assessment. In a recent venture we have established a system of peer-assessment of project reports within the foundation subject. To quote a conversation between myself and a team-member, 'These, after all, are practising University Teachers. If we can't trust them to assess the quality of one another's work, whom can we trust? They know more about teaching at the chalk-face than we (Staff Developers) ever will!' The experiment proceeds, as we try to overcome its enormous administrative complexities and deal with plenty of annoyance by participants who become frustrated, not by the process itself, but by the fickleness of their peers who among other crimes behave just like students and fail to produce work on time!

Autonomy

A recent venture has been to explore the potential of a self-directed workshop and self-directed reading programmes as steps towards recognizing and rewarding autonomy for adult learners. We interpret autonomy, however, as applicable to the learning group as well as to individual learners. In a three-day foundation workshop, whose process and materials were meticulously planned but whose direction and leadership were left entirely in participants' hands, we learned something very important about the strength of group cohesion and belonging that such an experience can create. Such innovations, instigated as a way of meeting some necessity (such as the course leader being absent for an extended period) have taught us much about how educationally powerful student autonomy combined with group support and cohesion can be.

Impact – personal and public

Many institutions have persistently criticized staff developers for being unable to produce evidence of lasting impact of their work. 'Why then should they be funded?' goes the tired, but still potent, argument. It seems to us at least hypothetically possible that credit programmes such as ours might make an impact in ways such as the following:

- The ripple effect: people who make a long-term commitment to their own professional development may have an impact on people around them.
- Even without the ripple effect better quality teaching and radically changed teaching practices may follow for at least those who do participate.
- A department having within itself people who have studied higher education in an award-validated scholarly manner will be likely to mark them as experts and ask them to serve on quality enhancement groups, curriculum committees, education working parties and the like. Their contribution may substantially raise the general level of discourse in those arenas.

- If mandatory induction programmes for new staff are to be instituted, credit-programmes like ours may provide the optimal model for what is needed. The certificate level of the UNSW programme, which can be completed in two semesters, might present the desired duration and academic level for induction programmes, provided that adequate time-release plus mentoring and other departmental support are provided. We discourage newly appointed and inexperienced staff from beginning our certificate programme unless they can be assured of adequate release and support, believing such study to be incompatible with the extraordinary personal and institutional demands made upon new staff in their first year. Customary tenure requirements such as the demand for a certain level of research achievements would also need to be reconsidered, perhaps allowing success in graduate certification studies to be counted as equivalent to a certain amount of research work.
- Institutionalized departmental or faculty-based course review processes can be effective only if their personnel are of high quality. It is too easy to merely rubber-stamp a faculty's existing courses as adequate and offer apologies for weaknesses without seriously remedying them. Graduates of good credit programmes may have a more forward-looking conception of evaluation, with a consciousness of the rich possibilities to which review can open the door (the 'what next?' perspective), rather than backward-looking.
- The design model of our programme could readily be used to develop parallel programmes in higher education administration or organizational development, whose participants could be non-academic staff such as middle-range managers. This would maximize the overall staff development impact of credit programmes across the institution. It is striking how many close similarities there are between the action research cycle and the Total Quality Management cycle.

Evaluation

As a matter of course, every subject is summatively evaluated by participant opinion questionnaire and formatively evaluated by familiar devices such as group discussions. However, these data are not normally regarded as having long-term impact status, their function being to feed back into progressive improvement of each subject. True impact-gathering to date has been of four kinds. First, evidence from within participant project work; second, anecdotal evidence from around the campus; third, a mid-term survey-based evaluative study; fourth, an intensive survey, plus interview-based study of a stratified semi-random sample of participants. Data from the latter are drawn from here to provide some preliminary evidence of the possibility that the six hypothetical impact propositions mentioned above may actually be realizable in practice.

- Interviewees do report changes in the perceptions and expectations of their colleagues which seem to derive from participation in the programme. Very often these lead to new roles and responsibilities for participants who on occasions have become identified as sources of information or as the departmental 'education person'. Some are asked to give seminars on the programme itself or on general educational issues.
- Interview evidence shows clear effects on the teaching practices of participants, a large majority reporting changes, even in the absence of changes to their conceptions of teaching and learning. Reported impacts extend to changes in attitudes of participants towards students, attitudes of students towards learning, reductions in failure rate, and substantially improved student evaluations of participants' teaching.
- Changes in the perceptions and expectations of colleagues very often lead to new roles and responsibilities for participants – being put on a teaching committee, or becoming a member of a course review panel, for instance, often despite the relative lack of seniority of the participant within the department.
- Growth in personal confidence as a teacher is the most often reported impact of the programme, and this suggests at least one strong argument in favour of using such programmes for induction purposes. However, the qualifications mentioned above are strongly borne out by interview evidence; namely, that participants working in aggressively non-supportive departments are likely to find even mild innovations being blocked, barriers being set up to communication with older colleagues, actual hostility being expressed towards the wastage of time on trivial matters such as teaching, derision at the idea that educational research can ever count as real research, and confrontation with rigid, unyielding structures and policies that prevent even modest action research from ever being carried out.

Academic motivations

This documented evidence of how Australian academics have responded to a graduate studies credit-based programme prompts perhaps the most interesting question of all: what motivates these people to commit all this time and energy in study that is in only rare cases actually supported by their departments, and which much of the academic world is certainly not yet ready to recognize as being valid or appropriate? The answer may lie outside the programme, inside it, or in both.

First, it may lie in the changing circumstances of academic employment. In Australia, as elsewhere, awards are offered for teaching excellence in most universities. In some institutions substantial weight can now be placed on teaching performance in promotion applications. There are more academic staff development personnel and units than ever before, and there is a growing availability of centrally-distributed funds for teaching development projects. Could a credit programme have succeeded before all these changes? One might conclude that we have done the experiment at the right time. But I hesitate to believe that external factors have been sufficient in themselves to explain the astonishing depth and breadth of acceptance of our programme. I think that if we can understand the nature of what underlies that acceptance, we will have achieved an unusually deep insight into the very nature of academic motivations – into what makes an academic tick.

Accordingly, the second possibility is that acceptance may lie in something inherent in the programme itself – something to which academics respond affirmatively. That may be its design, its style, its structure or its driving ethos and values. I trust that something of all this has been conveyed by the above account.

Implications for staff development

My present view, and that of my colleagues, is that there will continue to remain space for both the traditional short-course, workshop/seminar plus consultation approach to staff development and for credit programmes such as this. Our professional development centre continues both approaches in parallel. Our experience is that they fit very comfortably, supporting and complementing one another and operating synergistically. Clients in the credit programme become frequent attenders at other short courses which cover topics not included in the graduate curriculum. Participants at short courses meet colleagues enrolled in the credit programme and learn directly through conversation and comment how it may be helping them. Two recent developments, each an interesting instance of the synergizing effect of one programme approach upon another, remain to be tested in the long term but are already making a promising start:

1. The formation of department or school-based groups who meet regularly, facilitated by staff of the centre, to plan and execute reflective action research projects within their own teaching. Such groups will be doing the kinds of things we require of our postgraduate participants in their coursework projects. These will not be doing it for credit, but they may have an advantage not shared by postgraduate participants doing similar projects, in that they are working as collaborative groups within the one school and are, potentially, in a position to make a substantial impact on the school's approaches to teaching.
2. The replication, in the centre's non-credit programme of short courses, of a three-day introductory workshop which was originally set up as the start of our foundation subject (Introduction to University Teaching) within the postgraduate programme. Staff not presently intending to enrol for credit can attend this three-day event and have substantially the same introduction to the principles of effective teaching and quality student learning as do participants in the postgraduate programme. If

they should subsequently decide to enrol in the formal programme for credit, their attendance at the event is counted as partial advanced standing in the programme's foundation subject.

Not for the faint-hearted?

Credit study at postgraduate level is not easy; it demands a real commitment and can exact a considerable toll. It is demanding, time-consuming and in some departmental circumstances may not even be a strategic career move. One keen participant in the foundation subject recently complained how having to write up the projects interferes so much with the changes he wants to be making to his teaching, and there is never enough time to handle both. It can be personally disconcerting, generating cognitive dissonance as existing conceptions and departmental ethos alike are challenged. Participants have reported (with approval) experiencing their first sleepless nights since being appointed as academics 'I can't believe it; for the first time in my career I actually couldn't stop thinking about teaching the whole night – what have you done to us?'

Study can present a severe test of academic self-esteem as participants who have become expert scholars in their own discipline experience the ignominy of being mere beginners in a totally new disciplinary area of the social sciences, where the whole literary genre, way of arguing, approach to evidence and nature of data are unfamiliar, baffling and often frustrating. On the other hand, the experience of three years of this experiment confirms beyond our expectations that there exists a very highly motivated clientele waiting for such programmes. Those coming from hostile departments can find within the long-term learning community support, reassurance and confirmation of their intuitively felt value-positions about teaching and learning. We are confident that, provided appropriate approaches are taken to programme design and implementation, the participation of a wide range of motivated staff in such credit programmes will be not only personally rewarding but very likely to exert long-term and wide-ranging impact on institutional culture and practices.

4

Encouraging Reflective Practice Through Distance Education

Bob Ross and Jennifer Pittman

This chapter describes the origin and early development of a packaged staff development programme that was a collaborative endeavour between two institutions and two different orientations: student assistance and staff development. The packages represent a new approach to distance education that attempts to be compatible with much of the rhetoric current in higher education and, in particular, in staff development. The packages set out to use the experience of the participants and to meet their particular interests. They were also designed to incorporate current beliefs about adult learning and good practice in teaching, rather than just teach about them.

The programme described was produced for teachers in higher education, particularly those who had recently joined. However we believe that the approach taken would be easily adaptable to other related tasks. In developing the programme we explicitly attempted to follow the adage: 'practice what you preach', rather than retreating to the all too common 'do as I say; not as I do' approach. The chapter reports the first trial of the programme and raises issues that became apparent from that trial.

Background

Universities are facing increasing pressure for quality assurance. In Australia, industrial awards for academic staff now include staff development provisions, and proposals to link appraisal of staff performance to annual salary increments are being discussed. This is occurring in a period of considerable un-met demand for undergraduate places and declining real funding per student. Australia, of course, is not unique in experiencing this climate! Chapter 1 has explored the implications of changes such as these for staff development more generally.

In this climate an increasingly popular provision within staff development strategies is to offer award courses (Graduate Certificate; Graduate Diploma; Masters by coursework) in university teaching. This was a common strategy in the early seventies and some programmes from that period have survived (if only just) until the present; others have disappeared. At the close of that decade (1979) a major government-commissioned report recommended the establishment of a national award for university teachers, completion of which would be a condition of service for all new academic staff (Williams 1979). As an aside, the outcome of that recommendation was a report and set of recommendations from a working party established by the Australian Vice-Chancellors' Committee, but not a national award (AVCC 1981). Most of the recommendations had minimal impact. So, at present there is not even an informal requirement for such qualifications. The award strategy in the past has not resulted in wide acceptance by university staff, although it had some success with other groups. In the previous chapter, Lee Andresen dealt with one current programme that appears to be breaking that pattern and is highly successful.

As many universities in Australia have experience with distance education, it is not surprising that some have offered, or propose to offer, such award courses using distance education techniques. The usual approach to on-campus award programmes is to place a heavy emphasis on small group work and workshop activities. Teaching procedures in these programmes are heavily process-orientated and in the present climate are likely to describe themselves as employing action research procedures to produce reflective practitioners (see Chapter 3). Such programmes, at least *de facto*, recognize that teaching approaches vary between discipline areas and that this variation is legitimate – possibly reflecting the different types of knowledge in the different areas, or at least reflecting a different teaching ethos in each area.

Many of the approaches used in these programmes also explicitly attempt to rely on participants' previous and current experience. This reliance is based on two closely related sets of arguments. One of these arises from theories about learning, particularly adult learning; the other arises from recognizing the wealth of experience present in any group of participants.

All of the above features, reflected in the design of award programmes for on-campus participants, present interesting and difficult challenges for distance educators. Distance education programmes normally rely very heavily on structured didactic approaches. There are very few examples of programmes (in any subject area) that explicitly:

- incorporate the experience that students bring to their studies;
- take advantage of the different backgrounds and interests of students;
- and/or are process-orientated.

Yet it is probable that these are all requirements for any programme attempting to foster reflective practice or produce autonomous learners.

The project

This chapter describes a collaborative project between our two institutions: Griffith University and the Northern Rivers campus of The University of

New England (recently granted autonomy as Southern Cross University) over the last couple of years. The project has attempted to address the above challenges. Northern Rivers had a well established Learning Assistance unit. The unit had experienced consistently high numbers of students seeking assistance in some academic areas. This suggested to the staff in the unit that there were major problems with the teaching in those areas (this experience is by no means unique!). However, Northern Rivers did not have an academic staff development unit (at the time of writing this chapter) but had been involved in distance education for some years.

The task that we set ourselves was to produce self-instructional packages (i.e. using a distance education approach) for use by staff to develop/improve their teaching. In addition, it seemed necessary to produce packages that could be used by staff with a wide range of experiences and from a variety of disciplinary backgrounds. The process used in developing the materials and the trial of the first unit of the programme are described below. Analyses of both pose important issues for staff development.

Assumptions

One of our starting assumptions was that good teachers constantly seek to learn from their students (see, for example, Ramsden 1988). In modern terminology, as mentioned earlier, we would seek to produce *reflective practitioners*. We would also seek to have the participants in our programme develop procedures for encouraging their students to become independent learners. We took it for granted that our participants were themselves independent learners – but see later. We certainly believed that it was important to treat our participants as autonomous learners and for us to model the practice that we wished to encourage. We also make the assumption that our roles as staff developer and student assistance specialist are similar at the most general level in that they are to improve the learning experience that our institutions offer students. In staff development we believe that this is most effectively achieved by assisting staff to reflect on their own teaching and by helping them to learn from that reflection.

The approach we adopted, in the packages we were producing, was to attempt to structure student autonomy; a design problem that one of us had been considering for some time (Ross 1988). We wished to produce a distance education programme that gave participants the type of autonomy that open learning (or at least one interpretation) claims to offer. The interpretation of open learning to which we are referring is the attempt to give learners control over their own curriculum. That is, they are able to adjust their studies to their own needs and interests. One of the basic issues that we faced was that most distance education courses are considerably less 'open' in this way than many standard on-campus offerings in traditional institutions. In other words most distance education students have less control over what they study in their chosen courses, and how it is structured, than many on-campus students.

This is precisely because of the considerable effort put into structuring the teaching materials. In this respect the British Open University's 'systems approach' (Lewis 1974) has set the pattern for distance education for the last twenty years. There are a number of debates around the issues we allude to by implication above, about how open some packages claiming to be open learning really are; and what impact the usual approaches to producing and structuring distance education materials have on openness. See for example, those about distance education and open learning in Hodgson *et al.* 1987 and Evans and King 1991 and debates about Post-Fordism in distance education, for example, in Raggatt 1993.

The first assumption that we made is that all teaching staff have some knowledge and experience of higher education teaching (if only as consumers). Indeed, many staff will resent an approach based on an assumption of ignorance. (For a discussion of this issue in a related environment see Kelly 1987.) Of course we recognized that the level of such experience varies considerably. In addition, the range of techniques and teaching approaches with which staff are experienced and which they are likely to use is equally wide. Attempting to meet both of our additional goals, of utilizing students' knowledge and giving them some measure of autonomy, seemed not only useful, but necessary. It was our intention to explicitly incorporate aspects of the previous experience of teaching that staff have had, into our teaching and to give them the choice of teaching practice to examine and to help them to learn from their experience.

It is our belief that all higher education students bring some relevant knowledge and experience to all their courses. (The importance of prior knowledge in experiential learning is discussed in Wagemans and Dochy 1991.) Let us be absolutely clear: we are not, in this belief, referring to pre-requisite knowledge. By *pre-requisite knowledge* we mean those terms, concepts, etc., that students are assumed to have assimilated from earlier academic study. In contrast we are alluding to the knowledge and understanding that students acquire from their experience of life.

Like the approach described in the previous chapter, we also wished to work from the explicit recognition that staff participating in staff development are performing as learners; adult learners, if you like. Bowden (1988) argues that if teachers recognize themselves as learners and are treated as such, then learning is more likely to occur. By recognizing the roles they play, teachers can begin to examine their beliefs about teaching and relate them to their practice of teaching. This approach is designed to tackle the common discrepancy between *espoused theory* and *theory in action* (Argyris and Schön 1978). For example, staff frequently claim that their teaching is designed to encourage their students to learn how to learn but their practice may encourage their students to slavishly recall the formulations delivered by the staff.

Our assumptions required us to suggest ideas to staff about how their students learn and simultaneously to ask them to apply the same considerations to our teaching and to their own learning. If we practise what we preach then our teaching should serve as a model of one method of teaching. Having experienced this model, we felt staff would have a better understanding of the role of the learner and at the same time, begin to build a framework of ideas for their teaching.

The programme

An award at graduate certificate level has been approved, but this will be extended to a graduate diploma and masters degree if demand warrants the extension. This is a common pattern of development in Australia at this stage. The Graduate Certificate described here consists of four units; a total equivalent to one semester of work of full-time study, or a year of half-time study. We use the term *unit* in this chapter; common equivalents are *subject* or *course*. The projected graduate diploma will have twice as much coursework and the masters degree will add a research project of equivalent weight to the coursework of the graduate certificate.

The units included in the Graduate Certificate are:

Unit 1   Teaching for Effective Learning
Unit 2   Applying Theories of Learning to Teaching
Unit 3   Curriculum Development
Unit 4   Elective (to be selected from units available in other graduate
         programmes in Education)

We are concerned in this Chapter in the detail of Unit 1: Teaching for Effective Learning.

Unit 1: Teaching for Effective Learning

We were constrained by one of our institutions to produce the units as modules; that is, as more-or-less independent sections. We saw some advantages in this; one being that staff are busy and may be more prepared to commit themselves to a small segment of work at one time than to a whole unit. The modules for Unit 1 are:

Module 1   Examining Your Teaching
Module 2   Planning Teaching Practice
Module 3   Evaluating Your Teaching

These modules were developed to be sequential. An additional requirement that we set ourselves was that Module 1 should be able to stand alone. Our aim was for it to be useful for staff who wanted an introductory segment, but weren't interested in committing themselves to a longer programme of study. For similar reasons, Unit 1 was designed also to be complete in itself.

Extract

Activity 1: Examining teaching sessions

- Choose one teaching session which you have given that you felt was successful. Identify the session on top of the page opposite.
  We will be asking you to write about this session in the spaces opposite. You may like to begin by writing notes on scraps of paper and then transferring your ideas to the boxes opposite.

- In **Box 1** write, in point form, a detailed description of what you did in the session.
  How did you begin/end the session?
  What materials/equipment did you use? How?
  Did you use any handouts? How?
  What did you ask students to do?
  How did the students respond?

- In **Box 2a** describe any events that caused you to feel that this was a successful session.

- If you feel that the students thought it was a successful session, try to say what gave you that feeling in **Box 2b**.

- Now draw lines linking the features in your description of the teaching session (**Box 1**) to the comments (**Boxes 2a** and **2b**).

- What did you set out to achieve in this session? What role did you intend for the session? List these in the Box labelled Purposes (**Box 3**). After you have listed your purposes for the session, number each purpose in the session in the order of its importance for you.

- Now examine each of your purposes and then read your description of the session. Alongside any point in the description, place the number of any of the purposes that the described item was intended to meet.

- Is there any purpose that you could not link to your description in **Box 1**? Add more items to your description if you wish. If there are still any purposes in **Box 3** that you haven't been able to link to **Box 1** place a ring around those purposes in **Box 3**.

Unit/Course title: _____

Session (i.e. lecture, tutorial, lab): _____

1. Description of successful session	3. Purposes of successful session
2a. What made you feel this session was a success?	2b. What indications did the students give that the session was a success?

Module 1 is available on a non-assessment basis, but to complete the whole of Unit 1, that is the three modules, staff have to complete (but not necessarily submit) the assessment items for Modules 1 and 2 as their responses to the assessment tasks are used as part of the input to Module 3. We were conscious that many of the students would come to our programme expecting a 'bag of tricks'. We accepted that we had to meet that need, but decided that it was important not to start there, but first to begin to develop reflection on practice (see, for example, Boud, Keogh and Walker, 1988). This is an essential means of recognizing the context of a learner's past and current experience. Changes in consciousness and attitudes grow out of reflection and result in conceptual change (Brookfield, 1986). Another of the outcomes of reflection would be an understanding of the teaching–learning connection.

We wished to avoid a didactic approach and simultaneously produce materials that met the needs of a diverse group of participants and that also relied on their very different experiences. We achieved this by asking our participants to start the module by documenting part of their own experience and then, by posing questions about that experience to help them to reflect upon it.

We began by asking participants to choose a single teaching session for which they had been responsible and that they thought had been successful. They were asked to say why they thought the session was successful as well and were asked to describe what they did and what they expected their students to do. They then worked, under the guidance of our questions, on the material that they had generated. The first two pages of Module 1 are included to give you a feel for our approach. The rest of the module continues in much the same vein. One interesting aspect of this approach is that we could not anticipate what type of session any particular participant would choose to describe. We could, of course, guess most of the types of sessions that they would be likely to choose, but we were aware that it was always possible that they would choose something that we had not anticipated. In any case our approach had, at the very least, to fit the range of types of session from which we guessed that participants might choose. For example, some would choose a lecture, others a tutorial or problem class, while some might choose a field trip. While we hoped to extract many of the ideas in the modules from the participants themselves, it was obviously necessary to supply some ideas, at least for them to relate to their own content. To this end we chose a very limited number of readings. In Module 1 these concentrated on good teaching and the surface/deep learning approach distinction (described in Chapter 2 above).

We were consciously using our teaching (in the form of the modules) as a model (Bandura and Walters, 1963) and decided that it would be necessary to explicitly draw participants' attention to this fact. We also decided to attempt to use different approaches to teaching in the different modules, at least to some extent. This turned out to be considerably more difficult than one might imagine, particularly given our commitment to the ideas that we were trying to employ!

Module 2, we decided, needed to start on the 'bag of tricks'. So participants were asked to design a teaching session, while having access to 'the bag'. As in Module 1, we relied on participants generating their own material to work on. But, as part of the changed approach we altered the method of presentation to some extent. For Module 2 participants have a set book (rather than readings) and an audio tape on which we could be more discursive than we had been in Module 1.

In the third module we introduced participants to ways of evaluating their own teaching. They examine the different evaluation techniques that we had employed ourselves in Modules 1 and 2. And so, not surprisingly, in Module 3 we asked them to evaluate our teaching as part of their work for that module. In Module 3 we also introduced some of the issues in assessing student achievement and have a first tentative look at the relation between that and the evaluation of their teaching.

Units 2 and 3

These two units are less structured than Unit 1 (see the section on issues, below) without altering the general approach. Unit 1 is a prerequisite for Unit 2 and these two units are prerequisites for Unit 3. These prerequisite statements not only refer to the usual type of assumptions about student learning sequences, but in this case the teaching in the subsequent unit uses the material in the earlier unit as well as some of the student's own responses to the earlier unit. However, it is our belief that most of the former type of prerequisite assumption are hard to justify in practice. That is, students who have not completed the prerequisite may succeed nevertheless – and vice versa!

The trial

In Module 1 we asked the trial group to keep a diary which we had initially designed as an evaluation instrument for us. We wished to have an indication of the amount of time spent on each activity. The diary was also designed to give us feedback on the appropriateness of the language, content and approach that we had used. We later realized that this was, in fact, a valuable teaching technique to assist reflection (Walker 1988) and have incorporated it as such in the revised version of Module 1. In fact it was very clear from the diary entries that the process of writing comments for us assisted participants to reflect on their own learning.

In Module 2 we used a questionnaire for our evaluation so that different evaluation processes, as well as the teaching process, were modelled. And, as we indicated above, participants evaluate our teaching as part of their assessable work in Module 3. The assessment item at the end of each module also represents additional evaluative information. Achieving our objective of using our modelling of different teaching practices has proved to be more difficult than we anticipated. We found that the learners did not identify the teaching methods that we had used in the module. A quote from a participant's diary for Unit 1: 'I think this is here for your benefit, not mine.'

Although we have encouraged participants to reflect upon their practice we find that we cannot expect them to transfer that idea to reflecting on *our* practice. This is not an unusual problem. We have also encountered it during workshops that we have based on the modules – even those we have given to course developers and instructional designers! Lee Andresen tells us that teaching staff engaged in the programme for academic staff at the University of New South Wales, which was the subject of Chapter 3, report similar responses.

Boud, Keogh and Walker (1988: 9) identify three distinct stages in a learning activity – preparing for, engaging in an activity and processing the experience. In the preparatory stage the learners begin to explore what is expected of them. The anxiety level is usually high and students respond to it in different ways – either by over-preparing or not thinking ahead. Both of these responses were evident with our participants. Many of them stated that they came back to their session descriptions and added more after they had moved further through the module because 'I didn't give enough detail . . .'

During the second of Boud *et al.*'s stages learners can make so many observations that they feel overwhelmed and they can find the experience exhausting. These reactions can cause learners to withdraw, want to talk with colleagues or make notes to themselves in order to sort out feelings and reactions. Our participants exhibited all these behaviours, evidenced by the following:

'I stopped doing it . . . I found out I'm a terrible teacher.'
'I do everything that Ramsden lists as bad teaching!'
'Occasional gatherings of the group were a good idea. I tended also to discuss the module with another staff member.'
'I found myself making little notes to myself . . . especially on the *referring back* stages.'
'I made so many realizations of what I did wrong in the unsuccessful session.'

In the final phase of the process of reflection learners are usually required to report on their experience. To do this, they have to return to their notes and reconstruct happenings.

The problem with lecture 'S' (the one with the surface approach) is that I was giving it at the wrong time, when I hadn't properly covered principles and 'built the scaffolding' described by Eizenberg. This exercise helped me to determine that – so thanks! I learned a lot about making readings useful and relevant. In the past I've assigned reading but seldom given exercises that force students to link the readings to each other and to the lecture . . . and yet I expect the students to be able to do this in exams.

Although staff found it difficult and confusing at first, encouraging them to reflect on their practice in the module has been successful. In the diaries (and the workbooks we have been shown) we often see a comment which shows that some learning, or a connection, has been made during, or after, reflection:

I'm not too sure about your meaning of 'procedures' – in nursing a procedure is a major clinical intervention . . . However, talking, writing, reading, handing out materials, using audio visual and other teaching aids, structuring, demonstrating, using examples, enthusing, empowering, listening, attending, responding – I HAVE INTERACTED IN ALL OF THESE WAYS IN YOUR MATERIALS!

and 'I now realize that our role is to facilitate learning for students . . . to make them thirsty.'

Another issue we encountered with this audience is lack of awareness of themselves as learners. In some ways, like the participants described in Chapter 3, they demonstrate behaviours that are similar to their students. 'I wanted to be told when to read the rest of the Reading!' (This was also a warning to us to check the clarity of our instructions.) They had most difficulty with the activities which required them to be meta-cognitive – particularly identifying their reading method. In this, they are required to take the role of the learner and to describe the way they read a passage. The comments 'I found it difficult to analyse how I read,' and 'Difficult to write about my reading process . . .' are typical. As an aside, participants have asked the same questions about the assessment item that their students ask – how long does it have to be; when is it due and what is it worth? We had not supplied this information thinking that as experienced learners they would make those judgements for themselves!

The diaries have shown us that the participants are spending an intense 30–40 hours on each module, not including the time they would spend applying it to their practice. 'I had to think. I felt burnt out after an hour. Learning to teach is bloody hard work.' The effects seem to be long term: 'I keep thinking about the ideas and making connections with my teaching.'

Previous learning experiences and patterns have become apparent. This is the first time that some of the participants have undertaken an activity that does not have to be remembered for examination. Some have expressed surprise and pleasure when this realization dawns. Their comments also reflect their own beliefs about, and attitudes to, learning. 'Reading and learning are two different things,' and 'I always thought my view of learning corresponded with your 'deep approach' but my teaching certainly doesn't. In fact my own learning style is often surface – maybe I'm brainwashed and conditioned after so many years of school and uni – unable to learn any other way.'

Issues

The results of the evaluation were encouraging. We encountered a number of fairly predictable issues (some disappointing from this audience) which we attempted to address in the revised version. The results certainly suggest that further experience with the programme will establish at least one pattern for structuring student autonomy and simultaneously incorporating students' prior knowledge into teaching packages.

However, as with any staff development process, it will be important for us not just to rely on the evaluations that we have conducted at the end of each module (or, even worse, rely on the collection of satisfaction indices from the participants). We need also to try to determine what impact the programme has on the teaching activities of staff, particularly as viewed through the achievements of their students! But at this stage that is an issue for the future.

We are convinced that we have met our goals of having participants incorporate their own experience into their learning and them choose the teaching procedures on which to concentrate. However, the cost is, if anything, a more structured programme than most distance education offerings – perhaps a rather surprising outcome. This, in itself, poses further questions for distance education. After Lee Andresen drew our attention to the issue we attempted a much less directive approach in Unit 2, although we are willing to defend the approach in Unit 1. But we accept that there may be a problem for staff who don't proceed beyond Unit 1. In other words we need to return more control of the process, not just the content, to our participants if we are fully to meet our modelling goal.

The important question is whether this approach is satisfactory as staff development and results in improved teaching (as evidenced by improved student learning) by our participants. Participation in the trial of the materials certainly resulted in vigorous and interesting discussions between participants when they volunteered (in fact asked) to meet. This is a healthy sign and raises interest in teaching; a result that is, in itself, positive. Because the course starts from participants' own interest and experience, and builds on that experience, we believe that it has a greater chance than many approaches to influence staff in a permanent manner. However, inevitably the evidence for such influence is difficult to establish – particularly in the short term. So we are reduced to our own beliefs about such achievements that arise largely from what our participants say in the evaluations and their expressions of satisfaction, rather than what they subsequently do.

Acknowledgements

We gratefully acknowledge the enthusiastic participation in the trial of academic staff from a range of Faculties at Southern Cross University.

5

Releasing Staff on Projects

Joyce Barlow

This chapter looks at project work as a vehicle for staff development. It is based on experience of the Staff Release Scheme at the University of Brighton. The main focus will be on a set of six linked projects on Managing Independent Study which have recently been carried out by teams of academic staff. As coordinator of the scheme since 1982, I shall aim to bring out the nature of the role, in addition to giving a balanced picture of the potential benefits of project work, the conditions needed to maximize the benefits, and the pitfalls and limitations of such schemes.

This approach to staff development has acquired wide acceptance at Brighton, and the continuity and responsiveness of the scheme has enabled it to become firmly established and to give credibility and support to projects. The scheme at Brighton may well have been the first in the field. Nowadays it is by no means unique, and the principles and methods have been applied in many other institutions. Coventry, Oxford Brookes and Napier Universities were early examples; more recently the Academic Efficiency Fund at Kingston University has operated a scheme with substantial financial investment. Institutions with Enterprise in Higher Education (EHE) funding have also adopted project work very extensively as a means of organizing change.

Project work at the University of Brighton

Project work within the framework of a staff release scheme has been a key strategy for educational and staff development at the University of Brighton (previously Brighton Polytechnic) for nearly two decades. It is supported by the central service Department of Learning Resources whose mission is to work as closely as possible with academic departments and to give maximum support to teaching and learning activities. The coordinator has an institution-wide educational and staff development role, with the release scheme as a major focus. The scheme has survived far-reaching changes within higher education. It has been through good and bad phases, it has been criticized and favoured, and as a concept and strategy it has proved remarkably resilient.

The scheme has been described in detail in a paper published by the Staff and Educational Development Association (SEDA) (Barlow 1987), and booklets of guidelines are available on the way it operates (Barlow 1991) and on the evaluation of the outcomes (Barlow 1985). Only essential background will therefore be given here. Fundamentally the release scheme was designed as a strategy for ensuring that at least a modest amount of innovation in teaching and learning was happening on a continuing basis. The Learning Resources staffing budget provides for part-time replacement teaching to free academic staff for up to a day a week over a year. This funding covers approximately two projects a year in each of six faculties, and proposals are put to boards of study and faculty boards for discussion and selection on this basis. The coordinator plays an active part in the initiation and selection of projects, is responsible for monitoring their progress, helping them to reach a successful conclusion, and ensuring that the results are disseminated.

For many years, projects were very much individual initiatives, and it took some persistence to spread the benefits beyond the member of staff undertaking the work. Financial constraints have in fact served to strengthen the scheme in that its resources have become more highly valued, and faculties and departments are now concerned that projects should clearly benefit the learning of a substantial number of students.

Project schemes can readily be applied to other groups of staff than academics. Library staff, for example, have a very important role in supporting student learning. Their expertise in literature searching and organizing the availability of information to students can make an essential contribution to projects or form projects in their own right. Administrative staff also play a vital role in enabling student programmes of study to be delivered effectively. The importance of their role and the potential for job satisfaction through a fully recognized involvement is often underestimated. A separate scheme for projects to be carried out by staff in supporting roles has in fact been set up at Brighton, and an example of a project was the production of a handbook for administrative staff involved in the management of courses.

Linked projects

An important development within the scheme for the 1992/93 academic year was the addition of a coordinated network of six faculty-based projects, each carried out by a team of staff drawn from different departments. The six projects have been operating together to form one large strategic development project for the university; the theme which links the projects is the question of how to achieve a substantial shift towards student autonomy in learning. This has an essential corollary in the need for staff development for a changing role towards the facilitation of learning and the provision of frameworks within which students can identify and follow their own learning goals.

The main benefits of linked team-based projects are that they have a much greater critical mass: more staff are involved from more areas of the institution. The projects are less specialized and therefore of wider relevance. There is also wider awareness of the work being undertaken. Finally, the team process of the projects is in itself valuable, enabling working contact between staff who would otherwise know little of each other's interests and practice.

What project work has to offer

Project work has many strengths as a strategy for staff development, above all perhaps in the scope for choice and the way it links directly with current and future teaching. The process of defining and selecting projects has always been a matter of seeking a match between individual staff enthusiasm and educational development needs. Competition for approval and funding of projects implies a certain rigour, and it engages groups of colleagues in the defining of areas and methods for development. By this means projects are required to relate to departmental, faculty and institutional plans and are an investment in change.

Work within the scheme at Brighton has affinities to the action research described in Chapter 2 by Graham Gibbs in connection with the CNAA Improving Student Learning Project. The latter focused explicitly on encouraging deep approaches to learning. In that and in the Brighton scheme it is the lecturers themselves, rather than independent researchers, who are working on the processes of student learning, and many individual projects carried out at Brighton have similar characteristics of heuristic development. As an internal rather than national scheme, projects at Brighton are part of an established annual programme of development and as such may be seen as contributing to a continual process of change within the institution.

The most widespread adoption of project schemes must be in the context of the UK government's Enterprise in Higher Education (EHE) initiative. This involves some sixty higher education institutions in the UK. On the basis of competitive bids, they were awarded funding of up to a million pounds each over a five-year period. One of the conditions of receipt of the money was that they should complete a rolling programme of development throughout the institution to incorporate students' skills development as well as the acquisition of academic knowledge within all programmes of study. Another condition was that institutions should demonstrate improved links with employers and the world of work. Many EHE institutions operate a system of internal bidding by individuals and teams to carry out projects to meet these development requirements. EHE has increased the prevalence of this form of staff development very considerably. A directory of EHE projects is available. It is organized in broad subject areas and includes projects on developing links between employment and higher education (The University of Portsmouth 1994).

Another related development is the TRAC (Teaching Reflection and Collaboration) initiative at Queensland University in Australia which has already been mentioned in Chapter 2. This focuses on encouraging teaching staff to become reflective practitioners (Schön 1987). TRAC participants are committed to improving their teaching and students' learning; where appropriate they work collaboratively in this exploratory process; they join in group meetings to promote collegial discussion; and they write reflectively about their experiences, for the purpose of highlighting, analysing, synthesizing and publicizing them. Staff at Brighton are also being encouraged to adopt the reflective practitioner approach, and there are useful lessons to be learned from the methodology and outcomes of the TRAC initiative.

Project schemes undoubtedly have great potential for establishing an institutional culture of development in educational practice. This chapter is based on a wealth of experience of the management of such a scheme as a whole, and of the projects within it. There are undoubtedly many ways in which the scheme could be made even more effective and could be adapted to meet new needs both at an institutional level, for courses and departments, and for the learning needs of individual students. It is intended that the material presented in this chapter should stimulate debate and review. The focus will be mainly on the six linked faculty projects mentioned previously, but reference will also be made to the range of freestanding projects which the scheme has supported over many years.

Institutional coordination of teaching and learning

The coordination and exchange of information on developments in teaching and learning tends to be a problem in many universities. This is in spite of the acknowledged importance of avoiding unnecessary reinvention of the wheel, of enabling colleagues to benefit from each other's experience and expertise, and the desirability of achieving a coherence of development within the institution with regard to teaching and learning.

The linked projects at Brighton are part of such a strategy, but as the participants have pointed out, it requires support from management to complete the process of dissemination and to provide the impetus for cross-institutional change. Elton and Partington (1991) present a very cogent argument on defining teaching quality and gathering evidence of it. They concentrate on 'the individual teacher and what may lead him or her to pursue teaching excellence', and they stress very strongly the need for institutional direction, recognition, and development opportunities.

Faculty-based and institution-wide committees on teaching and learning have an important role to play. The absence of such a structure in many universities often hampers progress in this area. It is in marked contrast to the hierarchy of committees on research which certainly exist in former polytechnics and which indicate the institutional and individual kudos associated with this activity. A very significant recent development in the UK is the introduction of audit and assessment of institutional provision in this area. These procedures, as Chapter 11 shows, require appropriate committees and ask institutions to show evidence of teaching innovations. They are undoubtedly exerting an influence towards better coordinated provision and monitoring.

Setting up the faculty projects

As indicated, the idea of a network of faculty projects was a departure from previous practice. It required confirmation of additional funding, and agreement at dean and head of department level both with the idea in principle and in choosing the theme. To keep the latter process manageable only two choices of overall theme were offered: Managing Independent Study, and Using Educational Materials. They were obviously closely related, and consensus was quite easily reached in favour of the former, slightly broader option.

The coordinator of the scheme then undertook a relatively complex process of negotiation with the faculties in order to obtain a coherent set of projects. Deans were asked to consult with their heads of department and to identify a project topic which both matched their faculty's interests and needs and fitted within the Managing Independent Study theme. In practice the process was different in each faculty, reflecting the personalities and the politics. In all cases, however, the consultation stage was valuable in itself, and in some instances there were a number of competing bids.

A vital part of the negotiation of topics was the customary need to match staff enthusiasm and commitment to faculty priorities, first in order to find a convener, and then to enable the formation of faculty teams. The provision of time to carry out the work was essential, and the normal unit of funding had been doubled to enable the equivalent of two days per week to be spent on each project. The balance of funding for release hours was negotiated among the staff involved.

The process of decision-making and planning took place from January to June in preparation for projects to begin the following October. These were as follows:

• Group and Individual Design Projects (Faculty of Art, Design and Humanities)
• Innovation and Assessment (Business School)

- Student Profiling (Faculty of Education, Sport and Leisure)
- Supplemental Instruction (or student peer facilitation of learning) (Faculty of Engineering and Environmental Studies)
- Student Learning Contracts (Faculty of Health)
- Negotiated Independent Study (Faculty of Information Technology)

The appendix provides summary information on each of the projects. The focus here is on the processes of managing and carrying out the projects.

Management of the projects

The faculty projects were essentially designed for teamwork, wherever possible with representation from all departments, thus providing a natural networking mechanism within each faculty. The two most genuine team projects were in the Business School and the Faculty of Health, each with representation from all departments and involving up to eight staff. Responsibility for management within the projects was vested in a convener.

Each team organized itself and decided how best to carry out the project. The main organizational issues were: management of the team; forward planning; economy and focusing of effort; maintaining momentum and priority for the project in relation to members' other commitments; genuine release from teaching; cross-site working and the difficulty of finding suitable meeting times; coping with absence through ill health. Each project fared differently in relation to these issues.

Networking the faculty projects

Networking the projects across the university took the form of termly meetings run by the coordinator of the scheme and attended by representatives from each project. The meeting in the autumn term was concerned with information exchange including explaining their projects to each other and discussing them, looking for links between the projects and setting up contacts.

The spring term meeting was a rare occasion of very lively debate on teaching and learning, and strong opinions were voiced on what people felt it would take in order for student autonomy in learning to become a reality in the university:

> We need first a culture in which staff would attend groups for their own development.

> Independent learning forces students to use resources. Taken to extremes this could be a classic hands-off scenario (cf. Oxbridge). It is very important to distinguish between independent and individual learning. The former should foster group work and interactive support.

Independence need not mean isolation. It is not necessarily lecturer help which is needed; students can become a resource and support for each other.

The summer term meeting focused on the problem of dissemination throughout the institution, to ensure that the methods investigated and the findings of the projects were applied in courses as appropriate. There was a unanimous feeling that unless the process of dissemination had the active support of the directorate, deans and heads of department, nothing would happen.

Dissemination

Dissemination has always been one of the most problematical aspects of the Staff Release Scheme, and it calls for a variety of strategies. Staff doing projects report on their progress and completion to committees. Their reports are then compiled into an annual booklet which is circulated to all faculties and departments. One suspects that they are stored in office files and the idea of their becoming well thumbed through extensive use would be a fantasy. Much more easily digested and widely circulated forms of publicity are also needed, through, for example, a well designed, eye-catching, two-sided flier, or by using various in-house journals.

Another important strategy is to set up sessions or to link into events set up by others. It is extremely gratifying when a wide audience gathers and there is evident interest and lively debate. Heads of department have a crucial influence on whether an institution moves to a culture of taking part in such events. A very welcome development at Brighton is that all faculties now hold one or more faculty days each year. These are proving very useful as a context for informing colleagues about project work and encouraging debate.

The network of faculty projects, as an institution-wide drive towards changes in student learning, is in a special category, and greater effort and coordination is being employed for their dissemination. The purpose of this is to generate action and follow-up, with the intention of paving the way for further faculty or cross-faculty work to tackle large issues such as the reduction of contact hours, extending the use of technology in teaching, student peer support, and many others.

Staff development outcomes

In order to gather data on the staff development benefits to be derived from projects, participants were asked for their views on:

• the benefits and potential benefits of the network of projects for achieving institution-wide changes in teaching and learning;

- whether mounting the network of projects was likely to prove an effective mechanism for achieving a significant shift towards greater student independence in learning;
- ways of improving the individual working of the projects;
- their experience of working as a member of a faculty project;
- what staff development outcomes they felt were particular to group-based projects; for the individuals involved; for department/faculty colleagues; and for colleagues around the institution;
- how the coordinator of the scheme could help to ensure effective project work; effective implementation of the results; effective dissemination of the outcomes; and maximum institution-wide staff development from the projects.

The survey received a high level of response and has provided valuable data for both current needs and future planning for the scheme and for staff development more widely. Despite the variety of the questions and their differing backgrounds, staff respondents consistently identified a number of recurring themes across the range of open-ended questions.

Institutional culture

The culture of the institution and its commitment to the pursuit of improvements in teaching and learning was highlighted as a prerequisite for change in responses to all the questions. This means having a clear policy for the development of educational goals, giving due recognition and status to staff efforts in this area, and being willing to invest resources in terms of time and money. As in most institutions of higher education there is a justified perception that striving for excellence in teaching and learning is the poor relation compared to achievements in subject-based research. However, continued support for the release scheme at Brighton, and in particular the mounting of the network of projects on student independence in learning, was seen as evidence in itself of commitment to change.

It was felt that the situation could be improved by making involvement in teaching and learning development more mainstream, with many more people becoming involved. 'It appears to me that the same people are involved – probably because they are very pro a change. However it seems that an effort by each department is needed to see that everyone employed in teaching and learning should participate at some time.' This is one of the fundamental dilemmas for staff developers: how to reach beyond the 'inner circle' of the converted to encourage and support a wider group of staff, many of whom see change as unwelcome and threatening.

The support of heads of department and course leaders was seen as vital in order to provide an impetus for innovations in teaching and learning on a department and course basis.

Yes [the projects could bring about a significant shift towards student independence in learning] if supported fully by course management. Target heads of department – make them aware of the projects and what skills the staff need to implement the different projects!

A tendency within the present culture is for some staff to delegate responsibility for teaching and learning developments to certain committed colleagues. Several respondents referred to the need for links between the enthusiasts and those who do not normally volunteer to participate in strategies for change. From experience it seems that the principal elements needed for involving staff include the following.

- Staff need to feel that it is *possible* for them to change their approaches to teaching; often there is a fundamental willingness and desire to provide more effectively for student learning, but people do not know how to go about it.
- It also needs to be seen as *the done thing* to work on improving teaching. Importance needs to be attached to it in terms of status for the work, and support and interest from the head of department and colleagues.
- It needs to be *rewarding*. Student appreciation is a very considerable bonus in this, but a sense that investment in the area of teaching and learning can contribute to professional recognition is equally important.
- There also needs to be *leadership*; there are limits to what an individual can achieve as a lone innovator, and indeed her or his efforts can be negated by the conservatism of colleagues and students. If, however, the course leader or head of department is stimulating and coordinating a team effort, and students are receiving a coherent message about the way they are being encouraged to learn, then the picture is transformed.

A productive way of spreading enthusiasm and expertise is to have staff working in groups on innovative approaches to teaching. A team might be involved, for example, in managing a student project. A related example of this is provided by one of the strongest projects ever carried out within the release scheme at Brighton. It was, in fact, run within one of the most innovative departments in the institution and involved six staff, together with the subject librarian. They worked in sub-groups to prepare a range of case studies or projects in international accounting on topics such as the champagne industry, multinational conglomerates and take-overs, Japanese industrial culture and innovation, and the Third World banana industry. The case studies involved international travel and contacts for staff and students. The project itself was stimulating, fun, and highly developmental; it also created a team spirit among all those involved in delivering the degree in International Accounting and Finance.

If this quality of development could become endemic in higher education institutions, students would flock to them for the sheer richness of personal development and professional preparation offered.

Dissemination

Effective publicity was stressed as being absolutely vital to the effectiveness of the projects in bringing about a significant shift, institutionally, towards student independence in learning. The benefit of the network of projects 'could be enormous'. On the other hand it could be 'minimal unless the information is circulated and explained appropriately throughout the university. The information also needs to be seen in relation to individual courses. – How can they actually utilize the processes involved? Are they appropriate to their course?'

In order to do justice to the work done in projects, and particularly these faculty projects, deliberate and conspicuous action is needed to ensure dissemination. Clear communication is needed highlighting examples of good practice. Cross-institutional publicity could occur through regular newsheets or reports with wide distribution, and projects should feature more regularly as items on committee agendas and in informal discussions. All this would help to raise the profile of teaching and learning and to increase staff awareness of the issues. Involvement in the faculty projects was for many a disseminating experience in itself. Students also need to be aware of the purpose of changes in the way they are being encouraged to learn, to become conscious themselves of educational issues.

Teaching and learning

The system of projects was seen as a potentially powerful mechanism for raising the profile of teaching and learning within the institution, but as already indicated, the scheme needed to be given more prominence. Until the faculty projects were introduced, it supported a range of small scale developments. Around the institution, the scheme tended to be regarded as worthy but not of great significance. Its potential as a framework for important developments is now being increasingly recognized.

As in many institutions there is a dearth of information on ideas, experience and good practice.

'I would like to know what other people do! This is very hard to come by!'
'We need to do an audit of what is already currently going on and then try to establish areas that need to be further developed.'

Many of those involved in projects were agreeably surprised to discover colleagues who were also committed to improving teaching and learning, and who shared their goals. 'There are many who are concerned about teaching (and learning) and who are willing to put effort into advancing it.' The type of activity fostered by the scheme was seen as: 'Vital regarding the many issues facing us over increased numbers and needs for alternative teaching and learning and assessment methods.'

With specific reference to student independence, one participant said, 'I have always and especially now promoted a far more active role in students' own learning. Now study support groups get a lot of my backing; the more the student does, the better.'

The role of the coordinator

Personal contact and persuasion was seen as a very important function of the coordinator, generating enthusiasm, motivating people, and helping to set objectives and deadlines. The coordinator's role included ensuring that projects were realizable and where necessary advising staff on modifying their proposals. It was then important to check that the projects were properly set up; to oversee progress; to check that the process and the results were evaluated and reported, and that the staff played an active part in bringing their work to a wider audience. There is certainly scope for the coordinator to be very active indeed in support of projects and the networking between them, without taking away responsibility from those actually doing the projects.

It is part of the role of the coordinator at Brighton to brief faculty conveners and to negotiate and define their role as appropriate to each project. Faculty projects need a cohesive team. If a team is not working well, then the coordinator has to intervene. The coordinator also needs to set up networking meetings and to decide their focus and how they will be run.

Staff development

Faculty projects were seen as very valuable in providing for cross-departmental contact and creating cohesiveness and a sense of belonging. Very high among the individual staff development benefits was the motivating effect of taking part in a project, making new contacts and feeling part of a network of staff with similar interests and values. Colleagues wrote with considerable enthusiasm about the stimulus of exchanging ideas and finding out how other people do things.

The experience of team project work was summed up by one participant as:

Extremely beneficial and rewarding. Broadening one's perceptions – gaining views from other departments. Sharing ideas, knowledge and experiences. Motivation of working with new colleagues from other departments. Trying to improve and believing that the University is concerned with improvement.

It also brought confirmation of useful practice and the realization that 'somebody is interested in what we actually do! This gave me a great lift.' The fulfilment of the staff development benefits was again seen as dependent on commitment by course leaders and course team members to incorporating new ideas into the delivery of courses. The difficulties of spreading this type of staff development to the institution as a whole has already been discussed.

It is evident that in most cases staff showed high levels of motivation and commitment to the projects. Many of them found the work stimulating and fulfilling, and were very pleased to have the impetus of the scheme to become absorbed in researching a specific area such as student learning contracts. People also said how enjoyable they found it to be taking part in a team project. Such feelings are expressed both by staff involved in the faculty projects and in freestanding projects.

> My project has led to a deeper understanding in a global sense of how all foreign languages (not just my specialist language) are taught throughout the university. This has led to a sharing of ideas and the feeling that as a teacher I am not working in isolation.

> (The release scheme) provides an opportunity to do something different – perhaps in a different way, for example make a video, as well as providing something of value for the university and most importantly its students – it enables staff to 'lift their heads' and do something for them too.

Other colleagues summed up the personal benefits as follows:

> Extended my understanding of the subject of the project and of research methods. Benefits of working collaboratively with colleagues and teachers in schools. Professionally and intellectually stimulating.

> I am now actively involved in research and I am writing a book. Both these activities will bring benefits in the future and both arose from release projects.

Hazards and the vital ingredient of credibility

Running a project scheme is never a smooth ride. Even in ideal circumstances there are many forces working against the fulfilment of project goals. The importance attached to the work is a major factor, and academic staff often need to be very determined to pursue work on their project. 'It is yet another job to take on and it doesn't matter how committed the individual is if there is no departmental backing then other responsibilities will take over.' If a colleague is absent through illness or there is a meeting to be attended, it is all too easy to suggest that the time be borrowed from project work. This, added to the inexorable demands of a teaching time-table, can lead to a serious erosion of time and concentration.

Projects are inherently difficult, because they are breaking new ground. Encouragement is usually needed to help maintain interest and momentum and to steer towards a successful outcome. Colleagues may come to a progress meeting feeling rather despondent and apologetic, and then be agreeably surprised to discover, through talking about the project, that they have been making more progress than they thought.

Projects often work best when they are linked into the deadlines of teaching, for example, where a new development is being piloted within a current course and students actually need materials to be available at a particular stage. This must not be confused with regular planning and preparation for teaching. A strict criterion for project selection is that the work be innovative and that it be something which requires dedicated time and research to reach a stage where it can become part of the normal approach to course delivery.

The credibility of the scheme is vital as a support for the projects within it. When the scheme is seen to carry weight and accountability, then the staff doing projects will usually be accorded the departmental support they need to carry out the work. Conversely, if the scheme is poorly re-garded, it can become a resort for teachers whom heads of department and course leaders would like to keep out of the classroom. Some staff have even seen the scheme as a comfortable prelude to retirement! The reputation of a project scheme is enhanced when it addresses issues of central importance to the institution, as in the case of the Managing In-dependent Study projects. An extremely important task of a scheme's co-ordinator is to protect, and if necessary repair and build the credibility of the scheme.

The staff developer within the institutional context

This chapter has concentrated on a particular strategy for educational and staff development: a project scheme for promoting innovation in teaching and learning. The staff developer, in the role of coordinator of project work such as has been described in this chapter, has a change agent and catalyst role. A natural way of working is through a complex network among virtually the whole staff of the institution. They need to be politically aware and to tread a fine line in order to work both to management aims and to support academic staff. They need to be respected and trusted by all parts of the hierarchy, while fulfilling an essentially challenging role. The diffi-culties of the role are often compounded by the relative lack of status for their work. The following diagram is an attempt to portray their situation, but relating it to the project scheme example:

```
┌─────────────────────────────────────────────────────────────┐
│      Management steer: towards independent learning           │
└─────────────────────────────────────────────────────────────┘
                              │
┌─────────────────────────────────────────────────────────────┐
│   Teaching and learning development committee: oversight,     │
│      faculty perspectives, support and dissemination role     │
└─────────────────────────────────────────────────────────────┘
                              │
┌─────────────────────────────────────────────────────────────┐
│ Coordinator of Staff Release Scheme: managing activity        │
│   designed to implement institutional policy                  │
└─────────────────────────────────────────────────────────────┘
                              │
┌─────────────────────────────────────────────────────────────┐
│   Faculty projects: six teams working on facets of Managing   │
│                   Independent Study                           │
└─────────────────────────────────────────────────────────────┘
                              │
┌─────────────────────────────────────────────────────────────┐
│  Academic colleagues and support staff (resources and        │
│ administration) throughout the institution: project results  │
│  need to become a reality for them, in order to actually      │
│  implement the policy and use the fruits of the project work  │
└─────────────────────────────────────────────────────────────┘
                              │
┌─────────────────────────────────────────────────────────────┐
│  Students: the ultimate beneficiaries: awareness-raising and  │
│            information needed on policy                       │
└─────────────────────────────────────────────────────────────┘
                              │
┌─────────────────────────────────────────────────────────────┐
│ Student feedback (questionnaires; Consultation Exercise;      │
│   day-to-day contacts; personal tutor support)                │
└─────────────────────────────────────────────────────────────┘
```

Research is the arena with particular kudos. This is a fact of life, and staff developers need to play to this scenario. The staff release scheme lends itself to this. Several staff in their questionnaire returns referred to the research avenues opened up by their projects. The staff developer's goal can be to elevate pedagogical research to become a recognized and valued activity alongside subject-based research. For many higher education institutions this means a cultural shift, and this can only be achieved with the understanding and support of management. Academic staff will only believe in the shift when they see excellence in teaching and learning as a route to advancement. A rather encouraging sign at Brighton is that recently two engineering lecturers have submitted PhD proposals based on researching aspects of teaching for the education and professional preparation of engineers. Caution and scepticism were part of the initial reaction of at least one head of department, but this has been converted into support.

Conclusion

What this chapter has aimed to demonstrate above all is the power of a project scheme as a means of staff and educational development. It is particularly appropriate where the structure of the institution is quite devolved, and where there tends to be resistance to what may be perceived as institutional directives. Through projects, individual staff gain a sense of recognition of their work and are motivated to contribute to the achievement of institutional goals. Team projects are particularly valuable in encouraging contact between departments, and they are considered a more powerful and far-reaching mechanism than individual work. A logical progression would be to mount some cross-faculty projects.

To achieve its full potential, a project scheme needs to have a high profile within an institution. This depends on commitment and support at directorate level, giving the scheme the necessary status and resources. The work of projects will then be more highly valued, and it will greatly assist the process of disseminating results and encouraging wider participation.

Staff report great benefits professionally and personally from being involved in project work. They are refreshed by the opportunity to pursue an aspect of their teaching in depth, to see their work in a broader context, and to exchange ideas with colleagues beyond their own department and courses. Project work can make a most significant contribution towards an institutional culture of cooperation and shared goals and the development of its staff.

Appendix

Summary information on the six networked projects

Faculty of Art, Design and Humanities: project-based learning
Individual learning and creativity have always been central to art and design education, and the independence together with the one-to-one working relationship between tutors and students has been questioned in the context of larger numbers of students and reductions in the scope for employing practising artists as part-time staff. The project aimed to identify just what is involved in the individualized learning in these areas and to look at how students can both be independent and support each other.

The goals at each stage of the project were to:

- investigate and document the learning processes involved
- consolidate and create awareness of the method within the faculty
- provide examples of practice
- offer the methods and insights for potential application more widely in the University

The project drew on a range of student projects in the areas of fine art, design history, fashion and textiles, the performing arts, and three-dimensional design.

Students were observed and interviewed as they worked on the creative development of the design brief, and where group work was involved they were helped to
reflect on the way they worked together.

Business School: innovation and assessment

The Business School is notably innovative, and active learning methods are already
widely used. Student numbers have increased very substantially in the faculty, and
the real area of concern is the burden of assessment. It was therefore decided to
devote the project to investigating current practice and new developments in order
to make available ideas and information on good practice.

A project group with representatives from all the departments was convened, and
work focused on the following areas:

- continuous assessment: practice and problems;
- non-traditional assessment methods;
- independent study: assessing large groups;
- assessment in relation to the use of distance learning packages and the restruc-
  turing of contact hours in the area of business policy;
- a staff survey on assessment: practice and perspectives;
- assessment practices in language service teaching;
- student views on assessment;
- values and assessment.

Education, Sport and Leisure: student profiling

This project was selected in the context of changes in teacher training, with the
emphasis shifting to schools, and students having much less access to day-to-day
support from tutors. This is seen as an opportunity to emphasize students' own
awareness and sense of purpose over their professional and personal development
through the course. The means chosen to do this is student self-profiling with
personal tutor and mentor support and feedback.

As well as teacher training, the faculty is concerned with sports science and
leisure management, and self profiling is seen as equally applicable in these areas.
The faculty also sees profiling as having great potential for increasing student independence in other parts of the institution. It is relevant to modularization and the
consequent need for students to chart their way firmly through their own programme of study.

Engineering and Environmental Studies: supplemental instruction (SI)

Work in Engineering and Environmental Studies followed up a pilot project the
previous year in the Department of Civil Engineering. Supplemental Instruction, or
SI, is an American system of student peer tutoring. SI helps students consolidate
their knowledge, improves their study methods, gives them increased experience of
group learning, and the benefits in terms of improved marks spread to subjects
other than those covered in SI. The students who attend bring their own notes from
the class as a resource. The SI leaders themselves need initial training, and continuing supervision and training. SI Leaders are trained in group facilitation: not teaching, but helping students to work together on grasping important concepts, practising
techniques, and improving their confidence and skills. The SI Leaders themselves
gain markedly through the development of a wide range of transferable skills.

Faculty of Health: student learning contracts
The project researched the benefits and difficulties of student learning contracts, finding out what works, giving concrete examples, and providing a basis for decisions as to their potential usefulness, showing the benefits and advising on methods of implementation. Learning contracts, or learning agreements were already a feature of two smaller courses in the faculty, mainly involving mature students. A major question was how feasible they were for use with large numbers of mainly 18+ year-old students studying for a degree in pharmacy which requires mastery of a large body of knowledge.

The work has included a survey of all course leaders within the University on the nature and scope of existing practice in the use of learning contracts. Contact was also made with colleagues from other institutions to learn from their experiences.

Information Technology: negotiated independent study
The project used an existing course (FORUM) within the second year of the Mathematics for Management degree to investigate the problems of managing a negotiated independent learning module. The emphasis was on evaluating the processes involved in different models and the production of recommendations for wider application. The project had four phases:

- investigating the state of the art in negotiated independent learning;
- working with students on ways of formulating and negotiating their learning contracts for the spring term;
- implementing the process of independent learning and its assessment in the second term;
- evaluation of the project during the summer term, with students and staff involved in producing a final report.

Acknowledgement

I should like to thank Richard Kemp, University of Glamorgan, for his very valuable contribution to the working out of the ideas in this chapter and for his support and encouragement throughout the writing of it.

6

Getting and Using Student Feedback

James Wisdom

Introduction

Feedback can hurt your ears. When your friendly local pop group is setting up its equipment, a bad attack of feedback can lift the roof off the church hall! The early use of the word was among electrical engineers controlling circuits. Its use in education implies a self-balancing process, regulated and improved by the flow of information. Usually it describes either comments on students' work or students' views on the performance of their teachers. In both cases it has the potential to cause pain.

This chapter is based on the programme of student consultation meetings that the Educational Development Unit (EDU) at Kingston University has been conducting since 1986. It has been a programme of over 60 consultation exercises, covering courses on which over 6,000 students have been studying. Kingston is a newly-designated university, having been a Polytechnic since 1971 providing a vocational education in art, design, science, technology, business studies, human sciences and teacher training. However, the consultation exercise and the approach which brings it about are not specific to this background and have been repeated successfully in a number of other higher education institutions.

The core of this exercise has been to create a report which gives the students' perspective on how they have been learning the course. For the staff, the close-grained detail is as valuable as the broad outlines.

Approaches to gathering student feedback

In recent years there has been considerable public discussion of student evaluation in higher education. This discussion has laid out a range of techniques for gathering student feedback, together with warnings over reliability and suitability. In 1974, Flood Page reported on the American experience of student evaluation to the Society for Research into Higher

Education and rehearsed much of the discussion which today is being conducted in the context of appraisal and performance-related pay. In 1989 Gibbs, Habeshaw and Habeshaw published a manual of appropriate techniques and methods entitled *53 Interesting Ways to Appraise Your Teaching* (Gibbs *et al.* 1989). In 1991 McDowell at Newcastle Polytechnic (with support from the Council for National Academic Awards, 1991b) reported on initiatives being conducted throughout her institution and in the same year published the papers from a conference held by the Standing Conference on Educational Development entitled *Putting Students First: Listening to Students and Responding to their Needs* (1991a). These publications showed the variety of approaches, both well established and experimental, which were being adopted in the UK.

The CNAA also supported the establishment of a Student Satisfaction Research Unit at Birmingham Polytechnic (CNAA 1990), which in the main looked at institution-wide processes. A CNAA conference in 1991 (CNAA 1992) led to the commissioning of Silver to survey the Polytechnic sector. His report (Silver 1993) is a discussion of current practice written in the context of the economy of institutional processes which might play a part in the Quality debate. Meanwhile, the Enterprise in Higher Education initiative was considering how best to evaluate the student response to attempts to change institutional practices; this was reported by Sommerlad in 1993.

The Committee of Vice-Chancellors and Principals' Universities' Staff Development and Training Unit, sponsored by the Training, Enterprise and Education Directorate of the Employment Department, commissioned O'Neil and Pennington (1992) to prepare training materials for staff wishing to gain experience in evaluation in their series *Effective Learning and Teaching in Higher Education* (Cryer 1992) and have followed this up with *Student Feedback – Context, Issues and Practice*, edited by Partington (1993). Most recently, Knight (1993) has published a collection of papers for the Standing Conference on Educational Development and the Society for Research into Higher Education, with a particularly valuable bibliography. The background to all this work was the use of inspectors' (HMIs) ratings of teaching quality in the polytechnic sector to determine levels of funding. This initiative was followed by the Higher Education Funding Councils' current scheme to assess teaching quality in the whole of the University sector in every subject area.

As the literature now shows, there is a rich variety of mechanisms for gathering student feedback. Among these is a growing interest in fostering the skills and understanding that come from rigorous reflection and the development of self-understanding. This suggests that such vehicles as diaries, interviews, logs and notebooks, combined with a genuine spirit of enquiry and learning on the part of the teacher, are likely to develop into a very powerful suite of approaches. They could bring staff into a form of academic intimacy with students which they may have felt they were losing in the move towards mass higher education.

The most widespread method of gathering feedback (as Silver 1993 reports) is the use of questionnaires. These can be administered at the level of each module or unit of the course, of the course as a whole, or at institutional level. They can be brief or substantial, standard or bespoke. They can be used by individual staff for self-development or across cohorts of staff for management information and course or institutional development. As long as the normal caveats about gaining information for one purpose and using it for another are applied, there is no initial reason why they should not be seen as versatile and effective. However, they sometimes produce substantial amounts of data which can be hard to translate into action.

The other process which is almost universal in higher education is the course committee on which representative students meet their staff. For this to be a genuine and effective process, the representatives must be supported in a number of ways. They have to be allocated time during which they can discuss course matters with other students; they will probably need to be coached to handle (large) meetings to do this; they will need to be prepared to function successfully at meetings often controlled and sometimes dominated by academic staff; they might need practice at putting challenging or critical positions; and they have to have ways they can communicate outcomes of these meetings effectively. Often during student consultation meetings, the weaknesses of the student representative system have been revealed. One response has been to coach some student representatives to run 'pyramid' discussions (where participants work first on their own, then in pairs, then in fours and so on) ahead of course committees; it appears to be a development worth encouraging.

The process of both questionnaires and course committees is usually controlled by the academic staff. It is important to recognize the interactions of power and responsibility between teacher and student, especially when assessment is so dominant. Although the word *feedback* has connotations of equality and value-free openness, to some students it can appear to be no more than the acquisition of information within an unequal relationship without any guarantee of beneficial outcome.

Although students could generate the questions, the usual practice in the use of questionnaires is for students to be asked questions which the staff think are important. This is even more the case when the questionnaire is intended to gather comparative data between courses, or between staff. It is often used to focus on how staff teach and is therefore becoming more attractive in discussions about appraisal and performance-related pay. (For a debate about the introduction of institution-wide questionnaires, see Coomber and Harrison, 1992.)

The student consultation exercise used at Kingston has attempted to avoid some of the drawbacks of the questionnaire approach. The process signals to the students that the staff are interested in their (the students') agenda. The sequence of events gives the students many opportunities to consider their thoughts, and their ideas become clearer and stronger. The quality of the final discussion is often most worthwhile, and educational principles are often handled with care and respect. It is not unusual for students to end by thanking the EDU for the opportunity they have been given for such a discussion. The process is often taken one stage further when students see the final report and are invited to comment on it. This is usually the first occasion on which they can compare their thoughts with those of students from other years of the course. This can lead to a maturing of their understanding of the whole educational process. In comparison, the many hasty judgements made on a questionnaire form seem rather paltry. The act of evaluation is a learning experience in itself and one which academic staff should foster.

The question asked in the EDU's meetings is not 'How well have you been taught?' but 'How well are you learning?' The curious outcome has been the discovery that teaching performance is often not the most powerful determinant of the quality of the students' learning. Turning student evaluation towards learning opens many possibilities for developmental change and shows how, in both the design and the staffing of the course, the total experience is more than the sum of its parts.

Commissioning the student consultation report

There is no single best method of conducting the activity which is often called student evaluation, sometimes student feedback, monitoring or appraisal, frequently student assessment but at Kingston, when conducted by the EDU, student consultation. Nor should there be. (For a discussion on the importance of triangulation, see O'Neil and Pennington 1992.) There are, however, some practices which have been developed during the programme at Kingston which are robust enough to be transportable to other situations.

Central to most university quality assurance processes has been a critical evaluation of the course since its last review. One essential element in this has been the comments and opinions of students currently studying the course. This feature has been given new emphasis in the UK, in the Higher Education Funding Councils' Teaching Quality Assessment process. While the course leaders are free to gather and present those comments in any way they choose, the offer made by the EDU has been to prepare a report which would be returned directly to them. In this way, the EDU has been able to survey student opinion across the whole institution and this in turn has helped establish the Unit's staff and educational development priorities. This information has counter-balanced the weaknesses inherent in the training needs analysis approach which normally derives all its information from academic staff and their managers.

There are many in higher education who are interested in what students think of their courses and of the staff who teach them. One of the political features which has secured the course consultation process is that it is *only* the course leader (and the course team) who can trigger it off. If the process was commissioned by a head of school or department, a dean, the chair of the academic quality committee, a pro-vice chancellor or any of the other interested parties it would be a significantly different process; and the students' approach to it would also be different.

It is important to recognize the nature of the relationships between students and the staff who teach them. While in these relationships there is the constant presence of obligations based on assessment, there is also the presence of mutual loyalty, the recognition that both parties are working hard, sometimes in a difficult environment, to foster the personal growth and intellectual development inherent in the educational process. The relationship between a student and her or his teachers is a primary relationship. When a third party (such as the EDU) asks the students to speak of that relationship, the fact that it is a confidential conversation which is returned directly to those most closely involved enables the students to speak with a freedom, an openness and a respect which would be cast in a different form if the exercise was an investigation, commissioned by outsiders and owned elsewhere in the institution. There is, for example, no convincing evidence that most students wish to become involved in contributing to staff appraisal processes or to decisions about performance-related pay, though it has been assumed that students who pay their own fees are more likely to want to do so. Information gathered for those purposes will be significantly different from course consultation information, even if the same techniques are used.

The process of student consultation

The student consultation exercise is a structured group conversation which is sometimes called a *snowball* or a *pyramid* discussion. The course leader finds the times (usually $1^{1}/_{4}$ hours) when students in each year group will be available. The time of year slightly affects the outcomes of the discussion; the most popular time is the last few weeks of the teaching year (before the revision period has started) but this is the time of maximum sensitivity about the examinations.

Two members of the EDU staff conduct each meeting. When stretched, the EDU has asked for help from the library staff. This has been very successful. After introductions which point out who has commissioned the work and why, the students are told that the conversation will be confidential but that it will result in a record (being made on an overhead projector or a flip chart) which will be used for the report.

'We are interested in anything which is affecting the way you are learning the course' is the rubric which drives the rest of the meeting. The students are asked to create their own agenda by listing two sets of points. These are described quite carefully. On the one hand, anything about the course which has been successful, which should be retained in future years, about which students feel positively, anything which (or anyone who) the students might wish to praise. On the other hand, anything which has given difficulty, features about which the students feel negative or wish to be critical, but (and this is essential) the students are requested to offer these up with positive recommendations for change.

Through this opening discussion the focus is on student learning and how it is being helped or hindered. This has proved to be a more realistic focus than looking at student satisfaction and its associated notions of students as customers or clients, without obstructing in practice the inclusion of items of general or institutional importance.

After five or ten minutes the students are asked to compare their points in a small group and to try to prepare a common list, preferably in some order of priority. One of them will have to be a speaker but the process offers a level of anonymity as they will be representing the group, not themselves. Then the full discussion starts, in which each group in turn is asked to make a point. This is tested against the other groups with questions such as: Is it generally agreed? Do the other groups have similar points? Should it be expanded? Or developed? Or contradicted? Throughout this discussion one of the EDU staff is keeping a record on the overhead projector. This record *has* to be agreed by the students; it is constantly referred to, checked, confirmed. If the students cannot come to an agreement about a point, then the disputed opinions are offered up for the staff to consider. Most discussions usually last about 45 minutes, cover between five and seven sheets of transparency and result in about 14 points, half of them being major points which take up most of the discussion time and which have been dealt with in detail.

The EDU staff then prepare a report, either structured around the main themes which have emerged from the meetings, or by giving an account of each separate year group meeting. The purpose of the report is to give the students' perspective, which the staff can then use (with other perspectives or imperatives) to adapt the course in the future. They are not created or written as a series of student judgements against which there is no appeal. Students might be mistaken in their perspectives, or they may expect the impossible. The reports are written to help the staff make changes.

Absolute confidentiality is maintained by the EDU. One copy of the report is handed to the course leader with the very strong advice that they should put it back to all the students to check its contents and to use it as the basis for a dialogue. The students have often asked to see the whole report during their meetings. But it is completely the course leaders' to use as they will and for them to decide how and in what form it should enter the public domain.

Occasionally students have wanted to make a major criticism of a member of staff. The procedure the EDU uses is to hear the comments but inform the students that such material, if included in a report, might well be counter-productive and would certainly restrict its circulation. However, their views and suggestions would be reported to and discussed with the course leader. In no case has this information come as a surprise to the leader, though often they are perplexed about how best to handle the problem. It requires a very high level of managerial skill to ensure that such problems do not occur and even greater skill to deal with them when they do. Successful staff development in this area would release substantial talent and expertise into creative rather than destructive directions.

What do students say? The praise given by students

Perhaps the most important message the students give us is that in general terms they are pleased with the education which they are experiencing. They recognize that many of the staff are working hard to do the best they can for their students and that the qualification for which they are studying will be awarded on the basis of a real educational experience, rigorously assessed.

The words which students select to describe a good or successful course are often words like 'relevant', 'practical' or 'real-world'. This may be a function of the distinctive vocational mission of the former polytechnics. Much of the discussion during a consultation meeting will be about the relationship between the learning of theory in relation to practice, whether that be in the laboratory, in the workshop or during a field trip, and the order in which these elements should be studied.

When praising staff the key word which returns many times is 'enthusiastic', and many academic staff have also been described as 'approachable' and 'friendly'. When students describe the elements which contribute to their picture of the ideal lecturer they mention someone who is interested in them, who has up-to-date knowledge, who can organize the course well, who has a sense of the structure of the course and where it is going, who has a clear purpose to each lecture or seminar and an awareness of what it is like not to know the subject. The way staff solicit or respond to students' questions is particularly important. Students respond well to lecturers who build up an atmosphere of confidence. Other staff whose work often comes in for praise from students are administrative staff such as school or course secretaries and resources staff such as librarians.

Often during a student consultation meeting students will report the difficulties they are having with the course in greater detail than the successes. However it is very common at the end of a meeting for a student to say (with general agreement from others) that, although they may have discussed several negative features, it is important that we (the EDU) do not take away the overall impression that the students are unhappy with the course. They often affirm that the core activities of the course are good and worthwhile and that, if only attention could be given to the points they had raised, they would see the course as excellent.

Although it is important to recognize work which is exceptional or special, at a time when the staff in higher education feel themselves to be under great pressure from structural changes it is also important to recognize and acknowledge the success of staff who are quietly and successfully maintaining the quality of their work. This student consultation process has often been a vehicle for such praise and has contributed to creating a more positive climate for further staff development work.

What do students say? The difficulties which students discuss

There is surprising agreement between students over what aspects of their courses present them with difficulties. The following is a selection of concerns which are common between subject areas and institutions.

Assessment

Students need to stay on courses and in their final year the classification of their degree matters greatly. Marks are a currency and a form of communication, existing in raw and refined forms, scoring success and failure. As the proportion of students for which each member of staff has to take educational responsibility grows larger, the time taken to complete each assessment to a standard which is useful as feedback for the student grows longer. This problem is appearing in many consultation meetings and occasionally students have asked for a different form of testing; quick, short activities with rapid feedback, but without marks, to allow for learning while risking failure. Students are also aware of inequity and weakness in lecturers' assessment practices such as inconsistency of treatment or confused criteria. The growing enthusiasm for group work is producing its own difficulties with assessment, in particular with students described as 'passengers' in a group. Students have commented that it is hard for them to 'read around the subject' because of the heavy burden of assessed coursework. They often feel that all their attention should be devoted to the specific work upon which the academic staff have clearly placed the highest value.

The relationship between the role of assessment and the development of good and enriching forms of learning and teaching is one of the key tasks to which progressive staff development should address itself. The frequency and intensity of this concern expressed through the student consultation meetings shows that this is now an urgent necessity.

Styles of teaching

As much of students' time is spent in lecture rooms listening to lectures, this form of teaching comes in for very full comment. The students' ideal lecturer has already been described as a well-organized and empathetic individual. Although many academic staff feel that there may be peculiarities within their particular discipline which make the teaching of it especially problematic, the range of comments which students make about lecturing are common across all disciplines.

Often students describe the experience of being presented with too much detail for too long a period, usually while copying down notes from the overhead projector. In many cases they say that staff have unrealistic assumptions about what they already know or how quickly they can take in and understand the material. (This is becoming a very common matter for first year students.) Lecturers sometimes speak in a monotonous tone or use unexplained jargon or clumsy sentence structures. Students often suggest that staff should acquire basic lecturing, communication and explanation skills as part of the tools of their trade. This is a central and essential staff development obligation which goes beyond merely acquiring these skills once during the first, probationary year. They need to be maintained, refreshed and improved throughout a teaching career.

A particular intensity of comment is reserved for lecturers whose response to questions reinforces the feeling of inadequacy which the questioning was designed to overcome. Students often mention how reluctant they are to ask questions in large lectures and use up other students' valuable time. The silent response to the familiar end-of-lecture ploy ('Does anyone have any questions?') should not be taken as evidence of contentment. Lecturers who manage to encourage participation, either in lectures or seminars, and who respond to challenge without seeing it as criticism, come in for particular praise. There is a rich variety of styles of questioning and many activities which can be used to involve students in educational discourse; it is possible to detect students' disappointment that often their teachers seem content to use so few.

The management of the course

The single most important issue which the student consultation meetings bring forward, and the element which, in its many ways, most influences the quality of the students' experience, is the effectiveness of the management of the course. As this era is one in which existing processes are under pressure, the skill with which the staff manage the process of changing the course is also of central importance. In this context, *course* refers to the whole programme of study, within which there might be separate courses, modules, units, options or electives. Even in modular degrees, it is important to find a focus for consultation above that of the separate modules; a course is more than the sum of its parts.

For the purposes of presenting the issues which concern students, a course encompasses the design of the curriculum, the disposition of resources, the daily and weekly operational practice and the bringing together of what is sometimes a very large body of academic, administrative and resource staff into what is seen by the students as a course team.

Curriculum design

The design of the curriculum and its progress through the university's quality assurance procedures is, in institutions formerly under the aegis of the CNAA, a very thorough process resulting in a course document which is expected to have a currency of at least five years. During those years, with developments in knowledge, changes in staffing and pressure on resources, the course evolves and adapts. When the subjects on a course come together in an integrated way, the students will comment on the success of the course; they enjoy the experience of relating understandings gathered in the different subject areas. However it is common to find that, over time, parts have come adrift.

There are three aspects to the problem of integration which are commonly mentioned by students. The first relates to the differences between the optional or elective courses which students often take in their second and usually in their final year. There are often very great differences in workload, in the time required and in the standards which the various lecturers expect. The students perceive this as an issue of inequity as they prepare for their final examinations.

The second results from the 'service' teaching relationship, in which a school or department provides the staff to teach one part of a course being managed by another school. There are often differences in assumptions about some of the most basic aspects of the educational process, such as the criteria for assessment, the amounts of work students might be expected to do and the level at which they should be doing it. The language of the service subject is often unfamiliar and hard to grasp, the examples often do not relate to the subject matter of the rest of the course and the assessment is often perceived as more threatening. The lecturers themselves usually have an office elsewhere, possibly on another site, and there are often more failures over communication and personal tutoring. Similar concerns need to be addressed in modular courses.

When mathematics, statistics and quantitative methods are taught through a 'service' arrangement, there is an extra level of emotional intensity with these subjects which almost guarantees that, in whatever course or institution the student consultation process is conducted, they will generate discussion. Difficulties in this area are particularly common with first-year students.

Underlying the difficulties expressed over mathematics is the more major concern of how universities should design at least the first year of their degree courses to comfortably accommodate students with a wide variety of academic backgrounds and previous experience. This pressure can only intensify as the proportion of citizens entering higher education increases.

This development represents a major challenge to universities and colleges; the level of investment in staff development will be one of the critical factors in meeting it.

The use of resources

The disposition of resources is a matter which students raise in a variety of ways. One such is the way the library supports the course. While the librarians invariably are praised for their helpfulness, many students feel that there are insufficient books and journals on the shelves and that the stock is out-of-date. This is often a function of the pressure generated by the larger number of students without an equivalent increase in library spending. Some forms of course design have put very great pressure on library space and environment. Group research projects, for example, generate noise and the need for small rooms in which to work on reference materials.

What emerges from many course consultations is the quality of the relationship between academic and resources staff and in particular the many ways in which academic staff can unwittingly maximize the pressure on scarce resources. Examples of this pressure are: giving a reference to a single text, essential for an imminent piece of assessed coursework, to a whole class; failing to move essential texts into reference, short loan or project loan; dispensing bibliographies and recommended reading which bear little relationship to stock held on the shelves; failing to inform students in advance of the programme of assessed coursework or seminars; choosing major whole-class research topics without consultation with librarians; designing whole-class group work with short deadlines but dependent on reference material. When student-to-staff ratios were low, it was possible to ride such difficulties. Today, any failure to address such areas of course organization condemns students unnecessarily to work in a climate of greater competition for scarcer resources. Bringing library and other resources staff into an effective course team is now an essential requirement; good staff development will be needed to under-pin this process.

Operational practice

The quality of the daily and weekly operational practice of the course (such as timetable changes, work schedules and the communication of information) is another area which receives close attention in these meetings. Often at the forefront of students' minds is the difficulty so many have with the timetable for completion of assessed work. In a few courses, the year tutors or the course leader will have planned this so well that the students' workload is distributed evenly. In others, individual lecturers are left to decide the timetable for themselves and the inevitable result is bunching at the end of the terms and a crisis of uncompleted work due for submission just before the examinations. Often the students are asked to complete very great amounts of work; small failures in their heavy work programme can rapidly multiply into a course-threatening crisis.

The course team

The key figure in a course team is the course leader, the person who is ultimately responsible for presenting the students for graduation. The rest of the team will be those with ownership: the teaching staff of the parent school with administrative or managerial responsibilities; perhaps as year tutors, admissions tutors or industrial placement tutors and staff in the parent school who have only teaching responsibilities. Staff from other schools (service teachers) and part-time staff also have links, as have administrative staff (the course or school secretary), the resources staff (librarians, staff from the central computer unit) and the technical staff maintaining the laboratories or workshops; even the institution's facilities staff (rooming officers, caretakers) could be members of the team in certain circumstances.

If the concept of a course team is not one which is common across the whole of the higher education sector, the notion of a course team which is actively managed is even less so. Nevertheless, the central fact which emerges from student consultation is that students experience learning on the course as a single, whole interaction involving a variety of staff whom students might (within reason?) assume are in contact with each other. The students are not often interested in the managerial shape of this team but they do draw attention to problems which result from its failure to operate as a unit; conversely, when the group functions well, students recognize the success.

In courses which are constructed so that, in each subject area, the teacher has full autonomy to design and deliver their unit, it has been hard to respond to the challenges of recent years in anything other than an incremental way. There are a number of areas of academic practice which can best be addressed by a course team acting together. Three such areas which emerge from consultation meetings are the need to reduce the amount (and improve the quality) of assessment; to reduce the content of over-full syllabuses without lowering standards; and to adapt courses to foster the development of a range of personal transferable skills.

Many issues raised by students result from the responses that course teams have made to the struggle to maintain educational quality in the face of either an increasing number of students or the reduction of resources for teaching. Those responses have usually been modest shifts and accommodations to new circumstances, alterations which have maintained the basic form of the course design, sometimes in the hope that the status quo might soon be restored. But the cumulative effect of these coping strategies can be to distort the course beyond what students find comfortable, or even in some cases acceptable. Three examples will underline this development:

seminar groups which have grown too large, or which are held too infrequently, to successfully complement the lecture programme; laboratory programmes which are now designed for completion over the whole year and which, for most students, are out of synchronization with lectures; a personal tutoring system which was once the main interaction between staff and students but which has been reduced to seeing students only when they have problems.

The single greatest pressure for staff development which emerges from student consultation meetings is the need to improve the full range of managerial and communication skills. This is not to be interpreted as simply strengthening an hierarchical line management. There are many ways to structure the course team and many ways to handle the rights and responsibilities of working colleagues, and some which are particularly suited to an academic environment. There is also a substantial personal responsibility imposed on staff to ensure that their self-management skills are of an order which enables them to act effectively in their main educational tasks. There may also be a substantial responsibility imposed at institutional management level to ensure that staff have sufficient power to discharge effectively their responsibilities. Nevertheless, student consultation meetings show that improvement in this area will have a direct and immediate impact on the quality of the students' learning.

This finding also represents a challenge to some of the distinctions which have been made between staff and educational development. In many institutions one sort of staff development and training is provided for allied staff, educational development is provided for academic staff and management development and training is offered to senior staff. Working outward from the students' experience suggests that the barriers and differences inherent in this approach must be overcome and that our current notions of appropriateness cannot be sustained.

Conclusion

It is important to realize the limits of whichever consultation process is being used. There is one key question, unspoken but central to the whole exercise. Do the staff really want to listen to their students? If they do, then the students already know this. They have picked it up in the way the course is handled, in the way that the lectures, seminars, field trips or laboratory exercises are conducted, in the way that staff relate to each other and to them. They know their opinions will be heard and valued. The EDU's student consultation process gives a good vehicle for this communication, but even a badly-designed questionnaire would be serviceable.

With such groups of staff, the consultation reports become part of a continuing discussion about what the next range of staff development should be. Taken with exam results, comments from external examiners, outcomes of course committee meetings and other feedback, the reports, particularly as they contain positive suggestions and recommendations, are very useful in planning for educational change. They give strong guidance in a positive framework.

When, for whatever reason, the staff are not really listening to their students, it almost does not matter which approach is adopted. Often the focus of the discussion of the outcomes is on the tip of the tongue, the whole process being described as the students' assessment; as if it were a mirror image of the assessment activity of staff.

The political acceptability of the process at Kingston University has been assisted by giving the course leaders complete power to handle the report in the way which best suits them. The variety of responses can be very broad, ranging from written rebuttals of the facts which the students have got wrong through to the widespread circulation of the document and the holding of a series of meetings to discuss and debate the course and its future. Such action recognizes that ownership of the course can be shared. When the whole process is used to strengthen and continue a real learning conversation between staff and students, then any third-party activity which has deepened and enriched that process is enormously worthwhile.

Part 2

Staff Development for All

We are concerned in Part 2 with staff development for roles and responsibilities other than those involved with teaching and learning. The history of staff development in higher education is characterized by a tendency to treat the needs of different groups of staff in different ways. Staff development activities have grown out of these very different and sometimes apparently conflicting perspectives. From their varied traditions, each chapter in Part 2 helps to build up a picture of what staff development for the whole institution might look like. In bringing them together with the discussions in Part 1, one cannot fail to notice differences in language and culture. Yet there are similarities and it is these which are important for the future.

An important theme in Part 2 is the interrelationship between the individual's development and the institution's development which, as we saw in Chapter 1, is complex. Effective professional development must rely on the willingness of staff to engage in it. But it is also an essential tool for institutional change. If strategic plans are to be achieved then development must be geared towards particular priorities and targets. Chapter 7 outlines the present state of staff development in higher education for those who are heading for or who have already reached senior management positions in universities. In examining the current situation against some models and approaches to top management development in other sectors and in higher education in different countries, Robin Middlehurst suggests that heads of institutions should provide a model of development both by being themselves engaged in it and also by setting up structures and systems wherein development can take place in all areas. Staff development can assist vice-chancellors and pro-vice-chancellors in shaping the very environment which can support or encourage individuals in the institution to undergo training or development and the particular forms which this might take. Thus their professional development can be crucial in addressing the issue of balancing institutional and individual development. We have already seen that there is a need for support and encouragement for staff development right from the top. This is echoed throughout Part 2.

Despite the apparently different orientation in Parts 1 and 2 there is much common ground. There is in Part 2 an emphasis on providing a variety of learning opportunities, on taking account of individual differences in learning and on the importance of offering programmes which enable individuals to gain academic credit. These are all themes which were stressed in relation to educational development for teaching and learning.

There is too, again an emphasis on the importance of reflection on practice. Workplace learning is viewed as an important vehicle for professional development in many areas and at all levels in the institutional hierarchy. There is a strong link here with the action research approaches which were discussed in Part 1 in relation to the development of teaching and learning strategies. This theme is echoed throughout Part 2. In Chapter 8, the nature and variety of staff development available for heads of academic departments is considered and the relationship of this to the staff development work of their staff explored. In the changing higher education context, the chapter begins by asking why the training of heads of department is now a crucial issue. John Davies points to the problems of transferring learning to the workplace when training is undertaken away from it in formal courses organized elsewhere. There is clearly a role for such activities in raising general awareness and for the sharing of ideas and experiences, but heads of departments need, he suggests, to be actively involved in designing their own learning programmes and for this to be grounded in the day-to-day problems they experience.

In Chapter 9 John Doidge discusses the use of quality teams comprised of groups of staff who collectively attempt to solve problems in the workplace. Quality circles work on a cycle of action and reflection, theory being used as a vehicle for understanding the issues, not as an end in itself. The language is different but the links with action research are obvious. Institutions of higher education owe much of the success of what they do to the allied staff who work either directly or indirectly alongside academic colleagues. This approach serves to ground staff development in the immediate concerns of the staff themselves. It is also a way of empowering staff.

Chapter 9 also relates the growth in staff development activities in higher education in relation to wider developments in training such as, in the UK, the establishment of national training targets, national vocational qualifications, and Total Quality Management. These schemes for structuring, crediting and evaluating staff development in organizations are having an increasing impact in higher education. The chapter reminds us that there is much to learn from the experience of our industrial neighbours.

Staff development, then, is about the development of institutions as much as individuals and groups within it. As individuals develop their understanding of the influences and issues which drive their practice, so the institution changes. The form of organization of staff development which an institution takes is a measure of its stage of development. The history of staff development has taught us that the traditional piecemeal emphasis is going to be inappropriate for tomorrow's needs. As the institution grows and learns, new structures for the organization and practice of staff development are required. These new structures will themselves need to be revised and developed in the future as the university changes and grows. The challenge will ultimately be to establish ways of working which are capable of change as institutional needs and priorities are reassessed.

In Chapter 10, Liz Beaty describes the work of a group of staff consisting of people at different levels of the organization – including managers and those with the ability to design and run good staff development programmes. It was brought together to work on the problem of how to bring about significant change in the organization. Such a group has the potential to work across the hierarchy but also to do itself out of a job. For in the process of reflection and action, the institution develops its collective understanding of the nature of the development process. The chapter illustrates the essentially dynamic nature of staff development. It also underlines the role of dialogue in developing understanding in key individuals of the nature, purposes, functions and institutional potential of staff development. This is an important part of their own professional development. Here institutional and individual development are aligned.

7

Top Training: Development for Institutional Managers

Robin Middlehurst

Linking the words top and training is a provocative act, since it is commonly assumed that those who reach the pinnacle of their organizations no longer require further training or development. In this chapter, I argue that such assumptions are dangerously complacent in an environment that is constantly changing and in organizations whose core business is training and education. Instead, I propose an approach which embraces continuing and active participation in learning at all levels of the organization, including the top.

In developing the argument, a number of issues will be considered. When planning approaches to training and development, the context in which individuals operate and from which they rise to senior positions is of primary concern. Of parallel importance is the nature of the role and responsibilities that they are expected to undertake. As one gets closer to designing learning opportunities other issues are relevant, for example, individual backgrounds, skills and expertise; different models of development which might be appropriate; and the timing of developmental opportunities. Where new approaches are envisaged, it is also useful to consider and assess the range of provision that is currently available. These issues are addressed below, after giving brief attention to some conceptual matters.

Conceptual matters

The terms *education, training* and *development* of managers mean different things in different organizations. In their study *The Making of British Managers*, Constable and McCormick (1987) offer the following interpretation of the three terms:

* management education: refers to those processes which result in formal qualifications up to and including postgraduate degrees (i.e., education for management);

- management training: includes the formal learning activities which may not lead to qualifications and which may be undertaken at any time in a working career;
- management development: is broader still, job experience and learning from others are integral parts of the development process.

In many large commercial organizations, management training and development for senior staff will be built upon earlier foundations of management education. In universities, where institutional managers have had a variety of career experience (often predominantly professional rather than managerial), this assumption does not always hold. The general lack of formal management education among members of staff in universities, particularly academic staff, has implications for the design of management training and development opportunities since the notion of building these on common management education foundations does not apply.

Burgoyne (1988) offers an alternative perspective from that of Constable and McCormick when he describes management development as 'the management of managerial careers' and a managerial career as 'the biography of a person's managerial work life'. This conception has two important implications: first, that development is a broad concept involving formal and informal learning; and second, that responsibility for development rests both with the individual manager and with the organization of which they are a part. Burgoyne suggests further that there are two facets to managerial careers that can be managed. The structural facet includes the pattern of managerial tasks, roles and activities that the person is engaged in over time, while the developmental facet encompasses the processes of change, learning and development that affect how the person shapes and performs these tasks, roles and activities. Both facets need to be integrated into 'the management of managerial careers'. Burgoyne's interpretation of management development offers a useful starting point for this chapter.

A further conceptual matter concerns the distinction that is often made between management and leadership. For the purposes of our discussion, the theoretical distinctions between the two terms are acknowledged (Zaleznik 1977; Bennis 1989; Kotter 1990a), while recognizing that in practice, the two functions are closely linked. Individual roles at strategic levels may be more closely oriented towards either leadership or management, although an emphasis on both activities is necessary in order to relate strategy to implementation. The term management will therefore be used generically to include both activities and where necessary the finer distinctions between leadership and management will be highlighted.

Context

The external context in which UK universities have operated since the beginning of the 1980s will be a familiar one to most readers. This context is common to many parts of the public (as well as private and professional sectors) in the UK and has parallels with the economic and political environment of universities in other parts of the world, for example, in Australia, the US and parts of Europe.

A number of themes which are presently affecting UK higher education are important for the design of management development in universities. The first and most obvious is the change in the shape of higher education, from a binary (and elite) to a unitary (and mass) system. Institutions have become larger and their student populations more heterogeneous. These physical developments have implications for the structures, systems and cultures of institutions as well as for the patterns of their core business.

A second theme is the continuing squeeze on resources. Pressure on the public purse has produced political emphases on efficiency gains, cost-measuring and cutting, value-for-money and accountability in the use of public funds, as well as a focus on entrepreneurial and revenue-generating activities by universities themselves. Within this climate, a premium is placed on robust management systems within a framework of creative leadership.

A tighter financial environment has increased competition between universities themselves and between universities and other organizations. The growing prominence of the market in the affairs of universities has also brought with it a greater focus on the interests of higher education's customers. For strategic managers, these themes have required an emphasis on defining the institution's mission and market niche, and on promoting these assiduously. A new emphasis on quality management approaches has also been encouraged; an emphasis that is actively supported by the governments' desire – in the UK as elsewhere (Taylor 1987) – to scrutinise more closely the operations and outcomes of the institutions it funds.

In combination, these themes and the altered topography of UK higher education, have produced a dynamic operating context for institutional managers. Universities and colleges have had to adapt to external political and economic pressures as well as respond to the internal forces of disciplinary and pedagogical developments. In common with the rest of society, institutions are also subject to the pervading influence of technological change. Because of the nature of their core business, technological developments affect all aspects of university life, from teaching, research and academic support to administration and management.

Institutional managers have a particular responsibility to interpret and to manage the external context of the institution. However, they are also obliged to recognize and respond to the internal context: the nature and variety of institutional business, the diversity of staff; the traditions, values and cultures that permeate the university; the financial position, geographical location and physical condition of the enterprise. The management task is shaped by the particular internal features of the university as well as by the pressures from outside the institution. Both are filtered through the perceptions, attitudes, competence and past experience of senior managers and their constituents.

Internally, the university is a complex organization. Focusing on different aspects of the university, organization theorists have described the institution as a collegium (highlighting community, self-governance and consensus decision-making); as a bureaucracy (emphasizing defined roles and formal command structures); as a political entity (noting differences of power and values, competition and conflict); and as a cybernetic system (pointing to loosely-coupled units and to self-correcting mechanisms in the university) (Bensimon *et al.* 1989). Recently, an 'entrepreneurial image' has been added (Davies 1987) which depicts the university as a holding company for a number of semi-autonomous satellite units. All these perspectives reflect something of the internal reality of universities, whether in terms of present structures or past values which are still visible in the attitudes and responses of staff. An important part of the strategic management task is to interpret and to shape this internal environment so as to achieve optimum institutional performance.

The degree of change that has characterized universities in recent years as well as the range and complexity of the strategic management role suggests a need for new incumbents to senior management posts to undertake a variety of learning tasks. They will need to take time to brief themselves on the nature of their roles and the issues that face them in particular institutions. They will need to consider the ways in which other organizations have tackled strategic problems and will need to explore the particular environment in which they must operate. Since neither the environment, the institution nor the individuals will remain static, new managers will also need to develop analytical and practical tools to help them to diagnose and to create appropriate strategies for institutional change.

Roles and responsibilities

In order to design appropriate developmental opportunities, one must understand the nature of the role to be performed. The general context described above already begins to define some of the roles and responsibilities that institutional managers will be expected to undertake. A simple four-phase model, offered by Kotter (1990a), summarizes some of the key requirements more explicitly, in terms of leadership and management action.

The first responsibility of strategic managers, Kotter argues, is to create (or maintain) an agenda for the organization. In leadership terms, this will involve establishing a direction, a vision of the future and strategies for producing any changes needed to achieve the vision. On the management side, the complementary activities of planning and budgeting are important initially.

A second leadership responsibility involves aligning people, that is, communicating the intended direction by words and deeds to all those whose co-operation may be needed. Through this process, coalitions and teams are created that understand the vision and strategies and accept their validity.

Complementary management tasks in this phase are organizing and staffing. These establish a structure for accomplishing plans, allow delegation of responsibility and authority for carrying out the plans, provide policies and procedures which guide action and create methods or systems which monitor implementation. Together, this second tier of leadership and management responsibility develops a human network for achieving the agenda.

The third level, which Kotter labels execution includes the management activity of controlling and problem-solving (that is, monitoring results against plans, identifying deviations, and re-planning and organizing to solve problems). Leadership at this point, Kotter suggests, involves motivating and inspiring, energizing people to overcome major political, bureaucratic and resource barriers to change by satisfying very basic, but often unfulfilled, human needs.

The fourth phase depicts the outcomes that can be expected from successfully combining leadership and management action. Management will produce a degree of predictability and order and has the potential of consistently producing key results expected by various stakeholders. Leadership, on the other hand, will produce change and has the potential to produce useful change, for example, new activities that are wanted in the marketplace and new approaches to staff which can make the organization more competitive.

Kotter's model is both too simple and too rational to capture the untidy reality and the conflicting pressures that currently impinge on universities. It does not adequately reflect the flatter, less hierarchical and less tightly-coupled management structures of many universities compared with industrial or commercial organizations, the considerable dispersion of leadership responsibility across the institution or the autonomy of basic units, extended recently by greater devolution of managerial responsibility from the centre. None the less, the model does serve to highlight some of the management functions that are required even if their form requires modifying in the university setting.

Other authors draw attention to non-linear features of management, including its complexities and uncertainties. Mintzberg (1973) notes the speed and range of tasks undertaken by managers, while Birnbaum (1989) and others highlight the constraints on leadership in universities as well as the ambiguities and dilemmas which face strategic managers (Cohen and March 1986; Hampden-Turner 1990). A combination of rational and defined elements, with opportunities for challenge and breadth, for exercising flexibility and creativity and for developing intuition so as to respond quickly to a range of issues will clearly need to be part of any training and development approach which prepares or supports those at the top.

In looking more closely at the roles of institutional managers, it is obvious that functions differ (for example between the Finance Director and Director of Estates or between the Vice Chancellor and his or her deputies). The balance of leadership and management responsibilities may vary, as will the direct responsibility for resources, whether financial, material or human. The precise range of responsibilities undertaken by individual senior managers will also differ according to the requirements of the institution itself and the balance of roles needed at the top. Detailed discussion of individual roles is beyond the scope of this chapter (but can be found elsewhere, Green and McDade 1991; Middlehurst *et al.* 1992). What is more important to note for our present topic is that strategic management involves both an individual role (often as head of a department or function) and a collective role as part of a senior management team and a member of the wider institutional community. Green and McDade (1991), concentrating on senior managers in American universities, outline a range of responsibilities which are of general relevance to senior institutional managers. Building on their work and our own (Middlehurst *et al.* 1992), the following responsibilities can be identified, *inter alia*, as part of the senior management role in a changing world:

- providing leadership for varied and conflicting constituencies;
- overseeing or directing operations (leading the development and implementation of policies, designing structures and strategies to achieve objectives, planning for the most efficient and effective deployment of resources);
- securing resources and overseeing their use and development;
- marketing, and generating new business;
- establishing an appropriate working climate (through policies, systems, standards, support, communication, problem-solving, and the active modelling of values);
- ensuring smooth management (adequate and accurate planning, monitoring and evaluation of policies and procedures, co-ordination and delegation of tasks and activities, information management, decision-taking and arbitration);
- relating the institution (and its units) to external constituencies (through implementing legal requirements, representing and reporting institutional operations and outcomes, hosting and attending ceremonial events, liaison and intelligence gathering, interpreting, explaining and negotiating between internal and external worlds);
- building and developing teams, networks and alliances;
- promoting and managing innovation, change and institutional development.

This list illustrates the wide range of strategic responsibilities that will be faced by senior managers. Given the breadth of these tasks, it is obvious that narrowly conceived and short-term training will not be sufficient to prepare individuals for senior roles or to support them when in post, but it is also clear that some preparation and continuing development will be required. Those conceptions of training and development which take a broader view within a longer time-scale are likely to be most appropriate. The work of McCall *et al.* (1988) which identified 'the lessons of experience' and which suggests how to maximize their learning potential, or of Mumford and his colleagues (1987) which focuses upon helping directors to learn how to learn more effectively, provide some useful pointers for the design of appropriate management learning opportunities.

Capabilities

Outlining the general responsibilities of senior managers already suggests some of the task-related capabilities required for these roles. However, these are underpinned by other capabilities – intellectual, social, technical and professional.

Intellectual, cognitive and conceptual capabilities

Several authors (Bensimon *et al.* 1989; Streufert and Nogami 1989; Hunt 1992) point to 'cognitive complexity' as an important top-level leadership capability which enables individuals to create sophisticated mental maps of strategic interrelationships over time. This kind of intellectual complexity is needed to cope with the complexity of large, modern organizations within a dynamic environment. It has been variously defined as: the ability to differentiate and integrate large numbers and ranges of stimuli in the short run and across long periods of time; the flexibility to understand situations through the use of different and competing scenarios; the ability to combine rational and intuitive knowledge and skills; the ability to conceptualize complex and ambiguous relationships. *High level analytical skills* is often used as a short-hand descriptor for cognitive complexity.

More generalized classifications refer to the conceptual skills required at senior levels. Beyond analytical ability these include: logical thinking; proficiency in concept formation; creativity in problem-solving and idea generation; ability to analyse events and perceive trends, to anticipate problems and opportunities; deductive and inductive reasoning; the ability to process information, to plan and take decisions, particularly under conditions of ambiguity (Hunt 1992).

Other cognitive capabilities are related to personality variables such as those identified in the Myers and McCaulley and Sternberg Intellectual Style instruments (1985; 1990 respectively) and to certain predispositions (Hunt 1992). These cognitive predispositions are in effect inclinations towards leadership, evident in an individual's sense of competence, self-worth and self-belief (their self-efficacy) as well as their need for socially-oriented power. In combination with particular value preferences and ideologies (about organizations, people and their interactions), these cognitive dimensions help shape such critical leadership tasks as goal and strategy setting and organizational design.

Ensuring that new incumbents to senior management positions possess these intellectual capabilities is the task of search committees and appointment panels, but assisting individuals to develop their intellectual capacities further can be achieved through structured development opportunities.

Social capabilities

Within this category fall the familiar human relations and interpersonal capacities that are required of managers at all levels, but which are of particular importance for the teamwork required at the top of institutions. These social capabilities include knowledge about human behaviour and interpersonal processes; ability to understand the feelings, attitudes and motives of others from what they say and do (social sensitivity and empathy); the ability to communicate clearly and effectively (speech and written fluency, persuasiveness, the ability to give and receive feedback); the ability to establish co-operative and effective relationships (tact and diplomacy); the ability to mediate between conflicting individuals and to handle disturbances (conflict resolution). Political skills, such as the ability to understand and develop power relationships or to build coalitions might also be included (Pavett and Lau 1983; Kotter 1990a), alongside the capacity to deal with the ethical dimensions of strategic management (Cadbury 1992; Badaracco and Ellsworth 1989).

Interpersonal capabilities are paralleled by intra-personal capacities, for example the ability to understand one's own strengths and weaknesses, the capacity to be introspective about one's impact on others, the ability to organize oneself and manage time effectively, the ability to learn and apply learning successfully. Physical and emotional resilience, the ability to manage stress, to cope with ambiguity, setbacks or failure, to take risks and to embrace change and new opportunities – all these are also important aspects of intra-personal capabilities (Middlehurst 1993).

It is important for individuals to be able to assess their inter- and intra-personal capabilities in advance of applying for senior posts. It is also necessary for appointing panels to gain insights into candidates' strengths and weaknesses in these areas. Outside higher education, the use of assessment centres is common both to assist in identifying potential and to evaluate present capabilities. Aspects of these centres could usefully be built into developmental provision in higher education.

Technical and professional capabilities

Interpretations of technical capabilities differ between the generic and the specific, the latter usually relating to management capabilities. Hunt (1992) offers a generic interpretation; knowledge about the methods, processes, procedures and techniques for conducting a specialized activity, and the ability to use tools and to operate equipment related to that activity. If one associates this interpretation with management, then the capabilities identified by Kotter (1990a) above are usually inferred: that is, planning and decision-making; organizing and staffing; budgeting and operational control. Where management is undertaken in organizational settings, then the capacity to understand organizational structure, systems and culture will be needed. In organizations of professionals (such as universities) competence as a professional and understanding and appreciation of professional activities, values and culture are also likely to be prerequisites for senior institutional positions.

Individuals entering senior management positions will have had a variety of professional and technical experience which is valuable for their new post. However, for many individuals, the entry to senior posts involves a transition from operational to strategic management levels. Assessing the technical capabilities required and matching individual competence against these requirements is a necessary part of this transition. New skills and knowledge can be developed in tandem with this initial process of evaluation, and should continue as experience is gained.

Developmental purposes

Why should individuals and their organizations invest time and resources on management learning? At a basic level, the answer must be to ensure competence since higher education institutions are large-scale consumers of public money, they own valuable property and equipment, they are complex businesses serving a variety of important local, national and individual interests. Neither the nation nor the individual institution can afford incompetence.

Competence is usually interpreted in terms of the individual's level of technical or professional skill. In the case of senior managers, this may, for example, involve competence in financial, personnel, estate management or academic administration and services. However, a wider level of general management and organizational competence is also required since managers contribute significantly to the design and operation of the framework in which the work of the whole institution is conducted. Poor management at the top (or at other levels) directly affects the capacity and the motivation of individuals and groups to teach, research and learn to their fullest potential.

Besides competence, there are other purposes which may be served and benefits which may accrue through investing in management learning. Depending on the timing and nature of opportunities, some of the following benefits are available to institutions: matching individual needs and strengths to the institutional agenda (for example, matching people to jobs, maximizing strengths or reducing turnover); fostering shared goals and common understanding (for example, building teams, developing linkages across the institution or improving communications); promoting institutional renewal and achieving change (by identifying new leaders, by introducing new ideas and by supporting different styles and perspectives) (Green and McDade 1991). If a wider view of management learning is taken, then benefits will include contributions to policy development, to institutional evaluation and critical reflection on performance and practice.

At an individual level, other purposes are served. Developmental events provide an opportunity to acquire new knowledge and skills, to make contacts and build networks, to increase self-confidence, to reflect and gain alternative perspectives, to be stimulated and challenged. The information and knowledge acquired through formal events can be applied in the workplace, the major learning environment for most managers. However, through focusing attention on the learning potential of the work environment, other important lessons can be learned: how to set and implement agendas, how to handle relationships, insight into basic values and one's own 'leadership temperament' (Green and McDade 1991). In most higher education institutions which do not have a tradition of managing managerial careers or of making the job a learning experience, the onus for seeking developmental opportunities falls largely to the individual.

Outside higher education, investment in training and development is better established and for the most part, well-accepted (indeed, universities are involved in serving this market). The rationale for such investment includes many of the benefits outlined above, with the addition of some significant environmental factors. In an era of global competition and rapid change, where cost efficiency, quality and value are directly associated by most commercial organizations with increased profitability and market-share, continuous investment in developing the full potential of a company's human resource is seen as essential. These assumptions and principles are both espoused and put to the test in initiatives such as the Malcolm Baldridge Quality Award in the US or the European Quality Award which operates in Western Europe. As we have noted above, the current operating environment of universities is not dissimilar to that which faces businesses. This fact suggests at least one reason for an equivalent investment in staff and management development.

A further argument concerns the internal world of the university. We have already seen that this world is changing under the joint pressures of knowledge expansion, new technology and the imperatives of curriculum development and delivery. Yet at its heart, the *raison d'etre* of universities remains the same, they are institutions which provide (others with) learning. How much more dynamic and effective might they be as organizations if they were to capitalize on this mission for their own advantage? Developing a climate and a structure for maximizing institutional learning is likely not only to benefit those within the university through enhanced competence, confidence and creativity, but also to improve the depth and range of professional services offered by universities to their clients.

These arguments are relevant to staff development in general, but have particular significance for senior staff for a number of reasons. First, the conceptions of the organization held by senior staff, the ways in which they design structures and create and implement policies will have considerable impact on the functioning of the university. Encouraging a broader vision

of the strategic management task which encompasses competent management of the institution in its present form with an ability to assist the
institution's continuing development is likely to be of benefit to the organization as a whole. Second, as leaders, senior staff must create a climate in
which the development of individuals and the development of processes
and products/services is taken seriously and where opportunities for learning are maximized. An aspect of creating such a climate is 'modelling the
way' (Kouzes and Posner 1987) or setting an example to others of what can
be achieved through management learning. A further and more subtle
aspect of developing a learning climate involves encouraging initiative,
enterprise and the flow of new ideas within the university, as well as building trust and tolerating failure, where an evaluation of failure leads to
learning and to ultimate success.

Models and approaches

Two useful frameworks for thinking about management development or
for designing approaches to development are provided by Mumford *et al.*
(1987) and by Burgoyne (1988). Mumford and his colleagues provide a
model of three types of learning process which were identified in their
study, *Developing Directors*. Type 1 is labelled Informal Managerial and refers
to the accidental learning processes that occur naturally within managerial
activities. Type 2, Integrated Managerial, are the opportunistic processes
where natural managerial activities are structured in such a way as to make
use of the available learning opportunities. Type 3 includes the planned
processes which are part of Formal Management Development, namely
those planned activities which take place away from normal managerial
activities.

In higher education, perhaps even more than elsewhere, most attention
is given to formal management development through the provision of seminars, workshops, courses and other types of learning programme. Many of
these events take place away from the institution itself and may be divorced
in other ways from the main activities of senior managers. However, there
has been increasing recognition of the part played by informal, largely
unplanned experiences in the development of individuals (Middlehurst
1989; McCall *et al.* 1988). Work is being done to increase the potential
benefits of Integrated Managerial learning, for example, in the use of action-
learning in higher education, but there is scope for greater capitalization
of this area of learning.

The second framework describes how management development can
eventually be assimilated with organizational development. In this way,
business priorities can be integrated with the developmental needs and
interests of individuals. Burgoyne suggests that organizations pass through
different stages of maturity in terms of management development, depending

on a range of factors such as size, market position, culture and traditions. In the case of higher education, we might also include responsiveness to external pressures as an additional factor.

At the first level of maturity, Burgoyne records that management development is left to natural processes. For example, in a small or start-up operation, such as a new research institute or educational development centre, management learning can be achieved intuitively and naturally by having to acquire new knowledge and capabilities rapidly in order to be able to work effectively. At the second level, action is still taken in a largely unstructured way to meet *ad hoc*, usually individual needs, such as a requirement to update skills or knowledge. The third level is more focused, as action is taken to establish the kind of developmental approaches which best meet business needs.

Subsequent levels are still more structured and sophisticated. At level four, management development helps to implement corporate policy; at level five it feeds into policy making and finally, at level six, management development (in the sense of management learning) is the focal point in policy creation. At this point, integration between the learning of individuals and the development of the organization is achieved. Level six, which has not yet been attained by many organizations, Burgoyne reports, comes close to the ideal of the learning organization (Garratt 1987; Pedler *et al.* 1991) and to the principles of continuous improvement contained in the philosophy of Total Quality Management. Here, the ideal is for the actions of every individual in the organization to form part of a learning, improving and change process (Wille 1990).

Higher education institutions are likely to be at varying stages on Burgoyne's developmental ladder, with few institutions having moved beyond level three or four. While management development features in institutions' staff development provision, it is often geared more to individual needs than to the implementation of institutional strategy. The identification of management roles and responsibilities across staff groups is also largely unsystematic, so that management development tends to be associated with relatively narrow groups of staff or functional areas, for example, middle management (typically academic heads or administrators) or programme leaders rather than being spread widely, vertically and horizontally within the institution.

The notion of training and development is also either narrowly or negatively conceived. Too often, it is seen as a means of rectifying deficiencies, as unnecessary for already competent professionals, or as an add-on for the individual, specifically at levels below the top, with only indirect benefit to the organization (Middlehurst *et al.* 1992; Middlehurst, 1993). The connection between individual development and improved performance is now being made more frequently, prompted by such pressures as appraisal and performance review, but the link between institutional change and individual development achieved through the process of structured management learning has so far not been widely appreciated.

Current provision

In a recent overview paper (USDU 1993), the national Universities' Staff Development Unit listed the following features in the approaches to leadership and management development in UK higher education:

- provision is largely staff-category focused (mainly on academic and administrative staff, rather than being functionally based);
- provision is largely off-the-job (short, *ad hoc* courses);
- there is little appreciation within universities of the need to foster managerial and leadership competencies throughout a career and from its early stages;
- there is only limited evidence of provision being conceived in terms other than courses; shadowing, mentoring, job-rotation and other approaches are not happening either systematically or widely across the higher education system.

The kind of programmes that currently exist were also listed. For senior staff these included:

- national short courses and seminars (for example, an annual two-day seminar for vice chancellors and similar events for deputy principals and for senior administrators);
- locally organized in-house programmes on management themes;
- European programmes and conferences, usually of limited duration (up to one week).

The picture that is given here is likely to be a partial one since it does not capture the variety of development opportunities that exist within professional activities, for example, by running workshops or making presentations at professional conferences. There are also other current activities which, although not classed as developmental, have considerable learning potential, both for individuals and for institutions. These include: being an external examiner in several institutions; acting as editor for a learned journal; participating in external committees; or acting as governor or director for outside organizations; being seconded to the Funding Council as an assessor or acting as an auditor for the Higher Education Quality Council. In addition, the process of preparing for external review at departmental or institutional level is a potentially invaluable management learning opportunity. While these activities are not those with which strategic managers will continue to be directly concerned, they none the less contribute to the understanding of higher education processes and as such are a necessary part of institutional managers' background knowledge and understanding.

Developmental activities for top managers in UK universities, organized within the sector, are sparse and tend to be focused either on the transition to strategic management roles or on briefing events on topical issues. Outside organizations such as business schools or management consultancies offer a more varied diet and can tailor their activities, for example, to the needs of senior management teams or to specific institutional requirements. In other sectors and in overseas higher education, the picture is much more varied.

In the United States, for example, the American Council on Education has for twenty-five years been running a year-long programme for those interested in preparing themselves for institutional leadership. The programme is organized around an internship or attachment to senior management in an unfamiliar institution. One senior member of staff acts as mentor and guide and the ACE Fellow undertakes a management project on behalf of the host institution. In addition, Fellows attend three week-long seminars on aspects of management, leadership and higher education policy and read and travel widely to other campuses and to higher education conferences. The programme aims to instil commitment to the values of higher education, to develop an understanding of policy issues and to extend good management practice.

An example from Sweden offers a different approach. The aim of the Swedish senior management programme (organized at national level in the late 1980s) was to strengthen university leadership and to model 'presidential success' based on examples of an effective American presidency. A visit to a successful American university was planned for four university presidents – half the total Swedish population of presidents – and their registrars. In advance of the visit, detailed briefings were given on the US higher education system, the university to be visited; in addition, a study of current leadership at each of the participating Swedish universities was commissioned from outside consultants.

The visit to the American university included presentations by the president and his/her deputies, discussions with a variety of administrators within the university and with prominent national figures in higher education. Visits and discussions were also held with competitor institutions in the same locality. Topics discussed included strategic planning, fund-raising, internal communication and information processes, promoting quality in teaching and research, and methods of performance review. The visit was regarded as successful enough to warrant the organization of a similar trip for deans of the selected Swedish universities six months later. The impact of the US visit on university life in the universities concerned was considerable, according to the organizers of the event. Notable effects were a new interest in the quality of undergraduate teaching by the Swedish vice chancellors; the establishment of new Teaching Centres in the universities (directed by recognized 'star teachers'); the development of internal review systems for teaching; and the establishment of faculty development programmes. Current quality assessment arrangements at national level in Sweden can build on the foundations established through these early developmental initiatives.

The Swedish example of a round-table seminar has much in common with the week-long *live case-study* approach adopted by the Conference of European Rectors in their programme for new or prospective university heads. In this latter case, the university which hosts the seminar also invites participants on the programme to act as consultants on a management issue or project that the university wishes to tackle. Both participants in this exchange learn from the process; the 'students' gain insights into the realities of strategic management and the university acquires a range of disinterested expert perspectives on the issue concerned. The way in which the whole study is structured both ensures that learning takes place and is a learning opportunity in itself.

The pattern of using live problems from the work environment in a structured way so as to create developmental opportunities is one which is also favoured outside higher education. The Civil Service's four-week Top Management Programme, for example, includes a live case-study in either a public or private sector organization in which participants engage in internal research, problem-solving, and evaluation for the organization concerned. The case-study complements other elements in the programme which include theoretical sessions, for example, on strategy, marketing, economics, finance, managing people; national and international trends analysis (of economic, social, political and technological trends); presentations from senior practitioners; and approaches to self-assessment.

The Health Service's Top Management Programme, mounted by the King's Fund College, takes the notion of integrated managerial learning (Mumford *et al.* 1987) further still by alternating periods of study and reflection with time at work, supported by action learning sets formed from participants on the programme. The particular benefits of the Health Service programme are its length (it extends over a year, like the ACE Fellows programme discussed above); that it is participant-led and thus responsive to individual and institutional needs; that experience, analysis, experiment and reflection are combined and personal and intellectual challenge are linked with opportunities to extend knowledge, skills, attitudes and responses to strategic management.

In looking both at the provision available inside and outside higher education and the conceptual models which underpin existing or ideal provision, a number of important elements can be identified. These are likely to form valuable components in any approach to top management development. They include:

- a concentration on integrated managerial learning (through live case-studies, structured secondments, internal projects, and action or self-managed learning);
- bespoke programmes (where design and content are based on clear diagnosis of institutional and/or individual requirements);
- challenge and variety (where different perspectives, approaches, organizations, sectors, problems and types of participant are brought together);
- a key focus (such as strategic management, managing change or evaluating and promoting quality);
- opportunity for self and peer analysis as well as analysis of issues;

- a combination of reflection and review with presentation of new ideas and models, problem-solving, experimentation and structured evaluation of experience;
- an emphasis on high-level macro issues (economic, social, environmental, political trends) with input from experts in these areas;
- assistance in developing process models and tools (for example, for diagnosing organizational culture, for institutional self-assessment, for individual self-assessment and diagnosis of learning approaches, for managing change).

Stages of development

As was noted at the start of this chapter, management training and development are usually built on a foundation of management education. In universities such education will often have been haphazard and *ad hoc* since the management of managerial careers has not, in general, been undertaken systematically and formally. Management education will have been acquired informally through progressing to ever greater responsibilities and by extending the scope of one's role as an academic, an administrator or a professional. However, only in some areas (for example, among administrators and some professional groups) has management education been formalized and codified into different levels of knowledge, skill and capabilities, and even here, there is considerable adaptation in progress in response to wider structural changes facing higher education.

Given this relative absence of formal management education and the variety of backgrounds from which senior staff will have emerged to fill strategic roles, a starting point for any developmental opportunity will need to be testing and diagnosis of needs, interests, previous experience and knowledge. Even where generic programmes are offered, for example, to a group of new vice-chancellors, individual benefit will be maximized where self and comparative evaluation has been undertaken in advance. A stage of testing and diagnosis of this kind should ideally underpin any major transitions (including an assessment of whether such a transition is appropriate for an individual), and should particularly underpin the important transition from operational to strategic levels of management.

A second stage is that of preparation for undertaking a strategic role. Preparation can be divided into long-term preparation (which would come under the heading of management education and has been discussed above) and direct preparation. The latter form will be linked with appointment to a strategic position and many of the examples of existing provision given earlier fall into this category. Preparation for senior roles can take a variety of forms: from formal programmes to work shadowing, mentoring, working in an acting or deputizing capacity, or informal reading, discussion, observation and reflection. Many individuals will spend a considerable amount of time consulting with others in similar positions in other universities or in outside organizations. Internally, time may be spent on visiting different parts of the institution in order to become familiar with its operations. Time is also likely to be spent on team-building and getting to know the other individuals and sections that are involved with particular activities or functions at strategic and operational levels. Often, setting in motion a series of internal reviews provides helpful information which not only aids the development of strategic initiatives but also helps the individual to assess what the present state of the institution or unit is and what value can be added by their own perspectives, skills or experience (or indeed where there may be gaps in their portfolio of expertise).

A third stage relates to continuing development and here the pattern becomes more complex. Continuing development can be related to the needs of the individual, to those of the group or team and to those of the institution. The third group of institutional or business-driven needs can also be described as collective needs, although they may include different levels or groups in the institution with a different focus at each level. For example, a strategic need to improve university admissions will require developmental activities at several levels of the institution, from admissions' officers to registry staff, programme leaders, heads of department and those responsible for the framing of admissions policies. The need to develop institutional performance indicators may require developmental activities at senior level in parallel with activities in departments/units which may then come together in a management conference for both strategic and operational groups.

Within the category of continuing development, a range of potential needs can be identified which is based on our earlier analysis of the context of higher education and the particular responsibilities of those at senior levels of management. These needs (which may be in the form of a need for knowledge, insight, comparative perspectives, skills or attitude change) can in turn apply to any of the three target groups identified above: the individual, the team or the collective.

1. *Contextual needs*
   The first set of needs are contextual and will relate either to specific issues which affect the higher education sector as a whole or those which relate to particular institutions, for example: quality assurance arrangements in higher education; the impact of modularization or franchising arrangements at the University of Wessex. The motives for these kinds of developmental activities are many and varied, from introducing new policies to verifying that what the institution (or individual) is doing is in line with, or an improvement upon, approaches elsewhere.
2. *New approaches*
   A second set of needs relates to new approaches, for example, innovations within or outside the university, the need to acquire new skills, or the need to gain new perspectives or insights from other sectors.

3. *Process-related needs*

A third set of needs may loosely be described as process-related, that is, developmental activities which are designed to identify underlying systems and structures (for example, organizational culture workshops), that are designed to promote effective working relationships both within and outside the institution (for example, team-building events or external liaison), that seek to promote, gain acceptance for, to initiate or evaluate new developments (for example, strategic planning seminars or conferences) and those which are designed to give opportunities for evaluation, feedback and learning of various kinds (for example, action-learning sets, appraisal, consultancy advice).

4. *Renewal*

A fourth set of needs is of a different order to the other three areas. This set is not commonly expressed in relation to management in British universities (although it is recognized for academics in the form of sabbaticals), but is both recognized and formally catered for within the US higher education context. The need is for renewal which covers a variety of separate requirements including the need to remain intellectually stimulated and challenged, to maintain a breadth of vision and perspective, to achieve personal and professional refreshment (to stave off physical and psychological stress), to sustain outside contacts or to overcome isolation and institutional introversion. The nature of activities undertaken under this heading will vary from formal conference attendance to scholarship, reading, reflection, writing, study trips, public service and other personal development programmes and activities.

The timing of any one of these stages and the activities within them will vary from individual to individual and from group to group since the logical progression mentioned earlier (i.e., from education through training to development) is not always appropriate. The important point is that a variety of opportunities should be available in response to the needs of individuals, teams and institutions.

Towards a holistic view of management learning

Burgoyne's conception of management development mentioned at the start of this chapter, and particularly his two facets of managerial careers, the structural and the developmental, suggest that management learning needs to involve both institutional and individual effort. At the institutional level, care needs to be taken to ensure that the pattern of managerial tasks and roles undertaken by individuals offers sufficient scope for the development of relevant skills, knowledge and attitudes. Attention also needs to be given by institutions to the kinds of developmental support that they can and should make available to individuals.

At the individual level, managers or professionals seeking managerial responsibilities, need to identify the capabilities that they will require for senior positions. They will also need to assess themselves against these characteristics and be able to identify the kinds of projects and work-tasks that will assist their development. At both levels, the ability to capitalize on formal and informal development opportunities requires a positive and focused approach to learning, a clear understanding of the learning process and of individual learning styles, and a means of structuring the opportunities so that learning can be achieved. An institutional responsibility is to design systems of appraisal, performance review, shadowing, mentoring or career development which allow for the realization of management learning potential. For individuals, the task is to extend self-assessment exercises to include regular reflection and feed-back on practice in combination with a continuing search for new perspectives and analytical frameworks to extend management thinking and approaches.

Beyond these relatively straightforward individual and institutional responsibilities for management learning lie two further dimensions. These relate to the team and collective areas mentioned in the previous section. The first of these, the team dimension, is required since most activities at strategic level take place in the context of a team of functional specialists who bring different perspectives and skills to the management task. There is a need both for consensus to be built among the group and, at times, for conflict to surface. For teams to function effectively, individuals need to appreciate and respect each other's expertise, to understand individual strengths and weaknesses as well as group dynamics, and to trust individual and collective responses in joint problem-solving exercises. While these outcomes can be achieved informally and naturally in the course of day-to-day working relationships, particularly if guided by skilful leadership, it is by no means certain that they will be. In the same way that individual development can be made more effective through careful structuring of learning opportunities, so too can team development.

A second dimension can loosely be described as collective in that it involves structural and cultural features which affect the whole institution. It is important that opportunities are provided and frameworks are developed to enable individuals and groups within the institution to understand the operations of the university, to contribute to the shaping or evaluation of policy and to gain insight into the values and culture of the institution. The building of a collective spirit (if not a collective view) is needed if the institution is to develop a clear identity, internal ownership of initiatives and a continuing commitment to the institution's survival and development. The present context of higher education and particularly the pressures of quality, the market, scarce resources and inter-organizational competition point to the need for such a collective spirit and for an emphasis on collective learning to promote and underpin it. The task of building this kind of culture through the development of structures and systems, the development of appropriate management styles and principles and the cultivation of particular values, notably those which involve critical reflection, analysis and open communication, falls to leaders at all levels of the institution, but particularly to those at the top. And so we come full circle again to the need and importance of 'top training'. It is not just that those at the top need to be individually competent, experienced and creative. They also need to have the vision and drive to set in place a framework in which all staff (as well as students) are able to develop their own potential individually, in teams and collectively for the benefit of the whole learning community. The personal example of senior managers is an important component in ensuring the success of this institutional framework. For the future, the strength of a university may be judged by its commitment and achievement as a true learning organization, that is, an institution that strives continuously to understand and develop itself, its members, its clients and its environment in the direction of optimum benefit for all parties. This is a torch which must be lit at the top.

8

The Training of Academic Heads of Departments

John L. Davies

The topic of training academic heads of departments in higher education institutions is a relatively new phenomenon. Frequent attention has been given to the training of university administrators (Padley and Porter 1982), sixteen annual seminars for newly appointed rectors and vice-chancellors have now been conducted by me for the European Rectors' Conference in conjunction with the Organization for Economic Cooperation and Development (OECD). Given the turmoil in which institutions now find themselves, the management of the basic academic unit is now a pressing issue.

Drawing on the papers presented at the OECD Special Topic Workshop on this subject in May 1988, discussions arising therefrom, and my own experience as a consultant and researcher on university management questions in the UK, Western Europe, Australia and Latin America, the chapter examines, in comparative terms, why the training of academic heads is now a crucial issue; what the implications are of current management problems on training heads; the nature and variety of provision available for heads' training; and some general conclusions on future avenues of development.

Why is the training of academic heads of departments now a significant question?

It has become fairly clear, in the recent experience of most university systems in the western world, that heads of academic departments are being confronted with a range of challenges and threats which are certainly changing expectations of what the head's role should be and, in some cases, destabilizing the existing order quite fundamentally. If there is such a thing as a conventional view of the role of the head, it is probably best encapsulated in the recent thoughts of Clark (1987a and 1987b) where the primacy of the individual scholar and small clusters is affirmed, together with a very strong belief in decentralization and light managerial steerage, on the grounds of effectiveness, freedom, motivation, as well as more productivity in the academic sense. This implies a departmental management role focused on academic leadership and the defence of the basic unit. However, considerable are the pressures which are undermining this position. Let us examine them.

The now familiar phenomenon of financial reduction in higher education has created all manner of problems. Departments are being required to justify the cost effectiveness of their operations, both in terms of efficiency measures *per se*, and in value for money spent (Sizer 1987). Learning the vocabulary of performance indicators and the tactics of coping with their operational realities, thus becomes of considerable importance to the head (Davies 1980). Furthermore, the trend to contract funding in the resource allocation mechanisms of some governments gives rise to different ground rules in making cases to government, and also in subsequent accountability. Finally, the reduction in funding for some departments has stimulated a search for diversified income sources, to reduce dependence on government and its agencies.

Universities have always been competitive to a certain extent for good quality students, high class academics, and for funding. However, it was very apparent in the 1980s for students, research and contracts and, even more in the 1990s, that this trend will be exacerbated, given financial reduction, the effects of demographic downturn, etc. (Davies 1987). As whole institutions strive to enhance and proclaim the excellence of their reputation, to redefine their mission, and to analyse their distinctive competence and competitive advantage, this, in turn, has major repercussions for heads, in terms of marketing and public relations, chasing contracts, freeing colleagues for entrepreneurial endeavours, developing a coherent data base on the state and plans of competitor departments inside and outside the university, and redefining their own departmental mission.

All of these factors, of course, have changed the nature of accountability of departments, giving rise to a whole battery of performance indicators concerned with input, process, output and impact, and to a whole industry of departmental rankings (overt and covert; official and unofficial; government, market, professional and institutional). At a different level, staff appraisal is now becoming much more evident. Heads thus have not only to develop an accountability attitude, but also to acquire the political, technical and professional skills to cope with the pressures generated.

Again, on a market front, we see signs of shifts in consumer behaviour, expectations and preferences, whether by the student shopping for a place in higher education (and the drift to a buyer's market), or research foundations and companies seeking to commission research expertise. We are becoming increasingly aware of the likely problems and opportunities offered by the growing demand for part-time higher education, and all that continuing education implies in terms of access, credit transfer and accumulation, and inter-institutional collaboration in achieving this. For departments mainly used to full-time undergraduates and research students, the ramifications are enormous in terms of staff competencies and work patterns as well as methods of teaching and assessment.

Such is the speed of the creation of new knowledge, the shifts in the structure of knowledge, and the relationships between disciplines that static departments and disciplines are in some peril. Academic leadership of a high order is thus still a prerequisite of departmental management, but to this needs to be added the capacity to create new subject linkages organizationally (often across departments), to find resources to sustain new developments, and to phase out unproductive lines of activity. Of course, given this volatility, departments may be located on a spectrum of growth and development from excellent to negative. This, of itself, produces quite different sorts of stress for heads in different positions on the spectrum. The management of opportunity and also the management of insecurity thus become two inescapable roles for heads.

Finally, as if all this were not enough, institutions themselves are refining their own policy, planning and resource allocation policies and organizational structures to meet the above issues over the next 5–10 years. Among the common elements in such reformulations of institutional management, we see the creation of a formal top management team (rectorate, directorate, management group); distributive planning processes; strategic planning; reorganization into bigger concentrations of staff and resources in a quest for economies of scale; incentives for entrepreneurial activity; devolved budget responsibility to accountability/cost/budget/profit centres; and departmental reviews. It is clear that many rectors wish to define heads of departments as middle managers rather than as spokespersons for a particular academic grouping or as academic leaders *per se*. This clash between the cultures of managerialism and professionalism expresses itself over issues such as the terms of office, selection processes and succession planning of heads of departments. Any organizational changes inevitably provoke a redistribution of power, and outbreaks of internal competition and institutional micropolitics evident in coalitions of interest, bargains, etc. It would therefore appear that successful heads have not only to be effective academically, but also adept in ensuring that institutional processes deliver policies and procedures consistent with the health and survival of their departments.

Many will deplore these trends, and their consequences for the role of departmental leadership, arguing that they detract from the primary task, that of the development and dissemination of knowledge (Clark 1987a). They may well be right, but the problem remains as to how heads may be assisted to cope with these challenges, which seem to be with us for a while.

Implications for the roles of heads of departments

It will be apparent from the foregoing section that a considerable range of potential tasks, roles and training needs exist for heads of departments. It should be emphasized at the outset that not all heads will have to perform the same tasks or undertake the same roles, because there is a substantial variation in circumstances which we shall explore later.

Tucker (1984) gives a very comprehensive catalogue of the potential tasks which heads may need to perform beyond conventional academic leadership. These include, *inter alia*, departmental governance, departmental planning, instruction, staff affairs, student affairs, budget and resources, external communication, office management, professional development, and many more besides.

However, it is clear that, in the execution of these tasks, heads may operate in quite different ways from each other, according to personal style and predilection and particular circumstances. Tucker (1984), Middlehurst (1988) and Hurley (1988) provide a series of complementary portfolios of potential roles, which include communicator, mentor, researcher, entrepreneur, catalyst, problem solver, politician-diplomat and a whole host more. Each of these could constitute a major area of exploration in itself, both in terms of what constitutes good practice and how competence in these roles may be developed. Time and space does not afford us this luxury.

It follows from the above that, if roles and tasks differ from head-to-head, institution-to-institution, and discipline-to-discipline, then there must be a very wide range of training and developmental needs for heads. This is further complicated by a number of factors. Not all heads with similar tasks experience problems or difficulties. Some heads will not find problems difficult owing to existing competence; previous experience, personal aptitude and inclination; the frequency of the task (which should engender familiarity), support from the administration; adequate and programmed procedures; and through the provision of adequate information. Not all heads have similar authority or power to carry out their tasks. This will be a complex function of their personality (including political will); their legitimacy as perceived by rectorate and departmental colleagues; their competence in knowledge and skills; their position power (sanctions and rewards); their term of office (short terms tend to yield much less authority and achievement time); and method of selection (elected heads are likely to be weaker politically than appointed ones).

At first sight, therefore, the whole business of setting up developmental, preparation or training programmes for heads seems a very daunting proposition, especially since many heads are reluctant incumbents, do not view the role as at all important in professional or career development, do not perceive they have a need for systematic preparation or training (though they may well perceive it in others!), or believe sincerely that any such acquisition of skills can only be on the job itself. Arising from these somewhat gloomy observations, there may still be some general learning which should inform the design of serious developmental strategies in this field.

We should recognize that there are at least three different levels of needs:

• those which are essentially individual in nature in terms of particular personal or role problems, and may require assistance in coping with specific stress, feedback on managerial style and method, and clarification of role and authority, quite apart from technical or process competencies. Individuals have different settings in which to operate, different levels of personal preparation and different expectations of the role.

- those which are generic in nature, as perceived by heads as a group – based on discipline clusters or departmental types; membership of a particular institution (or just heads!). These may encompass technical and process competencies, as well as general management development. The former may embrace marketing, financial and personnel management, departmental facilities management, etc., and the latter, self evaluation, planning, coordination, systematic implementation, motivation of colleagues, and that more elusive aspect of leadership.
- those which are generic in nature, but may be perceived by those in an authoritative position over heads – vice chancellors/rectors; national boards, etc. These needs may very often derive from the desire to implement a national or institutional policy as efficiently as possible in a relatively uniform manner across departments or institutions, for example, performance indicators, budget systems, review of research capability, stimulation of entrepreneurial activity, implementation of management information systems, etc.

At the very least, developmental strategies and programme provision should encompass all three (with subdivisions) as being eminently legitimate.

Given the different levels of training, it becomes vital to base activities on a precise identification of needs, in order that provision may give as much assistance as possible. How this identification and diagnosis takes place is an interesting question, since one of the big issues is to achieve ownership and commitment from heads so that they are motivated to participate in the first instance and stick with it. To regard course design as a negotiated activity rather than a given by sponsor and provider would at least seem to be a helpful start.

There seems to be an overwhelming case for a very diversified portfolio of training activities for heads, since needs are likely to be different and cannot be met through the same vehicles. We shall discuss shortly the range of possibilities available, in terms of level in the system, content, style and duration.

Since the challenges outlined earlier are all about departmental survival and development, training presumably is about the improvement of departmental performance by the head. Here, an important point should be emphasized: in the experience of workshop participants, most heads view training as providing help with their current preoccupations rather than as preparing them for more senior responsibilities such as a deanship or rectorship. The expected orientation will be pragmatic – short, sharp and efficient, and it is likely there will be no particular desire to tie this in with a Masters or doctoral qualification. Here, we have a contrast with people at the same level in industry or government, for whom training (and associated qualifications) are linked with career development. This time may come in universities, but not for a while yet.

Training can clearly assist with a number of factors which influence personal performance at work. It can develop abilities and competencies in areas mentioned by Tucker (1988), it can help to motivate and give encouragement as a consequence and it can help in the clarification of role authority and tactics appropriate to this. However, it has distinct limitations in improving performance if rewards and recognition are inadequate, if authority to act is severely circumscribed or if top management views departmental training as satisfying only institutional needs. In short, there is a close relationship between training and other organizational processes in improving the quality of departmental management – staff appraisal, interactive planning processes, administrative support, etc. This should be borne in mind if only to provide a proper sense of modesty and humility as to the likely achievements of training *per se*.

This being the case, it seems logical not to view heads' training in isolation but, at the very least, to conduct part of the training together with senior administrators who have a parallel stake in good quality departmental and university management. The Swedish programme analysed in the OECD Workshop (Jalling 1988) admirably demonstrates the efficacy of this. Similarly, one should avoid reinventing the wheel for heads' training, but adopt, where appropriate, good practice elsewhere as in, for example, university administrative training, which has now been an established phenomenon in most European university systems for 15 years or more.

The nature of management training provision

There is now clearly a very rich range of evidence on current practices in Europe, North America and Australia, each designed with particular purposes and clientele in mind, and having unique characteristics of its own. However, it is possible to classify these into four broad categories which we shall discuss in turn. Some of these were analysed at the OECD Workshop referred to at the beginning of this chapter.

Programmes developed beyond the institution at national/regional level

As might be expected, the origins of these programmes usually lie with a national agency such as the National Board of Universities and Colleges in Sweden or the Committee of Vice-Chancellors and Principals in the UK. Such an organization would act as the sponsor and mentor of programmes, would assume responsibility for provision, possibly subcontracting the actual delivery and conduct to specialists in the field. The stimulus for such programmes would certainly come from a realization of the significance of the issues discussed in the earlier sections of this chapter, and that universities would not be able to cope with these issues without effective leadership at departmental level. There may be a particular focus which the sponsoring agency wishes to emphasize: in the Swedish case, recent moves towards university strategic planning have dominated these programmes. Elsewhere, a particular stimulus seems not to have dominated course design to the same degree.

There seem to be a number of common characteristics of these programmes:

- The mixed background of participants in terms of experience of headship, type of institution, discipline, etc., presumes a considerable belief in the value of cross-fertilization of different experiences and backgrounds, though the original Swedish programme for heads encouraged groups from the same university. Such cross-fertilization is certainly possible with a course group of not more than 40 for around two weeks, or 15 for around three to four days.
- One aim initially would be to create a climate where training would emerge as being helpful and worth pursuing further. In some cases, this would result in the adoption of low threat approaches, congenially pursued through the consideration of policy issues, general management questions and leadership topics, usually through lecture formats or non-threatening discussion groups. Materials and issues are thus generic, and non-specific to a particular institution represented. 'High status courses for high status people' (Jalling 1988) is a good description of the earlier stages of the Swedish programme.
- Whereas the design of such programmes would be variable, there would seem to be a broad framework for the exchange of experience on topics such as leadership roles and strategies; personnel management skills; budgeting and resources; general management and administrative topics (time management); planning; higher education policy (McDonald 1988).
- Such programmes tend to be stronger on information giving than on attitude challenge or skill development, and thus are not really geared up to action or problem-centred approaches to learning, demanding active analysis of real personal issues and the generation of real solutions. Thus, as a whole, they would be relatively weak on transfer of learning back to the job or on changes in individual behaviour and practice.

There is no doubt that national programmes are important in terms of raising the level of awareness of need, and politically demonstrating the commitment of sponsors. However, it is interesting to note that the Swedish programme's emphasis has now largely moved to the institutional level, and the expansion in the UK at present tends to be much more at the regional and institutional level rather than in national programme provision. None the less, national programmes clearly serve a vital purpose, especially in the start-up phase and probably for the very specialist modules which may be difficult to mount locally. Finally, cross-fertilization of experience between universities is neglected at the peril of the university community.

Programmes developed at the institutional level

The orientation and purposes of these programmes are rather different from the first category and, as may be expected, are much more geared to the culture, contemporary issues and operating conventions of the institution concerned. They may develop for several reasons. Senior management may wish, as a general proposition, to improve systematically the managerial capability and clout at departmental level and sees training in attitude change, certain skills and organizational knowledge as an instrument of achieving this. In a time of changing patterns of management and ground rules, heads, especially new ones, need speedy induction into a whole series of managerial expectations or procedures. Training is thus perceived as an instrument of both socialization and organization development. Heads themselves may well perceive a focused pragmatic training programme as a means of self-help, mutual assistance, collective self-defence and peer support. In this case, a formal curriculum is relatively unimportant compared with the informal agendas.

There may well be tensions arising from the coexistence of these different motives, which may express themselves in the design of the programme and its content; nominations/selection of participants; and the question of whether administrators or top management are central members of the programme, bystanders, occasional visitors, or *eminences grises* manipulating the process. Where these potential tensions are not resolved at an early stage, programmes generally have a very short life cycle.

The focus for these programmes does tend to reflect their institutional base. Thus, specific questions of institutional policy or change become overtly the main focus of the curriculum – staff appraisal; departments as budget centres; using performance indicators; stimulating continuing education or income generation. Even when the curriculum is laid out as a general management development experience, as described in Tucker (1984) or MacDonald (1988), the treatment and analysis of issues like role and authority; managing committees; effective use of time will inevitably be conditioned heavily by the current controversies, personalities, power groupings and culture of the institution. The challenge in the latter case is to achieve the development of general management skills without becoming a 'moanshop'. The challenge in the former is to use the expertise and experience of the group to develop real approaches to real problems in a constructive manner which is beneficial to participants and clearly helpful to top university management and administration, while still developing capabilities *en passant* (see Knudsen 1988).

The experience of internal programmes is varied, but some tentative conclusions may be advanced. Courses viewed as one-off events are usually viewed by heads as quite peripheral and are not valued accordingly. Training programmes conceived as a series of related activities at very regular intervals (i.e., drip-feed), on the other hand, tend to have legitimacy, demonstrate university commitment and tend to engender heads' commitment.

Simulations and cases are often helpful ways of getting started at institutional level, rather than some thorny real life aggravation containing considerable political conflict (Gordon 1988; Jalling 1988). The Strathclyde and Swedish programmes (at institutional level) have benefited considerably from a relatively low threat starting point, which has made it easier to move into more difficult real situations subsequently. The continuity referred to earlier is greatly facilitated by a formal/senior internal officer, who is able to act sensitively as an internal consultant without necessarily being part of top management. The handling of conflict generated by the discussion of real issues (either between departments, between top and departmental management, or between academic and administrative leaders) may well require an external consultant or facilitator, a point to which we shall return.

Programmes based on types of department

It can be contended that different types of department have different organizational, cultural and operating characteristics. Thus, the forms of training provided, it is argued, should be accordingly differentiated to be most effective (Becher 1988). The dimensions of differentiation between departments are likely to be size; maturity of department; maturity of discipline/subject generally; status of department nationally and within the university composition of budget; extent of diversification of income; extent of commercial activity; department buoyancy and growth potential; degree of autonomy, etc.

As Becher observes, experience in these differentiated programmes for university heads is limited, though, in the further education sectors, it is by no means uncommon, at least in the UK. One suspects that occupational hazards of such programmes based on disciplines would be a tendency to drift into discussions of a subject specific nature, rather than to concentrate on managerial issues, and a reluctance among participants to be open and frank about problems, strategies, etc., with a group of likely competitors. This would certainly inhibit the emergence of peer group support and exchange of ideas.

Such programmes might certainly be considered as more appropriate nationally, or through a regional consortium, rather than at institutional level. They may also be more effective as second-order training, after the initial preparation has occurred. Similar design issues could be expected as with the other categories.

Programmes based on individual need and provision

One of the legitimate developments which could be advanced as a result of concluding that there is a very wide range of individual needs (see earlier), is that individually designed and delivered programmes of study for heads have a great deal to commend them *vis-à-vis* generic programmes. The latter have limitations in the light of experience. They may insufficiently address real issues experienced by the individual, and may operate too much with cases, simulations and lectures. They are removed from the job, thus creating a significant transfer of learning problem. They tend to have a common structure, pace, timing and duration and do not necessarily deliver knowledge when needed or convenient. Heads' desire for knowledge of managerial techniques, etc., is mainly motivated by perceived need or frustration rather than by a wish to have a tidy predetermined package of study. Heads need individual counselling and guidance from a dispassionate third party (or friendly superior) as much as they need knowledge or techniques, and many individuals learn better by self-instruction methods.

We thus have a strong case for self-managed learning and counselling in the training of heads. This review of existing heads' programmes suggests that we do not have much systematic experience of this to date as a formally recognized development activity. This is perhaps not surprising for a range of reasons. The diagnosis of need has to be very specifically and sensitively done. To date, appraisal or annual review of heads is in its infancy in a formal sense, though certainly developing quickly in some places. (Gordon 1988; Hurley 1988). Appraisal, properly done, would ensure effective formulation of needs, but begs the question of who actually does it. Gordon and Hurley have useful pointers on this.

Programmes should involve the formulation of a learning contract to which head, superior and counsellor are ready to subscribe and adhere, and this presents a massive challenge to all concerned.

The accessing of individuals with needs to those with the resources to help is difficult. At one level, we may be thinking of learning packages: at another, access to a skilled consultant familiar with issues of departmental and university management. Flexible and possibly frequent contact is needed with the consultant/counsellor, as the timing of help may be difficult to predict, and thus efficient monitoring and dialogue is necessary. At some point, the support of a peer group may be most desirable and this is not easy to engineer in a system of self-managed learning. The nature of the triangular relationship between head, superior or institutional sponsor and consultant/counsellor is critical to the success of the venture in terms of shared expectations and responsibility, and the willingness to adapt patterns of behaviour in the light of experience. The costs of one-to-one contact, provision of support materials and packages, and consultancy help can be high.

In short, the demands of individual and action development programmes are considerable, and require a very particular type of organizational culture and top management to function properly. As a form of development, this relies on organizational processes more than most. As new experience of heads' training evolves, it may be that this will become a much more common and recognizably effective medium both of individual growth and organizational change.

Issues in the start-up of programmes

It is one thing to conceptualize a need for training academic heads; it is quite another to initiate a programme, since the forces of resistance, conservatism, or inertia will tend to be strong, and difficulties considerable. Various countervailing factors need to be taken into account. Conventional views on what constitutes the basis of good headship are usually associated with research and publications expertise and track record, rather than managerial prowess. There is a continuing suspicion of creeping managerialism and corporation in a collegial and scholastic environment, which values individual autonomy. There is a lack of availability of time for training in a crowded diary and a shortage of supporting funds and resources for all aspects of programme start-up.

What should be the elements of start-up strategies?

The role of government and higher education agencies is clearly critical in promoting developments and giving them legitimacy in a number of domains. Research is required into the generic needs for programme development, both in terms of content and design. There needs to be brought together the likely providers of programmes with the clients – or a representative sample thereof – of institutions and individuals, to formulate legitimate strategy and lines of programme development. A managing unit could be set up to commission, oversee, monitor and programme development. Start-up funding is needed for the development of materials and learning resources (especially in the case of distance learning efforts); for attendance of participants; and for the appointment or commissioning of specialist providers of courses or consultancy expertise. A continuing source of public relations and visible support for the programme needs to be provided whenever possible. Several of the on-going developments in Europe and North America owe a great deal to such support.

However, institutional support in start up is as important, for open national, regional and local provision. Examining the evidence presented, this would seem to consist of, among other things,

* *Programmes beyond the institution*
  Careful screening of relevance of programme; careful and persuasive nomination of participants; assistance with any project work (if appropriate); all financial burdens; structured debriefing and utilization of conclusions; review of effectiveness of initial programme.

* *Internal institution-based programmes*
  Tying in programme with any appraisal or review processes; personal
  counselling of individuals regarding expectations; designing the programme jointly with heads; creating a non-threatening climate; taking
  care of all financial burdens; guaranteeing remedial action on any issues
  of organizational change emerging from the programme; personal debriefing; support and participation of rector and director of administration; joint review of programmes.

All these may seem obvious, but they do not automatically happen. One
interesting line of argument is that heads themselves may not feel inclined
to participate unless they can discern a willingness on the part of the institution to change also. This clearly reaffirms the relationship between staff
development and organization development.

The continuation and institutionalization of programmes

It is interesting to note that there were some workshops for heads over a
decade ago, which seem to have had a very limited life. Maybe the environmental imperatives were not so pressing and maybe they were a novelty
which did not last. However, it is more likely that critical elements in the
institutionalization and 'bedding-down' of activities were neglected and, in
this current wave of heads' programmes, it is important that these are taken
on board from the beginning.

A clear and explicit process of sponsorship and support from government agency and institution is needed. In other sectors, this is pursued
through administrative regulation, contractual obligation on the individual
or at least through very strong moral pressure or expectation. Half-hearted
signals from above will certainly be interpreted for what they are. A clear
system of programme management is necessary, whether nationally or institutionally, indicating precisely the roles of sponsor, client and provider, in
a joint framework of governance and control, to secure the commitment of
all parties in a tripartite enterprise.

The position of expert provider (whether of process skills or technical
expertise) demands particular continuity, since providers, whether institutional specialist centres or individuals need to invest time and money in the
development of expertise, learning resources, research and ultimately, the
continuing credibility of the programme. This cannot just be sustained by
individuals in the administration picking up this role as a fringe activity,
because the primary administrative task will always dominate. Providers need
assurance that it is worth their while to invest in this area, and continuity
of professional satisfaction and reward is part of this.

It is important to make careful use of the providers indicated above. In
the case of internal programmes, external providers can play roles which

internals may not be able to. These include: specialist expertise in technical areas like state of the art knowledge; specialist expertise in organizational dynamics and process skills (especially useful if things get fraught because of conflict generated by real issues); provision of learning materials; consultancy skills as dispassionate observers, and finally, to act as important safeguards against institutional incest.

Parallel with external providers, we should emphasize the importance of an internal person at a senior management level, who will have sufficient authority and clout to make things happen over a period, with the backing of the rector and administration and support of heads as a body (through appropriate ongoing consultative mechanisms). They will (as the City University of Dublin and Strathclyde cases demonstrate admirably) very likely have responsibility and an expertise in human resource management and/ or the development of academic practice, and will thus be able to link this activity with related processes in the context of overall organization development. This officer will clearly be very active in assessing need and the relevance of programmes and providers to meet need; working with providers; counselling heads; designing programmes; and feeding issues needing remedial action to top management.

Continuing arrangements for the financial support of programmes needs establishing. If they are worth doing, they are worth doing properly. The Swedish case provides a good example of ongoing financial commitment over 20 years, with the current costs of a 20-day programme being US$3,000 per participant. Such funding would need to include continuing provision of learning materials and their updating. Bennett (1983) and Tucker (1984) are excellent examples, as is the range of simulations developed in Sweden. It is an interesting question as to whether finance is given to clients to shop around for courses or provision, to providers to conduct designated programmes, or a combination of the two. It is important at all costs to preserve quality through designated programmes and yet recognize that clients may have preferences, which may require alternative provision; a difficult dilemma. Continuing quality evaluation and control implies reviews closely linked with course and project development, with a proper regard to the desirability of giving innovative programmes a chance to settle down. Ceaseless changing of the ground rules, as has occurred with schools and college management training in the UK is not at all helpful.

The continuity of experience, of course, in the end depends on a perception of the quality and relevance of the programmes by clients and sponsors. We have already established that there is a case for a diversified programme portfolio, embracing national/regional efforts, institution-based activities and self-managed learning, recognizing the different types and levels of need and different provider expertise. We perhaps ought to add a programme sequence:

• an initial programme based on general departmental management encompassing leadership, policy formation, decision-making, budgeting and

planning, staff management, quality appraisal of programmes and research, time management, managing change, etc.;
- additional special topic modules/workshops in such areas as marketing
the department; staff appraisal; contract generation and content; continuing education, etc.;
- second level training for particular types of department, for example,
technology, humanities, etc.

This sequencing provides a continuing source of enrichment for heads,
as and when necessary, and avoids the notion that training is a one-off
or standard experience. One might also add that the needs of experienced heads, as distinct from new incumbents, could be met through this
mechanism.

We should also emphasise in relation to the above that programme design must give a priority to the structured transfer of learning to the particular job and department of the head concerned. Cases and simulations,
specially researched and developed are obviously essential elements in management development, but do not, of themselves, provide a learning process which helps participants to analyse their own specific problems, and,
using group expertise and experience, to develop approaches for subsequent action and review. Thus, institutionalization of heads' training is
clearly a complex process, if continuity is to be achieved in the longer run.

Conclusions

Some significant areas of general agreement are apparent, which offer
helpful agendas for those engaged in promoting these developments. These
include:

- the necessity of systematic training of heads in managerial areas to sup-
plement their existing expertise in academic fields;
- the desirability of a differentiated programme for different purposes and
different levels to meet the wide range of roles and tasks inherent in the
job;
- the dangers of viewing heads' development as just training courses. It
should be viewed as a developmental process for the institution and their
departments, as well as themselves; much of the work needs to be job
oriented, utilizing experience and problems, and emphasizing transfer of
learning;
- effective development needs close and structured collaboration between
client groups, sponsors and providers;
- a long-term commitment is necessary to make the initiatives work;
- standardized blue-prints for strategies at institutional level are likely to be
unproductive: instead, they should reflect the particular culture, organizational issues, micropolitics and interpersonal relationships and needs
of the specific institution.

Within this broad framework, clearly much experimentation and differentiation is possible.

The principal source of unease remains the concept of headship itself. A strong body of legitimate opinion holds to the notion that academic expertise and standing must still be the mainspring of effective departmental leadership, and heads must not be allowed to turn into middle-level bureaucrats in a top-down system. As such, the concepts of permanent career heads, or ones in position for up to 8–10 years is potentially a threat to collegialism as we have known and valued it. Headship, it is argued, should not be viewed as a career, but as an assignment undertaken on behalf of colleagues and the institution, as an interlude between sustained periods of research and teaching. The other view would be that headship needs to be much more professional and authoritative in order to undertake properly and effectively the tasks implied in the earlier sections of this chapter, and as such, it should be viewed, if not in permanent terms, at least as something like:

- a sequence of roles: vice-head for a period in preparation of a headship; the headship itself; and a period as past head to assist the new incumbent;
- appointment, not election – though the process would certainly be based on advice and consultation with colleagues;
- longer term of office, for example, 3 years;
- due salary recognition;
- sabbatical periods to keep up to date with subject developments;
- structured and obligatory training, appraisal and counselling.

Strategies for the management training of heads thus cannot be viewed in isolation from concepts of headship generally, and this is really the area in which the big choices have to be made. The more authoritative and managerial the position, the more attention to structured training seems to be required. One suspects, however, given the nature of universities, that an ambiguous and haphazard evolution of the concept of headship will proceed in parallel with a steadily increasing sophistication of training arrangements. In short, a small, but significant change has occurred.

9

Provision for Allied Staff

John Doidge

With an increasing focus on teaching and learning and on research, it is understandable that much staff development activity in higher education should be in supporting these key areas. This has meant, of course, that attention to academic staff development has been at the forefront of these activities. When seen in totality however, organizations owe much of the success of what they do to the allied staff, who work either directly or indirectly alongside academic colleagues and students in the pursuit of academic and business goals.

This chapter presents an overview of provision for allied staff regionally and nationally in the UK, and explores some trends and implications. It is important to note that much staff development does not take place in formal courses or workshops organized in house or externally; but through workplace activities. This chapter shows how, through the use of quality circles, staff develop problem-solving skills, gain a real sense of having some control over their working environment and are empowered to act to change their working conditions.

Institutional strategies

Two reports in the UK from the Committee of Vice-Chancellors and Principals (CVCP) committees under the chair of Brian Fender have been influential in developing strategies for allied staff development in universities. While it remains to be seen what effect the 1993 report *Promoting People* will have, the 1987 report on *Investing in People* expressed quite clearly the need to develop a constructive environment in which staff of all kinds could be motivated to maximize their contribution for the benefit of the institution and themselves. Fender was concerned with non-teaching staff. The report recommended that institutions should make a major new investment in staff development and training, produce a statement of policy and intentions leading to the production of a code of practice, and that each institution should appoint a staff development officer, backed by a network of support. *Promoting People* (Fender 1993) concentrated on pay and promotion systems and laid emphasis on developing people and teams, liberating their energies and promoting and harnessing their commitment. It emphasized that it is the collaborative performance of teams and the development of the individuals within them which makes the difference.

These were clearly revolutionary ideas for many universities, but for staff in the new universities sector, (previously polytechnics that lay under local authority management), it would not have come as a surprise. Indeed, the report drew on the experience and practice of other large organizations in the public sector and in private industry and commerce to establish their framework of recommendations. The report quotes the experience of local government in making extensive use of formal courses and qualifications provided both internally and externally, but it also drew attention to the resource implications for universities.

The *Investing in People* report (Fender 1987) was important in that it marked something of a watershed in the establishment of staff development units within universities and it recommended the formation of a national staff development unit as an agency of the CVCP. This unit, since its establishment in 1989, has been one of the key influences on institutional strategies for staff development.

Fender is not alone, however, in giving momentum to the national debate about appropriate strategies for staff development for allied staff. Within UK universities the Jarratt report on management (1985) and the 1989 technicians' pay settlement, which influenced national guidelines on appraisal in universities, are the most notable. However, government bodies have also contributed. Most recently, the government's Training and Enterprise Councils (TECs) have been at the forefront of the push towards national training targets. The National Training Awards are a reward for organizations – public or private, large or small – for excellent examples of training. National Vocational Qualifications (NVQs) are set to become the standard by which vocational training is conducted, and the Investors In People (IIP) scheme is likely to become the national standard and framework for staff development, giving a quality award for those meeting its rigorous standards. Investors In People, in particular, seems set to become a key feature in ensuring some equity in the provision of staff development within higher education.

Appraisal, personal and professional development

The 1987 Fender report was instrumental in focusing on the contribution that appraisal could give for allied staff, notably technicians. Again, it is worthwhile noting that many other organizations outside universities, which gave evidence to the Fender Committee, and other bodies, reported on the contribution that appraisal made in their organizations. It is therefore surprising that universities have been slow to formalize the extension of appraisal to allied staff, but for many universities significant progress has now been achieved.

In February 1993, the Universities' Staff Development Unit (USDU) published a Green Paper on managing the introduction of appraisal for allied staff (Hardwick and Greenwood 1993). In the foreword, the Director, Pat Partington, argued that on the back of all of the contributions that allied staff – which represent three times the numbers of academic staff – make to an organization and its aims, the investment in the professional and vocational development of these staff groups has been woefully inadequate by any comparisons. When introduced sensitively and appropriately with well defined aims, relevant to the goals and the culture of the organization, staff appraisal can provide the means by which enhanced communication between staff and their senior colleagues can lead to systematic identification of roles, tasks, targets and training plans for individuals, which support departmental and institutional goals. I would also add that all staff should be able to expect and to receive well informed and reasoned feedback on their performance, and an opportunity to be involved in discussion with their manager about those things which determine the way they do their job.

The Green Paper was prepared as a result of an agreement on the introduction of appraisal for technical staff. There are many examples of local appraisal schemes being introduced. The Green Paper argues that if the Fender Report (1987) had slanted emphasis more towards developmental as opposed to performance related appraisal, then progress towards its introduction may have been faster and smoother. Nevertheless, appraisal, in whatever form, must represent an essential first step and diagnostic tool for the staff developer and the manager in identifying and meeting training needs. To this extent I would argue that the most effective appraisal schemes are those which are developmentally based. In higher education institutions, this model is the one that is most likely to find favour. However, experience suggests that managers and staff are unlikely to accept that appraisal can only be developmental and it is essential at an early stage, if implementation is to be successful, to acknowledge the link between appraisal and a notion of performance. Managers should, if they are acting professionally, take every opportunity to assess individual and team performance. Appraisal represents an ideal opportunity to do this. What has been argued most effectively however, is that appraisal should not be directly linked to reward. Thus, issues of pay and performance-related pay lie with a different mechanism, separate in time from appraisal. Evidence suggests that allied staff are no different from academic staff in welcoming appraisal more openly when it is clear that it is geared towards development rather than pay. The guidelines on appraisal prepared and agreed by the Joint Technical Committee of the CVCP, stated quite firmly that appraisal should be entirely separate from salary reviews, grading reviews, and disciplinary procedures.

Personal and professional development and lifelong learning

Major structural changes in education and training by the UK government in the 1980s included the integration of enterprise elements within both school and higher education curricula, and a vehicle for support and delivery of investment in training through the establishment of a network of local Training and Enterprise Councils (TECs). Part of this thrust has been to develop the concept of lifelong learning. This is not new. The system of adult and workers' education was probably one of the greatest successes of the post-war years, giving opportunity for further education and advancement for millions. In a recent examination of the state of lifelong learning and personal development, Jowitt (1993) reported on the state of one increasingly popular aspect of the learning culture – employee personal development schemes. He found that there were major differences in approach between firms in a wide range of industries and very contradictory responses to education and training. I suspect this is no different in universities. In several very large companies (Land Rover is a notable example) the concept and value of lifelong learning is supported by an employee grant which may be used to buy courses in the company's learning centre. These courses may be on any subject and seek to promote the idea of learning being fun, and engender over time and as an investment, continuous learning which will be of lasting benefit to company and employee.

To put lifelong learning in context, many professional organizations now require their members to engage in continuous professional development, including further qualifications and evidence of involvement in updating schemes and attendance at seminars. There is also a growing demand for courses to carry a credit rating, and there may be a requirement to complete a portfolio of evidence, to be used as part of an application for upgrading of membership when appropriate. The use of portfolios to provide evidence is very similar to the requirements for NVQs. A good example of this approach has been developed for university administrative staff. This is known as a continuing professional development award (CPDA) (Guildford 1992). This has been developed jointly by the Association of University Administrators (AUA) and the Universities' Staff Development Unit (USDU). Its aim is to provide a coherent and accredited programme of professional development for administrators in their first five years of service. The CPDA provides, through a total of six modules of study, including compulsory and optional modules, a foundation course in the knowledge and skills which administrators need to do their jobs effectively, and to provide a platform for further staff development. It also includes an examined project and the production of a log book of activities and learning throughout the period of study. Participants have a designated mentor throughout the programme. The CPDA is seen as a complementary but core professional development programme within a framework of regional and national staff development programmes for administrators.

For other allied staff, such schemes for professional development are not normally available, and for this reason, a few institutions have developed schemes for personal and professional development which provide on a systematic basis, a programme of seminars aimed at developing knowledge and skills which can be applied in the workplace, but which also contribute to the development of the individual. They reflect a willingness to invest in the development of individuals which will equip them to continue with work related development, but also to be able to compete with others on a more equal basis for promotion opportunities. These schemes have been particularly valued by those allied staff who hitherto have not had an opportunity to attend professional or vocational qualification courses at college, who have not been able to secure time off from work for study, or for whom personal circumstances, including family commitments, have precluded the opportunity to undertake continuing development at an earlier time.

Regional and national networks

In the UK, regional staff development groups were set up in the 1970s and developed in the 1980s to provide for staff development where very little existed at an institutional level. For administrative staff, a part time appointment to an administrative training committee (under the auspices of the CVCP) provided a national course at introductory level and for middle grade administrators. These courses continue under the USDU framework.

Several regions, including the Midlands, England South and North, and Scotland, organized regional training committees for administrative staff, reporting to Registrars. These were very successful during the 1970s and 1980s in providing both a continuing series of one day seminars and development courses for senior managers (notably the Northern and Southern Universities' Management Programmes). Models of this type still continue. For other allied staff groups, provision is far more patchy, but in 1988, the Midlands Universities created a Support Staff Development Committee, embracing universities and polytechnics in the region. Its remit was to provide an ongoing programme of seminars and development courses which met the needs of particular (allied) staff groups. To this extent they differed from the more traditional provision for administrators in that they did not seek to provide one-off, one-day seminars and workshops, but a continuing series of courses designed to meet the professional needs of allied staff groups, including secretarial staff and security staffs. The success of these approaches has been furthered by the recent work of USDU in meeting the needs of other groups including catering and computing staffs.

These regional networks have been particularly instrumental in developing programmes for groups of staff where no development opportunities previously existed, and for whom attention to their training needs had not fallen as a priority to the institution. When linked to concepts of quality management, the relevance of training for these particular groups is clear.

Equal opportunity and fair employment

Equal opportunity legislation has informed some of the staff development work that universities have undertaken for allied staff. This legislation means there are legal requirements on employers in relation not only to recruitment and selection but also to the training and promotion of employees. To meet this requirement, more is now being done to develop training for disadvantaged groups of staff in order to enable them to compete for jobs on a fair and equitable basis with others. Perhaps the best example of this is for secretarial staff who in universities are normally precluded from competing for administrative posts which, within the UK, traditionally required a university degree as a qualification. Clearly most secretarial staff are not able to compete due to the absence of a degree, and yet in many respects have proved through their work and experience a competence in the major duties of some of the posts. In order to overcome these disadvantages, some universities set out to provide opportunities for secretarial staff to obtain degrees or other advanced qualifications, and provided an opportunity for time off for study or met some of the cost. Although many employers insist on job relation in order to give time off to study for a degree, for secretarial staff to do so clearly stretches the boundaries of this definition. Due to family commitments, or for other personal reasons, some staff may find it difficult to find time to study in the evenings, which for many is a traditional method of obtaining further and higher qualifications. In terms of fair employment, this is clearly something that many employers have sought to address, since it can affect women disproportionately.

Equal opportunity legislation raises several fundamental questions for employers in terms of the type of support that may be given. Clearly employers in times of limited or restricted resources will wish to ensure that what funds they have are focused and targeted in the most worthwhile areas. Notions of personal development, therefore, will need to be scrutinized very carefully. However, academic staff usually have an element of time for research and staff development built into their contracts. For allied staff, it is rare for such arrangements to exist. Employees depend on the goodwill of employers to follow the example of others, in setting aside proportional resources to meet training needs. At a time when resources and budgets are being devolved to local level, issues of fairness and equity are more clearly thrown into focus. The new universities, with a local authority background, and some of the older universities, have sought to overcome these problems by developing local guidelines, normally in agreement with the trade unions, on appropriate time off and financial support for employees undertaking staff development and training. These guidelines will normally provide a definition of courses for which support will be given; the amount of financial support; the amount of time off which will be given for periods of study (which may be up to 1 day a week); examination leave; and study leave for summer schools where the employee may be supported on Open University, open learning, or distance learning courses.

Where staff development and training budgets are devolved entirely to local level, agreements of this sort, to establish fundamental principles and a basis upon which rational decisions may be made within the context of allocation of resources, are clearly essential in meeting the requirements of the equal opportunity legislation. Where appraisal schemes are in operation, such guidelines become essential in enabling rational decisions to be made, and to balancing investment between staff groups. Like quality management approaches, this may help to break down barriers between allied and academic staff.

Quality management

Quality and quality management have received considerable exposure during the last few years and have now become familiar concepts within universities. Quality assessment of teaching and research are now being used to drive change and to inform funding within higher education.

Quality audit is becoming a routine external process which assesses an institution's processes and management systems. Quality management – as defined by the broad term Total Quality Management (TQM) – has been around considerably longer and has its roots in the Deming (1982) philosophy of continuous improvement. TQM encourages a focus on purpose, identifying customers' needs, and using feedback from them to pursue continuous improvement in products or services. The aim is to achieve better quality than competitors, innovation, efficiency, effectiveness and economy, and to do this principally through developing values of personal commitment, collaboration in teams and the development of individuals. The 1993 Fender report, *Promoting People*, which makes recommendations about institutional human resource strategies, also builds upon the concepts of TQM and team working. For allied staff, quality management can be a powerful vehicle for creating an environment in which staff at every level are motivated to provide timely and high quality results.

In the 1980s, the National Society for Quality through Teamworking (NSQT) acted as a focus for organizations wishing to develop the concept of teams and teamworking as major contributions towards continuous improvement and the achievement of quality goals. In the mid-and late-1980s, these concepts became major elements of staff development programmes. I was involved in the first of these in higher education, at Aston University, through the development of quality circles. These are voluntary, grassroots, quality improvement teams which meet on a regular basis to analyse and solve work-related problems. In particular, the strength and relevance of the quality circle movement has always been based on the concept of empowerment – enabling individuals at any level in the organization to be involved in generating ideas and solutions, and using initiative to meet the continuous improvement challenge. The difficulties, the successes and the mechanisms for setting up such a programme have been described in Doidge and Whitechurch, 1993. Evidence from a number of universities and from the wider public and private sector, suggests that while managing such processes is not easy, the rewards can be great. Not the least of these is the contribution that quality management including quality circles can provide to the development of individuals and the proper use of all their skills and knowledge in the improvement process. Evidence so far suggests that this is a worthwhile investment in participation and development which brings, above all, a major contribution towards a sense of shared purpose, self-esteem and valued contribution from all staff.

While no technique can be a panacea, it has been argued that quality management can also provide a framework for operational and strategic thinking. This can be of value to all staff, and is particularly so for allied staff where there is often less of an opportunity to gain an understanding of, or to be involved in, the development of a sense of strategy and purpose. Levels of commitment are enhanced where this is achieved. Institutions will need to work out for themselves where this approach to quality management fits, and care must always be taken in implementation so that managers are not alienated when this approach to involving individuals clearly threatens traditional management roles and styles. There is now good evidence to suggest that the use of quality teamworking approaches – whether management led or voluntary circles – can be a vehicle for embracing all staff groups in a department, in a shared sense of purpose and in joint activities to improve quality. It can also be a vital contribution to improving communications and cultures, the way in which people at every level are valued and judged by their colleagues; it can banish the 'us and them' syndrome!

Quality teamworking

The strongest organizations are built on a sense of teamworking and team commitment. Teams enable lateral and vertical communication and the building of understanding, commitment, purpose and involvement through team-building events. Quality teams are groups which meet regularly and, using a problem-solving methodology, identify, analyse and solve work-related problems and opportunities and implement solutions. Traditionally, the term *quality circle* has been used to describe the voluntary, grass roots teamwork operating in a particular workplace. *Quality improvement teams* also describes problem-solving through teamworking directed by management.

The 1980s was a decade when quality circles were used extensively in industry and more recently in commerce and the public sector as a means of providing grass roots involvement in quality in the workplace. As voluntary improvement teams, quality circles consist of small groups of people who normally work together in the same area. They voluntarily meet on a regular basis to identify, analyse and solve job-related problems leading to continuous improvement. These quality circles receive training in problem-solving techniques in order to research a work-related problem of their choice and make recommendations to management normally by giving a formal presentation of their findings. They follow up by implementation and review before moving on to their next project. The benefits have been described as follows:

> Whereas it may be obvious to state that quality cannot occur without people, it is important to understand that it is the willingness of the staff within an organisation to involve themselves in, and be committed to, quality improvement that is a prerequisite to success.

> Traditional features of public sector organisations in particular have been rigid hierarchical structures comprising individuals functioning within limited spans of control.

> Within such organisations there is a natural tendency for individuals to adhere to, and work within, the parameters of their job descriptions. Without a great deal of care and attention it is an environment that can inhibit the thoughts and aspirations of staff about their purpose, their overall contribution to the organization and their ability to innovate and communicate their ideas.
>
> (Doidge *et al.* 1994: 19)

Many household-name companies and a few universities have been operating quality circles for a long time: Wedgwood, ICL, Lucas and many health authorities to name but a few. Many thousands of small, incremental improvements have taken place, the immense overall contribution of which is difficult to calculate. Suffice it to say, however, that long-term success, quality of product and efficiency of production and service owe much to the incremental value of this step-by-step approach. Even more critical, perhaps, is the very real contribution quality circles make to the motivation of staff and their development by providing a mechanism for involvement at work in far wider respects than they might ever have otherwise been able to achieve or expect.

To operate successfully, circles usually need both support and training to enable them to work together effectively and use problem-solving skills and techniques. For this reason a staff developer who has or can win the trust of all members of the circle, will normally be involved in the early stages as a facilitator. This role can be crucial in enabling circles to operate effectively. Although enthusiasm is a key part of a quality circle's makeup and success, it is important not to get carried away on the euphoria of an improvement idea and find that without some solid foundations those ideas crumble into frustration. Training and communication lie at the heart of success. They will therefore need to:

- *Enlist management support* for the idea.
- *Arrange a briefing for all staff* on what a quality circle is and how it should operate; seek the help of an experienced quality circle practitioner, trainer or facilitator to help run the first meetings of the circle and to help everybody understand the methodology that quality circles use.
- *Identify projects* which are achievable, can be done relatively quickly and are likely to be successful – early success is better than frustration.

Circles will usually adopt the following practice:

- meet regularly once a week or fortnight;
- have short, timed, one-hour meetings that start on time and finish on time;
- use a continuous improvement methodology and appropriate techniques;
- have a leader who gives direction and co-ordination;
- use flipcharts for all their working sessions;
- produce notes (bulletins) only to keep colleagues who are not in the circle informed;
- report to and give a formal presentation of recommendations to management;
- implement and monitor.

From their experience of participating in a quality circle in their department at the University of Aston, two participants wrote:

Our departmental quality circle was given a free brief to examine any problem identified by the members and undertake research to the point of making a presentation of its recommendations for improvement.

The quality circle represented a new dimension to problem-solving and also marked something of a cultural shift in terms of the way problems were identified and tackled. The quality circle drew from non-managerial grades of staff who were thrust – many for the first time – into a collective problem-solving role. It resolved to meet for one hour on a fortnightly basis, and has used a full range of problem-solving techniques.

It would have been naive to have expected universal acceptance of the quality circle within the department, and we did not get it. Quality circles represent a different management philosophy – an acceptance that departmental administration is a joint effort and that solutions to problems can and should be resolved by those best able to do so. Managers need to see themselves as enablers rather than controllers of staff activity. Circle members undertook training which assisted in identifying and analysing problems and provided techniques for solving them. Gradually, the evidence and importance of the contribution made by the quality circle began to achieve wider recognition. The greatest hurdle was to convince all colleagues that what was essentially a voluntary activity was as important in terms of time and resources as any other departmental function.

(Doidge *et al.* 1994: 19)

The quality circle carried out some large scale projects including at least one leading to a major refurbishment of the entire department. There were, however, some less tangible (and perhaps immeasurable) important beneficial outcomes of the particular approach that was adopted.

They described the results of the quality circle as follows:

- Gradually, a *quality culture* emerged, and participants took a wider view of their role within the department.
- Colleagues were able to *identify the quality strengths and weaknesses* relating to their own jobs within the department.
- There are indications that some individuals have gained *confidence* through participation in the quality process, and this has assisted their personal development.
- Identification of customers has brought about the general recognition that it is *important to establish 'who the customer is'* and *'what the customer wants'*, thereby achieving quality is made easier by being in a position to meet customer demands.
- Very early on, colleagues recognized the importance of *good communication.* From the early days of the quality circle, colleagues have voluntarily produced a monthly in-house magazine which provided up-to-date information about a range of issues of concern to staff.
- Resolving problems in groups has encouraged a *team ethos,* and strengthened the loyalties that staff have towards their department.
- Colleagues have been able to *recognize problems* and identify them in a wider perspective rather than the narrow view from the work-station.

(Doidge *et al.* 1994: 19)

Staff development programmes

A fairly typical in-house training programme would include at least some of the following topics in addition to job (or team) specific training: induction, appraisal, networks (of technicians, secretarial and clerical, senior staff); personal and professional development programme; quality management/ teamworking; health and safety; management development; academic support services; information technology; equal opportunities; vocational training and qualifications. Clearly each institution will make its own decisions on what to include in its staff development programmes, determined by institutional priorities, individual needs and resources available. However, it is important to remember that much staff development – perhaps the majority – will not take place in formal courses or workshops but through workplace activities. Additionally, there is an increasing emphasis on team development and the importance of team development workshops (or 'away-days') including their contribution to quality management. Some development activities other than courses include: mentoring; job or task rotation; temporary exchanges; membership of working parties or project teams; involvement in quality teamworking/quality circles; visits to other institutions; observer in committees; self-paced open learning or distance learning packages; guided reading. The list is not exhaustive and will depend on the willingness of managers to embrace different, often innovative approaches to training and development – and much of this is free!

Investors In People

As mentioned earlier, Investors In People is a major UK initiative by the Employment Department which aims to encourage employers of all sizes and sectors to improve their performance by linking the training and development of their employees to their organization's objectives. It provides a challenging national standard for effective investment in people and invites organizations to commit themselves publicly to working towards attainment of the Standard; those that meet it can be publicly recognized as an Investor In People.

The Standard provides a model for staff development and for its monitoring and evaluation. It has now become the key strategy used by the UK government to encourage staff development within organizations. The Training and Enterprise Councils provide briefing packs, advice and consultancy to organizations and give help in its implementation. The Higher Education Quality Council (HEQC), and USDU, are collaborating in providing information and advice, including a network of support, to universities who have expressed an interest in Investors in People. A recent survey by HEQC indicated that over 100 higher education institutions had either expressed an interest in, or were deliberately working towards the achievement of the standard. Of these, at least three were likely to achieve the award in 1994.

Apart from the benefit which companies may get from using the award in their marketing strategies, the major benefit for organizations lies in ensuring that they have a rigorous framework for their staff development policies and plans. As the briefing document states:

> Investors In People is not just one more training programme, scheme or initiative, nor is it simply about persuading companies to spend more on training, it's about helping companies to realise the value of their most potent investment, their own people.
>
> (Employment Department 1990)

The focus of Investors In People is on action; what companies can do to develop their people in a way that contributes directly to the success of the business and how they can invest in their people to achieve real benefits which are visible on the bottom line. Investors In People will clearly be of value to universities, and particularly in the context of developing their allied staff. It will not be easy, however, for them to find the resources needed to match commitment with action. They will also need to ensure that some of the fundamental elements of staff development are in place – appraisal, management understanding and training, and a policy and plan covering all staff.

It is not inappropriate to conclude this overview of allied staff development in universities in the UK with the notion of Investors In People. Universities which make a public commitment to achieve the award will be aware of the value of the contribution that allied staff make to the achievement of academic and business goals. It may be that Investors In People becomes the key strategy in the next few years for ensuring that staff development opportunity for allied staff achieves the focus which they deserve.

10

Working Across the Hierarchy

Liz Beaty

Staff development is about the learning of individuals and the learning of organizations. The first of these is recognizable in the form that staff development takes – as training for the job or a broader more educational focus. The learning at organizational level is less obvious but no less important. This chapter describes a particular approach to the structuring of staff development that has helped an organization to understand itself and to develop an approach to staff development across the hierarchy.

The form that staff development takes within higher education institutions is varied. One question we might ask is how the form it takes relates to the phase of development for the organization itself. New organizations or those in times of rapid change are likely to look to staff development as one important way in which to guide and facilitate the development of the organization. As individuals change and develop so their needs for staff development and the form in which it is acceptable changes. So too an organization in different phases of its development will not only have different staff development needs but may well require different approaches to the delivery and organization of that development.

There are issues here about the status of staff development as well as about who organizes it and how. Arguments rage back and forward about whether control from a central unit or department is preferable to organization by the individual or their manager. The argument about the different benefits of central control as opposed to personal control is where some of the current debate lies and where confusion abounds. Two authors go so far as to describe the current diversity as a jungle (Smith and Smith 1993). If we want to ensure that our approach to staff development adequately develops individuals and the organization how is it best done? If we want to enable development through the innovation and motivation of individuals and groups rather than impose a solution from the top or from simple reaction to outside pressures, how can we do that effectively?

This chapter describes an approach to the design and organization of staff development in higher education that is informal, yet powerful. It describes a way to harness the energies of people from across the institution who have staff development as a concern and allow them scope to mould the needs of individual staff members and those of the institution into a programme of staff development. This is a group approach which has been used with some notable success at the University of Brighton since 1989. The chapter does not argue that this is necessarily the best way of organizing staff development, nor is it suggested that this approach would suit all institutions, rather the approach is described and evaluated alongside the strategic and practical context within which it works. My conclusion (as one member of the group) is that it is an approach with considerable merit, with some strengths that are missing from more conventional approaches but with some weaknesses that must be acknowledged and dealt with. The analysis of the group and how it worked is my own; the views contained in this chapter may not be those of other members of the group or other staff of the University of Brighton.

The group approach is a method which sits happily alongside many existing staff development systems and which can add to them by providing a think tank and effective evaluation and planning. It could be viewed as an early phase in the emergence of a staff development structure or it could be seen as a mature and enlightened approach to the organization of staff development. I have at different times seen it used as both of these. In the description below I have attempted to display the strengths and weaknesses of the approach so that readers may judge for themselves.

I have worked in higher education all my working life. I began as a researcher working on understanding how students learn then moved into an educational development unit as an academic staff developer. I now work half time on staff development including management development at the University of Brighton and the other half of my time is spent running a research programme for managers (from business and the public sector). My position at the university thus straddles an academic department and the central services of the university. I have learnt that the orientation to staff development is different from the two perspectives. This causes a tension in the system which may be difficult to overcome. How can staff development be organized to give ownership to the individual while enabling organizational development?

Models of staff development

Working from the top down – policy-led staff development

Many staff development needs are generated from the introduction of policies. The recent concentration on equal opportunities, for example, has been followed by staff development programmes to inform and train staff to deliver provision and processes within equal opportunities guidelines.

Another example is the introduction of information technology into the teaching and learning environment. Many staff found themselves under-skilled in this area and needed training in order to use the technology that had become available. As soon as institutions decide on a policy that all staff will have desk top computers and that letters and even memos will be word processed or that mail will be sent internally through an electronic mail system, the staff development needs become apparent and also may become a priority.

Staff development is an essential requisite of change management. Without it staff cannot be expected to practice in line with the policy's intention and cannot be blamed for this. Merely to inform staff of a new policy does not change practice. Even punitive arrangements for not changing cannot guarantee an effective changing practice. Staff development must be an integral part of the strategic planning of institutions unless the strategic plan is to remain a vague intentional wish list. To put policy into practice demands that staff be made aware of the policy, that they have the opportunity to question and discuss it in order to fully understand and tune it to their practice, and that they develop the ability to deliver it through a programme of training.

But staff development that comes only from the top down in this way is missing a great opportunity to build on the experience of professionals in their work. Policy-led staff development takes account of pressures from outside and from the powerful within but it does not harness and support innovation from the grass roots. Lone teachers innovating in their practice are unlikely, through that innovation, to affect policy decisions and yet their innovation may be the beginning of a new trend in learning which could generate the educational programmes of the future.

Working from the bottom up – innovation-led staff development

In any good staff development programme there must be cognizance of issues that affect the everyday working life of staff. Many individuals and groups, who alone are not powerful or influential, are together making the future of the institution. New ideas are leading to new courses and new approaches to teaching and learning and administrative systems. Of course, not every member of staff is innovative, some are retrograde and intransigent, but it is here on the ground where change in practice is evolving and where the future is being developed. It is also at the practice level where the intentions of policy can be interpreted in contrary fashion through the necessities of the moment. If staff feel that their ideas and problems are never listened to by leaders and managers in an institution they will become demoralized or will leave to find more conducive territory for their developments.

Enthusiasm and ownership are the two most important keys to successful change. While it is important that change is controlled, monitored and in some ways tailored to the strategy of the institution, if individual ideas are ignored the change will be sterile. Those who work in an area have an understanding of it that is difficult if not impossible to have second hand. It is the individual teacher, administrator or technician who knows best what will happen if this is done or that not done; who knows where the waste of effort currently is and where the workload is highest. If the knowledge of these people and their own ideas for development are used, then innovations are so much more likely to work.

The sandwich model of effective staff development

Staff development must work at the policy level because without this perspective developments will have no strategic direction. Staff development also needs to work from the individual level because without this there is no commitment and developments will not work in practice. Moreover, policies at the institutional level must take account of pressures and issues as experienced by individuals, and individuals need to develop their work in cognizance of institutional plans. The oil in this wheel can be staff development. The true place of the staff developer and for those organizing and designing staff development is in-between the institutional management and the individual members of staff. The head of department is in this position and therefore must have particular responsibility for the development of staff and for the information flow that goes both ways. However the head of department must also be partial, committed to getting the best for their staff and representing the view of their discipline/area of work. The staff developer must therefore be able to work with staff at this level to formulate and design programmes which further the policies and plans of the institution while nurturing and supporting the developments on the ground. He or she must be a conduit for good quality information in both directions and must be able to justify their provisions from both points of view. Staff development is the filling in the sandwich between the practical working of the institution and its strategic mission.

Policy development

Staff development programmes

Staff needs

It is not surprising, therefore, that staff and educational developers find their position within institutions both confusing and vulnerable. By the above analysis their location is to be at the centre but not of it, with the departments but with a consultant's perspective. I have come to the conclusion, after many years of feeling the unfairness of this, to believing that the mature staff developer must be prepared to be the invisible oil in the wheel of development as well as the occasional thorn in the flesh of the institution; needling and challenging, supporting and enabling but never quite being able to see the fruits of this labour except through the work of others.

Communication is a most important skill for the staff developer. As in all vulnerable situations group support is an invaluable requisite and encouragement for this communication function. In higher education staff development is also a multifaceted activity. If a group were to be formed to 'oil the wheel' of institutional and staff development what would this group look like and how would it work?

The above analysis demonstrates the complexity of the staff development task in higher education. This is not to say that it is unlike other organizations. An engineering firm has to balance the development of engineers alongside the development of these people as team workers and managers. The issue is one of balancing priorities and competing demands from the institutional and individual perspectives. Staff development is a complex task and needs to be embedded within the institution, both informing policy and encouraging innovation. It would be difficult to assign this responsibility to a person or to a single department.

A ginger group

At the University of Brighton we have developed a group approach to staff development at the institutional level which we informally call a ginger group. We use this phrase to capture the nature of the group as adding heat and spice to the debate about priorities and to the fact that the group's main task is to keep staff development needs and issues firmly on the agenda of faculties, services departments and the directorate. The ginger group at the University of Brighton is a group of people who are interested and have the ability to make staff development happen. It is not a representative group; it does not attempt to have membership from all areas of the institution or of stake holders. It rather collects together people who have been assertive in championing staff development as an issue and who want to spend time informing policy and offering implementation solutions.

The group has a small but stable membership (between eight and ten people). The meetings are held when required in the view of the group members and occasionally in response to requests from the directorate. They have met five or six times a year. The group consists of people who have influence in the institution on the issue of staff development. Many of these are from higher levels of the hierarchy. It includes people who deliver internal staff development and some who co-ordinate these provisions but it by no means includes all who have these responsibilities. The group has a Chair who manages the work of the group – sending out minutes and reports from the group – but it is not steered or dominated by hierarchy. The group has not attempted to become institutionalized; i.e., it has not taken the form of a committee, but it could suggest that a committee is needed. Other people are invited to the meetings to take part in particular discussions as necessary. Recently this has resulted in the group including both the deputy director and the assistant director for academic affairs as they have particular responsibilities for staff development policy and funding.

The group works on issues rather than beginning with policies or provisions. It asks questions such as: 'What are we doing about management development for heads of department since we have so many new people in post?' 'How can we enable administrative staff to develop their career prospects within the institution?' These needs are made explicit through many different channels of communication within the institution not specifically gathered for use by the group.

The group then acts as a think tank spending most time in meetings debating ideas and evaluating the position so far. Reports are made to the directorate as and when necessary to spur activity or policy. Sometimes these reports are requests for funding in relation to specific staff development activity suggested or developed by the group. At other times they take the form of analysis of needs or review of work to date. The group itself does not control a budget but rather makes the case for where staff development funds are needed in relation to implementation. As the group has evolved there is increased money earmarked for further staff development. When staff development activities become mainstream they are no longer funded by this money but assigned to relevant departments to fund as recurrent expenditure.

As the group is comprised of individuals from across the institution, the job of consulting with the appropriate people to investigate staff development is delegated to individuals within the group. The group members then work in other teams on these staff development programmes.

The ginger group in action

The Staff Development Group (ginger group) at the University of Brighton was first set up in 1989. The Dean of the Business School invited people to join and chaired the meetings. People who were invited were from different parts of the institution and although mostly senior staff this was not a prerequisite. The group was not intended to be representative and it did not have committee status. It was a group mandated to report to the director on staff development needs and to inform policy making in this area.

The group discussed its role and purpose from the beginning. It did not do this in order to come up with terms of reference but rather to be sure about its ability to perform a useful function. At regular intervals through the life of the group the Chair would ask, 'So have we done our job? Is there anything left that *we* need to do? What energy do we have as a group for doing these things?' It was important to question the existence of the group as we developed other mechanisms and approaches for the staff development work. It also proved to be an important review procedure, monitoring the effectiveness of the group. At one point, the group disbanded and stopped meeting. There had been a great deal of effort expended over a number of programme developments and the members felt less inclined to develop new ones. Second, and crucially, it was unclear how far the group's advice was now needed by the directorate. A number of suggestions had been turned down and the group seemed to be working in isolation. Within three months the group was asked to reform and to include in its membership two members of the directorate – to be true members of the group and not observers or managers. This re-energised the ginger group and the incentive to continue to work was re-established. At times other people were invited to join the group for some of its work. At one point work on a scheme to extend the educational development release scheme (see Chapter 5) to administrative staff involved two faculty officers. One member of the ginger group worked with them on developing the proposal and then the proposal was refined, incorporated into the development plans and passed up to the directorate for funding. This team worked to involve those who knew the needs, together with and to inform, those with the power to make this innovation a reality.

An important member of the ginger group has been an external management development consultant. Ian McGill, in this role, helped the group to formulate a programme from development needs of managers and, together with others, delivered the programmes. One example of this was the development of a staff development review programme which at Brighton now forms the basis of the appraisal system. The scheme was designed by a small team, including the personnel officer (who is a member of the group), a member of the Business School, (not a member of the group) and me. The documentation and training programme were designed and included a full day workshop for all managers across the institution. These workshops were run for 16 staff at a time and run over a period of 18 months by which time all managers had undergone the training in the particular form of interviewing necessary to make the scheme work. Simultaneously a pilot of the scheme was running in one faculty with discussion sessions held with all staff to inform and discuss the scheme. The scheme was evaluated through the faculty and refinements were made.

The ginger group was also responsible for steering the development of a Certificate in Teaching and Learning aimed at new academic staff in the institution. Over a three-year period this programme was designed, run and eventually made (normally) compulsory by incorporating it into the probation agreement for all new staff. This was possible because the group contained me as designer and eventual course leader, the personnel officer who found ways of working the required documentation through the recruitment of new staff, and deans who contributed to the development of the course from their perspective on faculty needs. The Certificate would not have been developed unless the funds to run it could be found to make it a staff development provision. The group's most important contribution was its ability to make the case for the spending of central funds for this area of staff development.

The group met at intervals of 8 to 10 weeks and had an informal agenda with occasional papers circulated in advance. The work of the group differed at each meeting. Sometimes the discussion would be a brainstorm of needs in a certain area, at other times the discussion centred around a particular group of staff. As the group became established more developed plans were committed to paper and targeted at management either directly or through an appropriate senior committee. Some of the developments were in the form of programmes or courses while others were procedures and policies.

The achievements of the group have included a policy on staff development which indicated how much a department should spend on staff development and how much time individuals should spend on their own development. This policy also includes a provision to allow free access to University of Brighton courses for members of staff. Staff members can constitute up to 10 per cent of the participants of the course. The group has also developed a number of courses as particular staff development provisions – The Certificate in Teaching and Learning in Higher Education and certificate language courses in French, German and Spanish. A number of programmes to support new policy areas including the staff development review scheme, the accompanying programme of training for interviewers and the intensive equal opportunities training, which again involved mainly senior staff and admissions tutors in three-day workshops. The administrative development release scheme is now running with six administrative staff per year doing development projects and gaining time within working hours, extra payments or overtime. The next development is an extensive programme of development for managers including heads of departments. This is currently under development steered by the ginger group but with the main initiative and development work coming from some of the heads of departments themselves. On the agenda is a focus on technical staff and a review of the use of the staff development review process for manual staff. A Diploma/MA in Teaching and Learning is in the planning stage in liaison with the Education Faculty.

Strengths of the approach

From the description above it is easy to say that this group has been successful in developing and organizing staff development for the institution. The strength has been the commitment of the people involved and their ability to span the institution informing on the needs and to liaise with others when necessary. A strength of the group is its freedom. It had a very general mandate, but within this the members could work on issues where they felt most strongly. Different members of the group brought different perspectives, which made for energetic debate, and yet there is an ease in the group's working which comes from the shared desire to produce useful developments and the lack of necessity to speak for a constituency. We also had fun in the meetings. There was laughter, and much drinking of coffee – a fight for the bourbon biscuits – and above all, a willingness to listen to others. I never went to a meeting that didn't produce some useful work and make important decisions. The frustration was not about the meetings but about what happened to our work when the papers were sent on. The power of the group in its working arrangements was not mirrored in its power within the institution. As a group with no direct mandate, no committee status and low visibility for most staff, it had no power of its own at all. This observation is not a complaint. It is right that the group should pass on its work to the normal processes of decision-making to those with the authority to act. A think tank or a ginger group is in every respect a servant of the organization and not a manager of any part of it. In this distinction there is a great deal of freedom as well as a lack of direct power. We were free to ask awkward questions and to make risky and unpalatable suggestions.

A strength of the ginger group approach is in the diversity of the people in the group. We joined or were asked to join because of a demonstrated interest and commitment to the development of staff in the university. We were from different faculties and bridged the administrative/academic divide and the management/staff divide. In the inclusion of the management consultant we also in some small way spanned internal and external provision of staff development. The group also mixed those who were responsible for the delivery of staff development with those who were customers for it (themselves or, as managers, for their staff). This provided a rich environment for discussions. What was also useful was that at different times these roles were reversed, for example, while in discussions about the development of the management development programme, I was a potential workshop tutor, at other times, for example, in relation to language course provision, I was a potential customer. This caused us to work in a more easy and co-operative manner than might have been the case if there had been no reciprocity.

The recent Higher Education Quality Council Audit Report (HEQC 1993a) commended the University for a number of aspects of its staff development provisions. Some of these are a direct result of the work of the ginger group, such as the Certificate in Teaching and Learning. Another commendation was about the numbers of people actively involved in designing policy and providing staff development. This again can be seen as a result of the ginger group approach.

Disadvantages of working in this way

At a recent audit meeting the questions about staff development were all about its co-ordination. 'How does information circulate around the place?' 'Who is responsible for co-ordinating the generic needs found from the staff development review process?' and so on. A quality audit is about the procedures and processes and whether they are linked. The auditors look to see if they can trace decisions and match them with practice across the institution. Do our quality control and assurance procedures work? With a ginger group approach to the development of programmes for staff development the question about co-ordination is difficult to answer. The group does not have committee status so its minutes are internal to the group or go to a particular audience for particular purposes. This is not the best way to demonstrate co-ordination.

The question of responsibility is also interesting. The group members do not represent anyone. How are people represented in this process? The ginger group recognized this as an issue, particularly the possible disenfranchisement of groups of staff technicians, manual workers and lower grade clerical workers. Who can speak for their needs within the group? It is perhaps no accident that much of the work and many of the resulting programmes have been aimed at management or academic staff.

It is also clear that when members of the group felt overloaded with work their enthusiasm for developing more work waned. It seemed to matter that the people in the group were substantially able to deliver some of the programmes from within the group. Without formal budgets and without a job labelled staff development there is a limit to what can be done. No one person was responsible for making these programmes happen. Permission and the budget to run things were given piecemeal and to different functional areas. The personnel department had priority areas that took the focus away from staff development so that some things that were meant to happen as a result of work of the group did not happen. One notable example of this was the appointment of a staff development officer within Personnel to co-ordinate the needs from staff development reviews. This post was first agreed as part of the staff development programme designed by the group, and even advertised once, but became a casualty of the need for other staff within the department.

From the staff point of view there is nowhere and no person or team who is identified as responsible for staff development. The result is that it is not clear who should be informed about a staff development need that might be met in house. The result is a wide variety of different approaches to meeting the needs of individual staff and an inefficient use of both internal and external provisions. The lack of a dedicated central budget for staff development has meant that each new programme has to be argued through the directorate and money found elsewhere from existing budgets.

The learning organization

We never stop learning and developing and, in that sense, we are all of us searching for the next expression and realization of our identities. This is one of the major functions of management and people-development activities and of the overall learning climate of the company. Just as individuals seek to extend themselves so the company as a whole, in its learning approach to strategy, seeks to find the next expression of collective identity and purpose – what we are here for now? The Learning Company does not arrive except temporarily.

(Pedler, Burgoyne and Boydell 1991: 32)

If I look more long term at the work of the ginger group, I could argue that, rather than a particular approach to the organization of staff development, it is better viewed as a phase in the development of that organization; as a stage in its learning process. Pedler, *et al.* (1991) describe the 11 characteristics of the concept of a learning company. These include aspects such as a learning approach to strategy, internal exchange, enabling structures, a learning climate and self-development for all, which could reasonably be argued as consistent with the ginger group approach to staff development. The University of Brighton and its predecessor Brighton Polytechnic have had structural arrangements for staff development in the past that have faded or died. The ginger group has filled a gap rather than started from scratch. The history of past provision is an important background to understanding not just the present position but how it would be possible to move forward. Another contextual feature of the university is the federal structure into strong and partially autonomous faculties. Third, with recent changes in the directorate team and pressures from outside to co-ordinate staff development, there is a new willingness to review and rework the relationships between different parts of the institution.

In describing the particular context at the University of Brighton, I am not suggesting that only here is the ginger group effective. By its very nature it is possible that beyond the next meeting the ginger group will cease to exist or change its constitution. This chapter is being written at a time of change, but it would be wrong to believe that in six months' time I could have described a new structure which would be a permanent one. Staff development is intimately tied to the learning of individuals and the learning of organizations. As such, it must change and develop its nature as well as its content and structure in line with the needs of the institution. For, as Pedler and colleagues, in describing the features of the learning organization show, it is difficult to capture the essence of a learning company through any description. It is perhaps not surprising that the approach to staff development at different institutions is diverse. To be so may match the needs of the institutions more effectively.

Staff development is an extremely important part of the effective functioning of an organization. If there is to be a truly enabling system of staff development it must be flexible, not only to individuals, but to the needs of groups and to the organization as a whole. It must also be responsive to changes as they occur. To be involved in staff development is at once exciting and exasperating. Just as I believe I know what I am doing, my role and function will change. Development is like that.

Part 3

The Learning Organization

We set out in this book to shed light on some fundamental dilemmas in the organization and execution of staff development in institutions of higher education. We have seen, in pursuing examples of educational development work and in our discussion of staff development for different groups of staff, themes emerging which suggest some important directions ahead. We have seen, too, the role of historical developments in shaping staff development practice and have observed some of the different traditions from which the current tapestry of arrangements is formed. But some important questions still remain.

Staff development is intimately tied to institutional development, which in turn is tied to demands for accountability. A major stimulus for staff development has recently been the need to meet the requirements of external quality assurance agencies. A demand for improved quality of itself does not increase the amount and type of staff development undertaken. Nevertheless, the process of quality assurance institutionalizes the principle of critical reflection. In order to meet audit and assessment requirements reflective practice takes place at institutional, subject-group and individual levels. In considering many of the consequences for staff and educational development brought about by the introduction of audit and quality assessment in the UK context, Chapter 11 demonstrates its potential to significantly shift institutions and individuals in a number of areas. Some of these are related to the process of quality audit and assessment. But there are far wider consequences. George Gordon shows how, in providing opportunities for institutions to reflect on their courses, structures and policies, staff inevitably engage in development across a broad spectrum of activities.

Earlier chapters, in pointing to the need for staff to be critically engaged in the process of reflecting on their practice, entering into dialogue with each other to elucidate and to solve problems and so working to improve what they do as individuals, as teams and as an institution have shown how these activities contribute to the development of a learning culture. The question which then arises is: What are the forms of organization for staff development which assist in the development of such a learning culture where each part of the institution is engaged in the development of every other part? This is an important question for, as Chapter 10 has already hinted, it is in the forms of organization which are instituted that the nature of the staff development task and conceptions of the continuing professional development of the university community are most clearly revealed.

Yet, if staff development arises from a number of different traditions, how are these to be organizationally reconciled? In addressing this question in Chapter 12, Lewis Elton tackles perhaps the most contentious issue in relation to staff development: namely, where is its specialist expertise to be located in the organizational structure? The question of the location of a staff development unit is intimately related to the question of what kind of activity staff development is seen to be and also, importantly, to what kind of institution a university or college of higher education is considered to be. It is also tied to the question of the special expertise of staff developers. Clearly it is important to relate the organization of staff development to the institutional context. While we must be cautious of assuming that models can be transported from one context to another, there are none the less some general principles which should inform choices. Lewis Elton explores some different organizational models which have emerged and discusses the way in which these have arisen from the different traditions of staff development, considering the issues involved in deciding between different arrangements.

The whole of this volume has repeatedly emphasized the importance of the role of critical reflection in staff development. The questioning, self-critical approach which is being encouraged in many examples in this book also carries over into staff developers' own work. This includes bringing to their work an attempt to understand the reasons for what they see and so continuing to develop their understanding and practice. It means they are always in the process of learning. It also means taking steps to ensure that staff development is meeting the needs of its clients and the institution. Evaluation assists in this process. It is one of the tools for informed reflective practice.

Although staff development has become more visible and been given a higher profile in recent years, a question which is often left out of discussions is to what extent it is having a real impact on attitudes and behaviour. It is surprising that this question is so rarely asked. Those who participate in workshops, in quality circles, in action research projects and so on, are often in no doubt as to whether engaging in such an activity has, for them at least, been effective. It is surprising how often managers take the effectiveness of staff development on trust, or how often it is criticized for not meeting unobtainable demands, many of which may not have been spelled out initially. Staff development is often talked about and written about without any evidence of its effectiveness. There is no good in having models and theories of staff development if they do not bring about the desired changes. The impact of staff development could be considerable. It could affect individuals. It also may affect the course team in which they work, their department or faculty, or the institution as a whole. On the other hand, inappropriate means may be used to achieve desired ends.

How, then, do we distinguish good from less good staff development? If we are to claim that examples in this book represent good practice what makes us say so? Chapter 13 considers how we tell whether staff development is effective and the different kinds of questions which those with an interest in it are likely to ask. While not neglecting the most frequently evaluated one-off workshop, David Baume and Carole Baume draw attention to some often neglected aspects of staff development evaluation: policy and overall strategy. They present a practical, systematic model for evaluation which provides a template for checking the appropriateness and adequacy of different kinds of evaluation instruments according to a range of different needs.

Perhaps one of the major difficulties with staff development in higher education is that many people want very many different things from it. The problem is there are many clients. Satisfying them all is likely to be impossible owing to a significant number of contradictions – many of which have been discussed in this book. Chapter 13 considers who the stakeholders are and to what uses staff development evaluation can be put.

Finally, there remains the question of what the future for staff development will look like. The themes and directions explored in this book provide some important clues. But, as we have seen, it is a dynamic, growing scene. Staff development, by its very nature, transforms the people and the organizations who engage in it. It therefore changes itself in the act of being. Organizational structures are needed which are capable of transformation as needs and demands grow. But in this kaleidoscopic landscape, there are some directions about which we can be clear. In the final chapter, David Boud looks at what we can say of the future of staff development and its relationship to institutional development. Many of the themes stressed throughout the book are consolidated. We are able to see where current trends are leading us and to anticipate the challenges which lie ahead.

11

The Implications of Quality Assurance, Audit and Assessment

George Gordon

This chapter is concerned with the challenges, opportunities and issues for staff development arising from the segment of initiatives associated with quality assurance, audit and assessment – initiatives which staff in higher education tend to view as imposed and driven by agendas set outside the academy. I am aware of the fact that many countries have not, as yet, been affected by these, or comparable initiatives. Indeed, it is important to recognize the range and variety of higher education at the international scale and how systems vary on dimensions such as primary source of funding, degree of government regulation, internal organization or participation rates. As systems of higher education grow in size and complexity, however, there appears to be a general tendency for governments to seek to shift towards methods of indirect control. Often that has been manifested in governments seeking increased levels of institutional accountability for the expenditure of public funds. It is important to recognize that the push for accountability does not appear to be attributable to a specific ideology. For example, broadly comparable measures have been introduced in Australia and Britain by governments of different political traditions.

These trends have been represented (for example, Trow 1992) as a break-down of trust between governments and institutions of higher education. In my experience many members of staff object to the intrusiveness of accountability measures and dislike the lack of trust which they believe lies behind them. However, it is unlikely in the countries affected by this trend that trust will be restored simply by arguing that the academy knows best and should be left alone without offering evidence to substantiate that view. Quality audit, accreditation, validation and quality assessment are procedures intended to address particular aspects of accountability.

Warren Piper (1992) argued that only once academics were properly trained could they truly claim to be part of a profession. Another view is that of the academic as a reflective practitioner. Effective reflection is facilitated when the practitioner has developed the necessary skills and knows how to use suitable tools of analysis and how to relate them to existing knowledge and theory. Effective staff development should equip individuals to perform that role. Effective quality assessment and/or audit could assist by requiring that the process of reflection/self-evaluation takes place and suggesting frameworks that could be used in that activity and issues to be considered. If such reflection is set within the context of fitness for purpose and an examination of the aims and objectives of programmes and/or policies and procedures, it should be helpful and meaningful provided individual members of staff recognize the relevance and potency of the procedures, how these fit into their continuing personal development and to the development of activities and programmes in which they are involved. If achieved it would secure commitment from every individual member of staff to the processes of quality assurance and enhancement sought either by quality audit and assessment, or by alternative approaches such as that advocated by the Engineering Professors' Conference in Britain, (Tannock and Burge 1992), or that favoured by the proponents of Total Quality Management (Crawford 1991; Deming 1982), in a manner which the individual members of staff deemed appropriate to the needs and purposes of higher education in general and their subject/programme/activity in particular.

Staff development in higher education is often perceived in relation to change, be it the acquisition of new knowledge or skills, (or increased levels of proficiency in skills) or the use of new tools, such as those used for evaluation, or changes in behaviour. These activities and experiences are captured in the word learning, which lies at the core of the culture of institutions of higher education. The point needs to be made simply because staff development in higher education is sometimes opposed as inappropriate, unnecessary and unwanted. In part that situation may reflect differing perceptions of priorities. It may also be based upon views about the relevance of the policies and strategies for staff development and the quality of the provision. However some of the tension, even conflict and opposition, stems from the association of staff development activities with various changes currently affecting and impacting upon systems of higher education, such as the appraisal of staff, the quality assurance of programmes and courses or the evaluation of performance. Thus staff development can be viewed by some as an agent of change rather than a means of assisting staff to learn about, develop and modify new initiatives, procedures and policies. This poses substantial professional and practical challenges to staff developers who must handle such situations with integrity, dignity and sensitivity. In doing so they often need to possess high levels of personal resilience in addition to good facilitative and reflective skills. It also requires policy-makers to be aware of the possible sources of tension and conflict which may underlie some criticisms about staff development and to find ways of successfully achieving institutional policies related to the continuing professional development for both academic and allied staff.

Quality audit, assurance and assessment

External interest and involvement in quality assurance is not a new phenomenon in certain systems of higher education or in certain disciplines. For example, in many countries professional bodies accredit relevant programmes in higher education as a means of assuring entry standards to, and training for, that profession – medicine, law, engineering, dentistry. Commonly the process involves the preparation of substantial documentary evidence about the nature of the curriculum and methods of assessment and evaluation supported by indicators of output and outcomes. Invariably these are scrutinized by panels of experts. Additionally, the panels often visit the institution and meet with the teaching staff and students from the relevant programme/discipline. Failure to gain the seal of approval from the relevant body could threaten recruitment to the programme and would disqualify the students on that programme from automatic entry to the profession or exemption from some of the necessary qualifying examinations.

For many years regional groupings of institutions of higher education in the United States have collaborated in voluntary processes for the accreditation both of specific programmes and of institutions, (Adelman and Silver 1990). Several weaknesses in the American system of accreditation have attracted attention. Concern has been expressed about the long intervals between visits, the lack of means of enforcing conditions attached to accreditation and problems in recruiting members of panels (Arnstein 1979). Kells rang a more disturbing note when he concluded that self-evaluation for accreditation was not viewed by academics as being 'a central process of ongoing improvement and change in most American institutions' (1988: xiii). Kells was commenting upon the relationship between organizational procedures and processes and generalization about the perceptions of individual academic staff in American institutions in terms of how they saw effective ways of working to achieve improvement and change. If procedures and processes are widely considered by the academy to be either irrelevant to the task/issue or to be seriously flawed in their design, then it is likely that these factors will influence and limit the learning or development accruing from operating the procedures and processes.

It is important to recognize that different individuals and interests hold differing views of and criteria for defining value, appropriateness, effectiveness or difficulty, as recent research by Loder (1993) on the respective perceptions of staff and students in British higher education has illustrated.

The remainder of this chapter focuses upon the introduction of quality audit and quality assessment in the United Kingdom in relation to educational programmes and provision. Broadly comparable procedures have been, or are being, introduced in an increasing number of countries. One important indicator of effectiveness of these initiatives might be the extent to which they facilitate reflection on the educational process, i.e., the cultivation of reflective practitioners, teams and institutions. Other critical tests might be the contribution to promoting people, all staff and students, and to the enhancement of learning partnerships and the learning environment.

Quality audit

In *Higher Education: A New Framework* (Department of Education and Science (DES): 1991) the term 'quality audit' was introduced and defined as the process of ensuring that quality control arrangements in an institution are satisfactory. Prime responsibility for quality audit was vested individually or collectively with institutions. The totality of quality assurance in institutions was interpreted as including staff development and curriculum design.

Subsequently, the ideas and proposals in this document were embodied in legislation enacted in March 1992 which led to the ending of the separate funding councils in Britain responsible for the universities and for other institutions of higher education and the winding up of the Council for National Academic Awards (CNAA) which had accredited and awarded the degrees for many higher education institutions in the non-university sector. In order for institutions to collectively assume responsibility for quality assurance a new body was formed, the Higher Education Quality Council (HEQC). A significant and substantial constituent division of that body is the Division of Quality Audit, in effect the successor to the Academic Audit Unit which had been founded some two years earlier by the Committee of Vice Chancellors and Principals (CVCP).

The Higher Education Quality Council has defined the terms of reference for the Division of Quality Audit to be: to consider and review the mechanisms and structures used by degree-awarding bodies; to monitor, assure, promote and enhance their academic quality and standards in the light of their stated aims and objectives; to undertake a similar consideration and review in respect of other institutions of higher education, at their request; to comment on the extent to which such procedures in place in individual institutions reflect appropriate good practice in maintaining and enhancing quality and are applied effectively; to prepare and publish a report on each institutional audit; to prepare and submit to the Higher Education Quality Council (HEQC) an annual report; to liaise with the other divisions of the HEQC, drawing their attention to such matters and findings which the Division considers may be of interest to the higher education system and which may merit further research and development – likewise receiving benefit from the work of the other divisions (HEQC 1993b).

The formal process of audit commences with the arrangement of dates for the visit by auditors and the institution supplying a range of briefing documents about quality assurance policies and procedures with particular reference to: the provision and design of programmes of study; quality assurance of teaching, learning and communication; the recruitment, development and performance of academic staff; means of acquiring and evaluating the views of students, external examiners, employers and professional bodies; the practices operated in respect of the validation of programmes taught in associated or affiliated institutions. The visit, normally of three days duration, is conducted by three academic auditors, supported by an audit secretary (usually an academic administrator). During the visit the team of auditors will commonly meet with some 150 to 170 staff and students. The institution is supplied, in advance, with a detailed programme specifying the times of each meeting and the individuals and groups which the auditors wish to meet and the broad topics which they will be pursuing. Institutions are encouraged to nominate a person to act as local co-ordinator. That task primarily involves co-ordination of the local arrangements for, and during, the visit.

The programme for a visit might involve meeting the vice-chancellor; each of the senior academic committees with a quality assurance role; a sample of middle tier committees with a quality assurance role such as at the level of schools or faculties; a small sample of departments/course teams; undergraduates from these departments/courses; postgraduate students; members of the promotions committee; the staff development director and/or committee; a group of non-tenured (probationary) staff; a group of experienced non-professorial staff; the directors of academic services, for example, the library, computing centre; other distinctive areas/activities in that institution, such as work placements, year abroad programmes, Enterprise in Higher Education, etc.; and the senior management team.

After the visit a report is drafted and sent to the institution for correction of factual errors. Thereafter it is finalized and published. The whole process spans at least several months from the initial discussions about the dates for the visit to the publication of the report.

The staff development implications of quality audit

The staff development opportunities associated with the process of audit are substantial. Direct involvement as one of the founding group of auditors leads me to suggest that a considerable amount of staff development and organizational development has taken place.

In the Report for 1990/91 of the Academic Audit Unit, the Director, Peter Williams, commented:

> whatever approaches are being followed within universities, the Unit is in no doubt that a considerable amount of time, energy, and effort is now being spent in them by a large number of people, to address the questions raised by quality assurance. This level of activity goes well beyond any immediate requirements occasioned by an impending visit by the Unit (although we are frequently told that our visits have a galvanising effect in forcing institutions to face difficult questions head on).

> (Academic Audit Unit, 1992: 20)

Williams added:

> the opportunity is not infrequently being taken to develop an integrated and systematic approach to quality assurance; another is that regulations, codes of practice and notes of guidance are being reviewed and revised, again sometimes for the first time in many years, to take account of current standards of good practice. The resulting compilation of documents may form the basis of a quality assurance manual, which offers an efficient and economical tool available to all those in the institution with a stake in quality control and assurance.
>
> Other valuable strategies now being widely adopted include the establishment of academic standards or teaching committees, a more thorough consideration of external examiners' reports, the development of more explicit course evaluation and monitoring mechanisms, a willingness to be more open and direct about the aims and objectives of study programmes, and the communication of these in an accessible form to students. Moreover, attention has begun to be given to ways in which good teachers can be identified and rewarded, and to the means of obtaining useful information from (e.g.) students, about the courses they are taking.
>
> (Academic Audit Unit, 1992: 20)

The Academic Audit Unit produced *Notes for the Guidance of Auditors* (1991). These have been updated on several occasions and are being rewritten to reflect the terms of reference of Quality Audit. Institutions were informed that they could request copies of the *Notes* from the Unit and these have become important sources both of dissemination of information about audit and also of foci for staff development. The *Notes* provide illustrative detailed questions for each facet of audit but they also state some simple overarching questions that can provide a penetrating reflective framework for the review and evaluation of any activity. Those questions are:

- What are you trying to do?
- Why are you trying to do it?
- How are you doing it?
- Why are you doing it that way?
- Why do you think that is the best way of doing it?
- How do you know it works?

Audit has encouraged institutions to review, and frequently revise, their policies and procedures for quality assurance, their means of co-ordinating them, of ensuring that they are operating evenly and effectively and that they match with the needs and objectives of the institution and with current views about good practice. Examples of detailed strategies include the production of manuals to guide good practice, the conduct of internal reviews or audits and of a largely 'bottom-up' approach in institutions with substantial devolution of academic responsibility. Invariably these activities are supported by administrative actions such as the rewording of regulations and by enhanced programmes of staff development.

The fact that the topic of staff development features on the agenda of audit has caused institutions to review their strategies and policies with respect to staff development and reconsider how these assist quality control, assurance and enhancement. In many institutions part of the response has involved clarification of the responsibility both for activating personal development plans arising from individual appraisals/career reviews and for identifying and addressing the staff development needs of departments and/or course teams. This involves close dialogue between staff developers and heads of department or their nominees. The resultant provision includes centrally organized generic and targeted courses, seminars and workshops, the dissemination of resource materials on teaching, learning, assessment and evaluation, and, where staffing permits, and increasingly that is so, by sustained collegial developmental work by course-based/discipline-based groups supported by staff developers acting in the specialized role of educational consultants.

The staff development opportunities associated with quality audit are not confined to academic staff. In my experience many administrative staff are integral to the quality assurance systems of institutions as are staff in a wide range of academic and student services. Reviewing policies and practice in all of these areas is part of the preparation for, and experience of, audit. Ensuring that the whole community of staff are actively and appropriately involved and developed is a major challenge for staff development policies and practice.

Many institutions (see Cryer 1993) have taken the opportunity to amend their existing systems of occasional reviews of courses/departments to regularize and formalize the process as a central part of the quality assurance procedures. As a consequence cyclical reviews – commonly five yearly – of curriculum, methods of assessment, etc., often involving a degree of external peer review, are supported by annual reporting and monitoring of indicators, external examiners reports, evaluations of student feedback and statements of intended adjustments to address problems and issues that have arisen. Another outcome has been the publication of handbooks such as the one for external examiners by the Universities' Staff Development Unit (Partington, Brown and Gordon 1993).

Institutions have developed or revised codes of practice for a number of activities, such as supervision of postgraduate students. Attention is increasingly being devoted to the assembly and evaluation of feedback on courses and services and to the monitoring of consequential actions. Likewise promotions committees are seeking means of identifying outstanding teachers, often through the use of materials collected to form teaching portfolios (see Seldin 1991; O'Neil and Wright 1992). Other strategies designed to promote and encourage good teaching which have been adopted in institutions include grants for innovation in teaching and opportunities to publish reports on developmental work on curriculum design, methods of assessment or experiments with a change in the method of instruction.

Additionally, the briefing of academic, administrative and allied staff about audit is, in itself, an important potential source of development, as is the direct involvement of those who meet the team of visiting auditors. In my institution, a post-audit questionnaire to staff and students (Mellows and Roy 1992) elicited generally positive reactions to the experience although students were divided on the extent to which they thought the process would lead to improvements. In part that result may represent a healthy scepticism in the student body, but it does support the research by Loder (1993) which indicated that staff and students tend to have different agendas and priorities.

The learning benefits from the process of audit should not, and in my experience do not, stop with the publication of the report. Every report concludes with a number of items which receive commendation and a corresponding list of things which the institution might wish to review or resolve. In the case of the report on my institution, a number of the suggestions related to co-ordination, monitoring and the desirable level of consistency of policy and procedure in a devolved structure of academic responsibility which had vested considerable authority with the faculties. This led to the formation of a new small sub-committee: the Academic Quality Assurance Group, with membership drawn from the chairs of the appropriate faculty committees, the student president, the academic registrar and the Director of Academic Practice. In the eighteen months of its existence much work has been done to resolve the points raised in the audit report. The resulting dialogue between members of the Group and between individual members and their constituencies provides another example of the varied and complex ways in which acceptable and effective staff development ensues from the process of audit. It has also led to dialogue with representatives of the students about ways of enhancing their contribution to the procedures for quality assurance. Activities being discussed include training of student representatives on staff student committees and the preparation of supporting handbooks.

Finally, an important and specific strand of staff development has involved those serving as auditors, as audit secretaries and the permanent staff of the Academic Audit Unit/Division of Quality Audit. All of these individuals have learned a great deal both from developing and operating the process and from the unique detailed insights which they gain of the institutions which they visit. Much can be learned from the documentation which institutions provide, especially the illustrations of the policies in action, but this is greatly enhanced by the discussions which take place during the visit. At best these meetings can be significant developmental activities for all concerned, genuinely stimulating professional discussions about issues of common concern (Davies 1992). That said, auditors and audited both recognize that the purpose is to learn about policies and procedures, ascertain if they operate effectively and consider whether there is scope for enhancement of particular facets of the systems of quality assurance functioning in the institution. Auditors are not charged with acting either as consultants or staff developers.

Prior to the present system of Quality Audit, every institution had its own internal procedures and policies and were all to varying degrees exposed to aspects of external scrutiny. Indeed those institutions with awards accredited by the Council for National Academic Awards had extensive experience of institutional and programme-based evaluations of quality assurance and control. None the less, the requirements of audit with the publication of the reports has acted as a catalyst for review and change. I am inclined to the view that all institutions and most members of staff have experienced some learning benefits from the process. There remains scope for further developmental gains as the system and the majority of individuals move through the diffusion cycle of the innovation, albeit at differing rates. Ultimately the potential for further gains will diminish unless a new catalyst is provided or the majority of individuals accept and continue to operate the concept of continuous and continuing improvement (an unending innovation).

Quality assessment

A further catalyst has been provided by the inclusion in the 1992 legislation relating to higher education in the United Kingdom of the requirement for the three new funding councils (for England, Scotland and Wales) to put in place ways of receiving guidance about the quality of the actual provision of educational programmes. Subsequently inter-funding council differences have developed in the progress with, and methodology for, quality assessment (Gordon and Partington 1993).

The Scottish Higher Education Funding Council (SHEFC) has made rapid progress with the implementation of quality assessment. In 1992/3 assessments were made of the provision in Economics and in Electronic and Electrical Engineering. Several cognate areas are being assessed in 1993/4 and an indicative schedule for a five-year period has been published along with the framework for assessment and the guidelines for preparing self-assessments (SHEFC 1992c). In England and Wales the first round of assessments commenced in 1993 and involves different cognate areas from Scotland (Law, History, Chemistry, Mechanical Engineering).

The principal inter-funding council similarities in purpose and approach to quality assessment are:

• the intention to inform the relevant funding council about the quality of educational provision in higher education;
• the encouragement of improvement in the quality of education through the production of reports of assessments;
• the use of cognate areas as the unit of assessment;

- the initiation of the process through the submission of self-assessments which make and substantiate claims about the standard of provision;
- the evaluation of such claims by individuals appointed by the funding council;
- the training of these individuals;
- the role of the assessment committee of the funding council in overseeing the development of the process;
- the provision of guidance to institutions about the process and feedback to them on assessments;
- external evaluation of the first round of the process.

To date the principal differences appear to surround the articulation of purposes, the degree of specification in the guidelines to institutions, the selection of cognate areas, the detailed timetable, the grades of assessment, the role of visits to institutions in the process, and the consequence for funding.

In document QA/1 the SHEFC (1992a) listed as one of the purposes of quality assessment, 'to inform students and employers on the quality of provision, thereby promoting competition and choice.' That function did not feature in the purposes stated by the Higher Education Funding Council England (HEFCE 1993a).

The quality framework adopted by the SHEFC lists eleven key aspects as foci for the scope of quality assessment whereas the equivalent HEFCE document indicates eight topics. However, in this case the apparent numerical differences principally reflect detail of labelling and classification because there is substantial inter-funding council agreement over the main topics to be covered by the quality assessment of educational provision in higher education.

Substantial divergence exists on the role of visits to institutions. In Scotland, to date, visits have been made to all institutions offering provision in the cognate area being assessed. The Higher Education Funding Council Wales (HEFCW) has indicated that institutions will be visited (1993a). Conversely, the HEFCE has decided that assessment visits will be made when either a prima-facie case is established that an institution is providing excellent education in the subject/cognate area concerned or when the assessors consider that there are grounds for concern that the quality sought be at risk. Additionally, a sample of institutions providing satisfactory quality education would be visited. Thus in England the evaluation of self-assessment claims is a crucial stage which alone can decide upon the judgement by the assessors of the standard of provision. In Scotland and Wales, in effect, it is a preliminary stage of analysis which is elaborated by a two or three day visit to observe teaching, see accommodation, talk with staff and students, visit support services and look at examples of the work of students.

Reference has been made to inter-funding council differences in the selection of cognate areas for assessment and to details of the timetable for

assessment. At present the HEFCE and HEFCW are following similar schedules which differ from that announced by the SHEFC. Not only is the latter
seeking to progress more rapidly with a five-year programme but the structure of the programme appears to be constructed on a different basis from
that in England and Wales. In Scotland most of the several cognate areas
being assessed in 1993/4 are drawn from Science and Engineering. Other
groupings of disciplines feature in each year of the programme. By contrast
the HEFCE and HEFCW appear to favour an annual pattern which involves
a wider spread of cognate areas.

In the initial round of assessments three categories were used for the
purposes of self-assessment and reporting, namely excellent, satisfactory
and unsatisfactory. In 1993/4 the SHEFC has introduced an additional
category, highly satisfactory. Finally, the HEFCE has still to decide upon the
funding consequences of quality assessments whereas the SHEFC adjusted
the funding for 1993/4 for institutions which were adjudged to be providing
excellent provision in the cognate areas evaluated in the 1992/3 round of
assessments. The HEFCW (1993b) is currently consulting on the future use
of quality profiles. It hopes that such profiles would provide a sound basis
for self-assessments and external assessment by peers, thereby possibly ob-
viating the need for any hint of an inspectional approach.

Reactions to the assessments which have taken place have been varied. In
part this reflects the newness of the approach and also the differences in
the methodology, notably the validity of sampling in England. Generally,
where visits occurred, assessors appeared to have been perceived as thorough and dedicated peers who wished to assure all interested stakeholders
(government, students, parents, employers, university staff) of the level and
quality of educational provision in specified subjects/programmes. Some institutions have questioned the suitability of the framework for their academic
structures, arguing that the approach presumed subject-based academic programmes and corresponding organization of academic affairs which did not
match comfortably with the increasing presence of interdisciplinary or multi-
disciplinary programmes, or the growth of modularity or of student-centred
learning.

The staff development implications of quality assessment

The introduction of quality assessment has provided a further catalyst for
staff development. Indeed, it may be more powerful than that provided by
academic (quality) audit because it relates more closely and centrally to
matters of concern to staff and students, i.e., the specific academic programmes provided by institutions. Both parties have shared interests in the
quality and prestige of these programmes. In that sense it is easier for them
to identify with quality assessment than it is to associate with an audit of
policies and procedures. Assessment is vitally concerned with the content of

the curriculum, the extent to which aims and objectives are appropriate and achieved and the quality of the students' experiences.

The comparatively speedy introduction of quality assessment has shortened many developmental schedules and in the initial phase abbreviated some learning experiences derived from participating in the process. None the less, I have heard many staff observe that much was learned from undertaking the self-assessment of their programme. Further learning, possibly more subtle, occurred during the exchanges with assessors in the visitation and a third phase was initiated by the consideration of the published report.

A report of research on the longer established system of assessment in Dutch Higher Education (Frederiks, Westerheijden and Weusthof 1993), suggested that the quality of education had gained an important place on the agenda of university decision-makers with institutions having special committees or specific staff dealing with the topic. That research also indicated that self-evaluation was a particularly powerful developmental tool. The SHEFC reports in 1993 commented upon the existing provision for, and effectiveness of, staff development and identified unmet needs which should be addressed.

With reference to staff and professional development the advance guidance provided to institutions by HEFCE suggested that 'Assessment should include opportunities for professional development including research, consultancy and professional liaison activities.' Illustrative questions of what that might entail included:

> Is the teaching establishment suitable and sufficient to deliver the curricula? Is there adequate support from library, technical and administrative staff? Is there systematic identification of staff development needs in relation to institutional, curricular and individual requirements? Are lecturers engaged in research and other scholarly activities? Are staff encouraged to maintain links with employers, professional bodies and other educational establishments? Do research and liaison activities have a positive influence on curricular development and teaching?
>
> (HEFCE 1993b)

Illustrative items in the SHEFC framework provide clear possibilities for staff and educational development, as follows: teaching and learning are based on explicit objectives which are consistent with course aims; teaching methods are innovative, varied, appropriate to the stated objectives and make effective use of available facilities, equipment, materials and aids; teaching is well planned and prepared and effectively performed, taking account of the needs of all categories of student; the pace of teaching and learning takes due account of the nature of the curriculum, students' varied abilities and prior learning, and the special needs of the very able and weak students; teaching approaches encourage independent learning and students take responsibility for their own learning; learning is enriched by appropriate reference to cross-curricular links, current research, industrial applications and development of generic skills such as communication and teamwork (SHEFC 1992b).

In the first rounds of quality assessment most of the staff development has been associated with the preparation of the self-assessment submissions and, more recently, with the actions arising from consideration of the reports. However, now that the funding councils have indicated that assessment will continue and cognate areas to be assessed have been identified, earlier preparations are being made by departments/course teams and by academic and student services. Simultaneously adjustments have been made to the managerial structures in institutions to accommodate quality assessment and ensure that it is co-ordinated and overseen by specific senior individuals and/or senior committees.

In the search for economy, efficiency and effectiveness, institutions increasingly, with the support of staff, are seeking ways of integrating quality assessment into existing procedures both for the approval and review of programmes and for the review and development of staff. In my experience there has been a rapid and marked movement, led by heads of department and senior postholders in faculties and schools and service areas, to prepare for forthcoming assessment. Such activities include learning from extant assessment experiences, reviewing policy and practice, seeking insights into successful practices in other institutions/disciplines and receiving briefings and advice on a range of educational matters, such as methods of assessment of students' work, methods of evaluation of programmes and components thereof, teaching methods, writing objectives, integrating transferable skills into the curriculum, integrating the use of new technologies into curriculum design and promoting effective independent learning.

Amongst developmental matters identified in the first round of reports by the SHEFC were the provision of training for part-time staff and for postgraduates acting as tutors, increased familiarity with, and use of, a wider range of teaching aids, the addressing of institutional needs in departmentally-based activities and greater use by staff of the developmental services and support offered by central staff development units.

In addition to intra-institutional staff development accruing from quality assessment, there is also the substantial developmental experience of the cadre of assessors. In effect, once every five or six years, a group of academics from each cognate area will have an opportunity (for some, across funding council boundaries), to gain detailed insights of educational provision in other institutions and to reflect on standards and on each of the key aspects and elements of the quality framework used to guide their judgements. A small number of individuals will be involved in a more sustained role either as lead or core assessors on temporary secondment to the respective Quality Assessment Division.

Quality assessment seeks information about the standard of provision over a wider range of matters. Within cognate areas central concerns surround aims and objectives, the link to institutional mission, the design of the curriculum, the methods of delivery and of differentiation and assessment, the effectiveness of learning and the robustness of systems of feedback, evaluation and review. Integral to these concerns are interest in resources (staff, accommodation, equipment) to support effective learning and the systems operating in the institution for supporting staff and students, (for example, staff development, student counselling). Quality assessment also considers matters such as approval of curricula or monitoring of student progress, components which feature prominently in quality audit of systems of quality assurance.

Thus the staff development needs relating to quality assessment are many and varied and, to date, probably inadequately understood and addressed. A substantial task is that of assisting the various parties involved both to prepare for assessment and also to meet and share information about policies and practices and define agendas for further action in the light of these conversations and analyses. In devolving the ownership of quality assessment to the specific cognate area under scrutiny, institutions will need to ensure that wider co-ordination occurs if they are not to miss an important developmental opportunity and also possibly prejudice the external assessment of the standard of educational provision. Assessors commonly visit libraries, computer centres, student services, audio-visual services and staff development centres as an integral part of the assessment of educational provision of specific cognate areas. In my own case that is likely to involve visits from seven assessment teams in 1993/4. Clearly that has implications that I must address within my own Centre, with others in a similar position within the institution (and even in other institutions), with the key contacts in each cognate area being assessed in the institution and with senior colleagues charged with overseeing the preparations for, and reactions to, assessment within the institution.

The newness of quality assessment means that much work has still to be done in many areas of staff development arising from, and associated with, the process. To a considerable extent this is likely to involve supporting immediate needs, sharing experiences, aiding reflection, promoting good practice, contributing to the refinement of policies, the development of staff and the enhancement of the educational experience. It may also require staff developers to revise their *modus operandi* and revisit models of staff development and adjust the range of provision to integrate the needs arising from quality audit and assessment.

Concluding remarks

While the focus of staff development related to quality assessment will, and should, be on departments or on course teams, every activity and function of the institution contributes in some measure to the quality of student experience and, consequently, should be touched by the implications of, and developments associated with, quality assessment. Whether it is the information provided to potential students, the quality and effectiveness of careers guidance, the efficacy of registration or student counselling, the quality of teaching accommodation and study space or the standards of the performance of staff in their duties, each in its distinctive way contributes to the quality of the students' experience and is a proper subject for inclusion in the quality control, assurance and enhancement policies and procedures of the institution. To be successful, quality assessment should be conducted in such a manner as to facilitate, encourage and enable enhancement. Securing that goal may require some refocusing of the process of quality assessment combined with closer attention being paid by the funding councils to the enhancement and staff development sections of institutional plans. In the current structure there is a danger that institutional plans become detached from the process of quality assessment with the latter inadvertently fractionalizing and compartmentalizing intra- and inter-institutional evaluations of educational provision and experiences.

Academic (quality) audit in Britain has recently been evaluated and that report (Centre for Higher Education Studies 1994) will be considered by the Higher Education Quality Council. It is possible that it may lead to changes in the conduct of audit. Certainly many, including the Minister for Higher Education, would like to see a streamlining of audit and assessment in order to avoid excessive intrusion and unnecessary duplication.

At some juncture, preferably sooner rather than later, there will need to be an evaluation of the cost effectiveness of these initiatives, of the contributions that they have made to the maintenance and enhancement of standards and to the developmental benefits which have accrued. Meanwhile they provide extensive opportunities for staff development initiatives for academic and allied staff and substantial organizational and cultural challenges to those charged with determining staff development needs, structuring how these will be met, providing the support and evaluating the effectiveness of the endeavours.

12

An Institutional Framework

Lewis Elton

Over the past twenty years, the history of staff development has been very different in the two sectors of British higher education, now at last united, and this is reflected in the very different current staff development arrangements in what were called universities and polytechnics and have now come to be called the old and new universities. It is important to be aware of these different histories in order to understand the present and move towards what ought to be a more unified future. At the same time, the new situation, created by the abolition of the binary line which had divided the two sectors from each other, provides an opportunity for change. My plan in this chapter, therefore, will be to start with the past in order to illuminate the present, then move to what may be considered to be a rather utopian future, and finally attempt to outline ways of reaching this future. In relating the historical developments, I shall inevitably have to concentrate on major trends and omit those developments, good or bad, that were confined to just a few instances. Although I shall draw essentially only on experience of the UK, the problems are very similar in other countries with similar structures of higher education, i.e. most Commonwealth countries, and appropriate solutions to the problems may also then be similar.

History

The history of staff development has been significantly different in different countries, but nowhere, except possibly in Australia, have there been two quite separate histories, as has been the case in the UK. While this is not something that anyone would want deliberately to engineer, it is useful in retrospect to take advantage of it. Thus in the UK, a major impulse in the old universities towards putting staff development on the map was the agreement in 1974 between the University Authorities Panel and the Association of University Teachers, which linked the introduction of a three year probationary period for new lecturers to universities providing a) an appropriate introductory training; b) a 'senior colleague' for each new lecturer; and c) a reduction in the teaching load during the probationary period (Matheson 1981: 12). Of these, it is fair to say that b) and c) rarely, if ever, happened, but short introductory training courses were established in many universities. This had the good effect that a start was made on the training of academic staff in their teaching role and the bad effect that this came to be seen by the majority of those in authority as associated purely with inexperienced staff, i.e., it was thought to be something that could be acquired more quickly by such training than simply by experience, but not more effectively. It also fitted in with a culture in which the real business of academics was research, and time spent on improving oneself as a teacher was by many considered to be misspent time.

In some universities, such initial courses were provided by staff from within the university who had taken an interest previously in the improvement of teaching and learning and had done research and development work in this area. However, there were not many of these, and most universities either sent their new academic staff to one of the few national courses available or appointed a coordinator/organizer, often placed in the personnel department, who bought in training from better placed universities or commercial providers. In parallel, but mostly rather later, personnel departments in many universities started to generate staff development activities for what at the time was generally called non-academic staff and more recently has come to be called support staff or allied staff in an attempt to create a more positive image for such staff. Such superficial attempts at reassuring less privileged groups always hide deeper difficulties and are rarely successful in removing these. I shall have to come back to the tensions that arise from this division between different kinds of university staff.

At the same time, staff development in the polytechnics had a very different meaning and was largely associated with the disciplinary development of the academic staff through taking higher degrees, attending conferences, acquiring industrial experience through secondments, etc. Although the staff were no more likely to have been trained as teachers than they were in universities, the much stronger teaching traditions of the polytechnics paradoxically made training less important, since it at least meant that new entrants to the profession were inducted into a culture that considered teaching the most important task. On the other hand, the polytechnics under pressure from the Council for National Academic Awards (CNAA) were forced to pay increasing attention to teaching at the curriculum rather than the individual level and many in consequence set up educational development units to meet CNAA demands. In due course, this led to the concept of staff development being extended to the improvement of the teaching abilities of individual academic staff and this has increasingly led to quite substantial training courses. The staff development of allied staff, on the other hand, developed much less than in the universities, since there was no pressure for it from the CNAA (Cryer 1993). Neither in the universities nor in the polytechnics had the training of academic staff in their managerial roles gone much beyond short training events, although the importance of such training is now increasingly recognized.

Following from this history, it is possible to identify a number of issues:

- Should academic and allied staff be treated largely separately for staff development or in a unified manner?
- How should the organization and administration of staff development be divided between the academic and personnel areas?
- Should academic staff development continue to concentrate in the main on the teaching function, or should there be corresponding developments in the areas of management and even leadership which have come to the fore more recently?

The future for staff development in universities

By speaking of the future *for* rather than *of* staff development I want to indicate the slightly utopian nature of what follows; only however slightly, because in formulating it I draw on research and evaluated experience. The latter comes in the main from experience at the University of Surrey (Elton and Gilbert 1980) and with the Enterprise in Higher Education Initiative (EHE) of the Employment Department (Elton 1991). The latter, with its many evaluations, has provided insights for those involved in it of a quite exceptional kind and I refer readers to a recently published article (Elton 1994) for the substantiation of some of the claims that I shall make and the conclusions which I shall draw.

The collegial institution

The rapidly changing environment within which universities will have to work for the foreseeable future and the effects that these changes will have on the quality of the life and work of their staff and students imply that staff development will have a primary function as an agent of institutional change. While one of its concerns must always be to meet the legitimate personal needs of staff, its main concern in difficult times will inevitably be to meet the needs of students, in their learning experiences, in the services provided for them and in the environment in which they spend three or more very important years of their lives. It will be concerned in different ways with changes in knowledge, skills and attitudes of all staff and at every level, right up to that of the most senior administrators and the head of each and every university. Furthermore, because of the interlocking responsibilities of different staff, the development of different categories of staff should not be kept organizationally separate from each other. Staff development should move from being topic driven to being problem driven, with different categories of staff engaging jointly or separately in staff development activities on the basis of what is needed to solve the problems. This may mean that much of it will still be conducted separately, but it will be done on the basis of a wholly different and much more unitary philosophy of staff development.

Universities have always prided themselves on the collegial nature of their society, but this has in the past been confined to that of their academic staff, and even there has been eroded by managerial developments (Middlehurst and Elton 1992). In future, it will be necessary for all staff to feel that they are, and are accepted to be, collegial members of this society, contributing to the best of their ability to the common good of their institution and its students. This extension of the concept of collegiality comes close to what is of course one of the fundamental tenets of what has come to be called Total Quality Management.

Such collegiality does not equate to the abolition of hierarchies, although it should lead to their loosening. Within those hierarchies it requires all staff to accept a degree of personal responsibility for their work, both up and down in the hierarchies in which they find themselves, that may be unfamiliar to most. At present academic staff are apt to over-stress their academic freedom at the expense of their institutional accountability and loyalty to their discipline at the expense of loyalty to their institution. Allied staff are apt to see themselves as secondary citizens and are indeed seen as such by many academics. Changes to genuine and all-encompassing collegiality will not be easy and will require remarkable leadership qualities from vice-chancellors and their teams. Most staff will initially be suspicious and will want to see genuine evidence that such a development amounts to more than lip service. They will look for signs that their efforts are appreciated and rewarded in their annual appraisals, that their expertise and skills are recognized in the departmental and institutional plans into which their own work plans must fit, and that opportunities are provided for personal development and possible promotion. To recognize and satisfy their needs and demands will in turn require staff development not only at their level, but at every level above and below them, for the changed institution will require aspects of management and leadership very different from that of the past (Middlehurst and Elton 1992). In this connection, it is important to distinguish good management, designed to make the institution more efficient, from effective leadership, which produces useful change (Kotter 1990).

These considerations lead in turn to a tentative agenda for the most important areas of staff development. In a strange way, they have been based largely on the experience of EHE: the first three, and in particular the development of personal and transferable skills, because they have been pursued there with considerable success; the last three, because this very success highlighted their absence:

• The didactics of higher education
• Personal and transferable skills

- Staff appraisal and promotion
- Institutional management and planning
- Academic leadership
- Application of organization theory to higher education institutions

In the kind of collegial society which I envisage, all academic and allied staff require some aspects of all of these topics, although different staff obviously require them to a different extent and in different ways.

The role of research

No mention has so far been made of the research function of universities and this is not the place to again rehearse the critique of the funding policies of the funding councils (Elton 1987a) which still actively discourage teaching efforts. In line with the argument that the major aim of staff development is to meet the needs of students, I see the role of research in the following:

1. The research and teaching nexus, which argues that teaching at university level is enriched by accompanying research. Although this is a much debated question, the inclusion of the concept of scholarship appears to strengthen the nexus (Elton 1986; 1992a).
2. Research in the pedagogy of higher education, which ranges from fundamental research to action research, where research, development and practice are closely integrated.
3. Institutional research, which ranges from fundamental research to research that directly informs decision-making in the institution in which it takes place.

The first of these and increasingly also the second are becoming recognized as, in significant parts, an appropriate concern for staff developers. The last two are obviously directly relevant to the maintenance and enhancement of teaching quality and I shall make a case later in this chapter that either or both are suitable research areas for the personal research of staff developers (Elton *et al.* 1994).

Models of staff development for change

Smith (1992) has recently reviewed a number of models that have been put forward in the literature and these are summarized in the table below. (The references in the table are to Rutherford 1982; Tavistock Institute of Human Relations 1991; Harding *et al.* 1981; Boud and McDonald 1981; Main 1985 and Hewton 1982. The terms used are taken from their papers). What emerges is that, although they use different categorizations and terms, they consistently lead to one of five distinct roles for staff developers, except in

Table 12.1 Models of staff development practice

Role of Staff developer	Rutherford	Tavistock	Harding	Bond	Main	Hewton
Provides service	product			professional service		
Dispenses advice	prescription	provider	medical and public health			
Acts as counsellor	process	process		counselling	personal growth	
Acts as collaborator	problem		athletic	colleagual		
Acts as controller			authoritarian			
Negotiates, using a variety of methods		broker		eclectic		diplomacy

the last row of the Table, where the staff developer may use some or all of the five roles.

What has come out of the EHE experience in this connection is that the most acceptable form of staff development and the one that probably has had most success is that in which staff developers and academic teachers collaborate with the aim of improving the student learning experience. Staff developers and academic teachers both play active parts in the process. In the light of what has been said earlier about collegiality, such collaboration should, of course, include all relevant staff and not only teaching staff. While this makes the collaborator role dominant, it does not prevent the inclusion of other roles (except that of controller!) by negotiation, when they arise from a mutual understanding of staff needs. In all four roles, staff developers have also to make judgements as to when they may be considered as experts by the staff, when a more equal stance is indicated and when the main expertise lies with the staff. What is to be avoided are the extremes: at one, staff developers consider that they have all the necessary expertise, and at the other, they disclaim all special expertise and act merely as facilitators who bring out the expertise which academic teachers are supposed to have as a result of their teaching experience. The first leads to the delivery of *all* staff development at the action level through formal training events and short courses by trainers who have themselves been trained by trainers who have themselves been trained by trainers . . . This *cascade* model, which is inherent in a recently advocated approach (Glover 1990), assumes that knowledge and associated skills and attitudes can be transferred unidirectionally, rather than that they arise from the mutual interaction of all concerned in the teaching-learning process. Not surprisingly, it has been shown, for example, in EHE, to be comparatively ineffective (Tavistock Institute of Human Relations 1991), quite apart from its well known dilution effect. The second, in its pure form, has not been used in EHE, probably because the frustration it causes to academic staff who often 'just want to be told' is by now well known.

The model which has proved to be most successful in EHE (Elton *et al.* 1990) is a feedback model, which is based soundly on learning theory and had been proposed previously quite independently (Elton 1987b, section 2.6). In this model, a small group of central staff developers liaise with designated departmental staff developers in departments who in turn liaise with staff in their departments and also, via the centre, with each other. All links are two way, so that this is neither a cascade model nor one in which there are no people with special expertise. It obviously has aspects of both, but any cascade effects are modified by feedback and it allows both for the feeding in of previously acquired expertise by all parties at all levels and of the development of new expertise, again at all levels. The same approach can also be used for the training of trainers and in this form is often referred to as a *bootstrap* model, since in it trainers pull themselves up by their own and their colleagues' bootstraps. In this way it overcomes the problem inherent in the infinite regression of the training of trainers.

This model of staff development, which is based on the ideas of 'facilitative reflection' and of the 'reflective practitioner' (Schön 1983) in order to analyse and consult on processes, is increasingly used in education. In many cases, the role of a critical friend is played by a colleague as part of an agreed process of reflection that encompasses all the members of a department or unit. The model is also particularly suited to the involvement of staff from the world of work outside academia. In the cascade model, these are brought in as experts, although they frequently lack an adequate understanding of the academic world. In the inexpert model they feel even more frustrated than academics. The feedback model provides the opportunity for them to be in a position where they simultaneously provide and receive training and development.

Much experience has shown that the feedback model often works best, if it is initially centred on the department and usually on the course board concerned with the creation and delivery of a particular course. Other activities such as formal training sessions and courses are added, as the need for them is identified. This approach has been exemplified by one of its practitioners:

> The management of the EHE project has changed from one where the focus of concern was directly with the *task* of ensuring that the contract was being met to one where it is recognised that the task is best met by a focus on the *process* of change and on how staff are involved.
>
> This has meant giving much more responsibility for the EHE project to staff in faculties and departments. The EHE Unit then becomes much more of a support unit, coordinating activities rather than determining them.
>
> (Heycock 1991)

While the model, outlined above, has proved very successful in the area of the didactics of higher education and for the general body of academic staff, it has not been tried in the other areas that have been postulated above and which aim primarily, although not wholly, at the more senior staff. The methods employed there have tended to be much more formal, partly because this is what such staff perceive as appropriate for them and partly probably also in deference to the increasing levels of stress and anxiety in staff, when put into genuinely participative training situations, as one ascends the academic hierarchy (Middlehurst 1989). Further examples have been discussed in Chapters 7 and 8.

Institutional structures for staff development

It has to be admitted that much of staff development is at present moving in a very different direction. Many universities now have not staff developers, but staff development officers, who see their task as mainly organizational and administrative, buying in staff development expertise, rather than providing it themselves. I believe this development to be wrong on four quite separate grounds:

1. Such staff development officers will tend to remain marginalized in personnel departments.
2. Since much of the expertise is brought in from outside, it finds it difficult to respond to specific local needs and it is also difficult to provide appropriate follow-up activities.
3. The process consumes expertise without creating any. In a situation in which the need for staff development is rapidly increasing, this leads very quickly to a shortage of staff developers.
4. Staff development cannot be readily related to and integrated with institutional research.

All this is extremely relevant to what has become perhaps the thorniest problem in staff development over the past decade, i.e., where the staff development organization should be placed within the institutional structure of a university. Should it be an academic entity, should it be within the personnel office, should it be both, should it be neither? The debate has gone on for a long time without an acceptable solution having been found and what is usually the case in such a long-standing situation is that it is the formulation of the problem that is invalid. In practice, the answer in any one university has been predicated on both the organization of the university and the history of staff development in it, but nowhere has the answer been satisfactory.

I have already rejected the simplistic solution of replacing staff developers by staff development officers, who inevitably are placed in personnel sections. I now believe that the problem has to be seen in the light of traditional academic values, which have the following effects:

• the supremacy of research;
• the prestige of award bearing courses;
• the low esteem of service teaching, particularly when farmed out to outsiders;
• the split between academic and allied staff.

From what I have said earlier, I believe that these traditional values need changing and that staff development is the way to change them. This means that we have to change the most entrenched of academic attitudes, using a currently very low prestige approach – not an easy task. However, in the spirit of a not wholly utopian utopia, let us outline what the ideal might look like and defer the problem of getting there to later in this chapter.

A not wholly utopian utopia

One of the most interesting features of the EHE Initiative has been its success wherever it went with the grain, i.e., it modified existing practices rather than opposed them. If research is supreme, staff developers will not change that. What they can also do is research and they have two ready-made areas in pedagogic and institutional research. They should take heart from the support they have received in a recent report:

> Educational innovation would be greatly assisted by the recognition that the creation of improved teaching methods and materials is an intellectually demanding activity, providing great scope for originality and scholarship. It must be seen as fully equivalent to conventional discipline-based research in terms of its intrinsic interest and its academic value.
>
> (MacFarlane 1992, section 5.1.1)

Similarly, if prestige goes with award bearing courses, they should be part of the remit of staff development. By now we have the basis for a quite normal academic department, whose service function will be the provision of staff development services as demanded. Its survival will no longer depend entirely on the services that it provides, which is not an easy way to survive in the academic jungle, but in the first instance on the value to the university of its research and of its award bearing courses. Just as for a normal academic department, both research and teaching would be in a special discipline, which, in line with the MacFarlane Report, would be the discipline of higher education. Remember, this is utopia, but not entirely, because I ran just such a department for twelve years (Elton and Gilbert 1980) and one of the new universities is at present planning to make staff and educational development one of its schools. Also, after many years, when Australia seemed to lose its head start in staff development because it was not linked to research, it has now largely regained this lead exactly through allying staff development to research, for example, at the University of New South Wales, at Griffith University and at the Queensland University of Technology. In all of these, staff development is firmly in the academic area.

The solution which I have put forward in terms of academic values, fits the first three of the values, but it does nothing about changing the fourth, which is, of course, the one that we particularly want to change. This is not surprising. When I ran that department, I regret to say that I accepted the fourth as it stood and we confined our activities to academic staff development. What would I have done to alter the work of the department, had I seen the light in those far off days?

First, I would have felt under an obligation always to think of collegiality to extend to all staff and hence bring representatives of all staff into all planning. Second, I would have looked for ways to unify staff development for different staff categories through common themes and common needs. There are two ways of doing this. The first, which is frequently practised now and which is fine, although it is hardly central to staff needs, is to look for themes that are wanted by all categories. Time management and information technology skills are favourites and provide staff development events.

The second is to turn staff development inside out and to start with problems that are looking for solutions which require staff development. Such problems – from a new curriculum to car parking – invariably require a mixture of staff categories for their solution and the staff involved will see the relevance of the required staff development. Such a problem-oriented approach has been very successful in student learning (Barrows and Tamblyn 1980) and has been suggested for a distance programme for academic staff training (Cryer and Elton 1993a). The quality circle approach in Chapter 9 and the ginger group approach in Chapter 10 represent other examples. While under present circumstances, a personnel office would be likely to have a service role rather like that of an audio visual services unit, in the utopia, where all staff are equal (and none more equal than others) this would become a partnership. More realistically, the status of the personnel office might approach that of the university library or computing unit.

And how do we get to utopia?

Everyone is likely to agree that, given a choice, they would not start from where we are. The weight of history, different in the old and the new universities but equally weighty, is not helpful. The fact that they are different, however, is helpful, for it means that the two sides can learn something valuable from each other. In the new universities the existing educational development units could be upgraded into academic departments – many of them are already providing substantial courses and are engaging in pedagogic research and development with staff who successfully complete the courses being accredited by the Staff and Educational Development Association (Baume 1992). At present, more fundamental research is carried out more in the old universities, where the existing strong research culture also provides a better basis for the development of new kinds of research.

To foster and develop research programmes of the kind indicated in a large number of institutions will not be easy. One way forward might be through a National Higher Education Development Centre, which I have advocated before (Elton 1992b). I do not envisage this as a large building, teeming with people, or having as extensive a remit as the Teaching and Learning Board, put forward by MacFarlane (1992, section 5.3.4), but rather as a small organization – not much larger perhaps than the current Division of Quality Enhancement of the Higher Education Quality Council, out of which it might well grow – which would coordinate and stimulate diverse activities, as well as carry out some activities itself.

The really difficult problem will be that of creating genuine collegiality throughout a university (Elton 1994b). However, if it is recalled that it is not so very different from what in industry is called Total Quality Management, it may perhaps appeal more to those in authority. Indeed, the more we can link staff development and the need for institutional change (see Cryer and Elton 1993b) to the demands for quality, the more likely we are to be successful. One way to break down the differences between different staff categories and at the same time increase the efficiency of the institution as a whole is through greater flexibility in job descriptions, particularly of academic staff. The following suggestion has been put forward by the Senior Pro-Vice-Chancellor of the University of Surrey in his personal capacity:

> All academics are involved in teaching, in administration and in research. Rather than segregating the community of academics into teachers or researchers or even administrators[!], it must be recognized that there will be a difference of emphasis in each individual's commitment and aptitude for these diverse roles which can change as their own career progresses.
>
> (Butterworth and Goldfarb 1993)

If we add to this the many allied staff who could have research as part of their remit and the many more who are at present involved in supporting research without always getting the credit that they deserve, and the many who have a teaching function (careers advice, counselling, etc., quite apart from staff development), then the rigid division between academic and allied staff begins to look artificial, hide bound and even snobbish. Let us make a start towards utopia by getting rid of it!

13

A Strategy for Evaluation

David Baume and Carole Baume

> Before you go I'd like to find out what you thought of the workshop;
> how it went, what you got out of it, what you think should have been
> different. If you could just fill in this questionnaire for me . . .

The feedback questionnaire, or its neighbour the feedback round, is as
much a part of the staff developer's workshop repertoire as the ice-breaker
and the goal setting exercise. The obtaining of feedback provides some
essential data for the reflective practice of staff development. But how do
staff developers plan feedback questionnaires and rounds? How do they
decide what to ask? What do they do with the responses? How else is staff
development evaluated?

Moving back a step; who are the current audiences for the evaluation?
What uses do these various audiences make of the results of the feedback?
Moving back still further who should be the audiences for evaluations of
staff development? What are their legitimate interests? Against what should
evaluations be conducted?

And returning to the vicinity of our starting point for each of these
audiences and purposes, what are appropriate methods for gathering,
processing, and disseminating the results of evaluations? During 1993 we
conducted a survey of practice in the evaluation of staff development in the
UK. In summary, this showed that, while evaluation of staff development
events and programmes was widespread, much less evaluation was carried
out in respect of policy. This finding suggested to us a need to develop a
systematic approach to the evaluation of staff development which would
embrace policy and strategy as well as methods and processes.

It may be argued, more often, it may simply be felt, that an evaluation
system such as the one we outline here is over-elaborate. What problem is
this evaluation system designed to solve? In the messy reality that is often
the working environment of staff and educational developers, where goals
may be unclear or even incompatible, surely all this is a bit idealistic? So
why bother?

- *A principled reason*: it is surely better to start with an ideal model process, in this case of evaluation, and then where necessary make compromises as a conscious and informed act rather than as a fudge.
- *An opportunistic reason*: the moves towards increased accountability sweeping the public sector will in due course reach even into corners such as staff development, and staff developers had best be prepared.
- *Two political reasons*: staff developers can contribute much more to the work of lecturers on the evaluation of their teaching if they have current and first hand experience of evaluation. Further, staff developers' insistence on the importance of their clients evaluating teaching and learning will be more credible if their own house is seen to be in good order.
- *A personal reason*: in the wee small hours, or when arguing for a budget, or when making the case for staff development as a respectable profession which makes a real contribution to the quality of educational provision, it is good to be able to go beyond assertion and some way towards proof.

The examples in this chapter are mainly concerned with the evaluation of staff development in direct support of teaching and learning. However, the approach we describe is applicable to all forms of staff development.

Questions about evaluation

We start with some questions about educational evaluation. We then move on to develop a grid or framework within which the various identified stakeholders in the process of staff development can develop, undertake, make use of the results of, and finally review and improve, an appropriate evaluation process.

One difficulty with systems is that they can feel too systematic, dry, mechanical, denying of imagination and serendipity. The system developed in this chapter could indeed lead to dull evaluations; evaluations which miss the life and spark which characterize good evaluation as well as good staff development. A systematic approach to evaluation is needed. The increased pressures for quality, accountability and efficiency all require it. But how do we avoid the lifelessness?

One of the ways we can do that is by remembering that, as well as meeting requirements for accountability, the underlying purpose of evaluation is to understand and improve, in this case staff development and hence the quality of the student learning experience. Evaluation systems and methods must finally be judged in these terms. Human learning, by whoever, remains a complex, fascinating and only partly understood business. In leading to an improved understanding of this learning, the evaluation of staff development should never become dry and dull; it should never miss the surprises from which progress comes.

Questions and initial answers

Nevo (1986) suggests ten dimensions along which evaluation can usefully be considered. He expresses these dimensions as questions, which he then answers in general terms. After listing the questions we modify and extend Nevo's answers to apply to staff development. At the same time we identify the main stakeholders in the evaluation of staff development. The purpose of all this is to establish a framework within which any individual evaluation can be located, and thus to make it possible to devise a valid and locally appropriate evaluation method. Nevo's questions are:

- How is evaluation defined?
- What are the functions of evaluation?
- What are the objects of evaluation?
- What kinds of information should be collected regarding each object?
- What criteria should be used to judge the merit and worth of an evaluation object?
- Who should be served by an evaluation?
- What is the process of doing an evaluation?
- What methods of enquiry should be used in an evaluation?
- Who should do the evaluation?
- By what standards should evaluation be judged?

An evaluation of staff development should comprise a systematic description of the staff development *object*, followed by a systematic assessment of its merit, worth, value, cost-effectiveness, or other characteristics of interest to the stakeholders.

Three functions can be identified. Formative evaluations are intended to improve the staff development process. Summative evaluations may provide accountability, proving that resources were properly expended; may inform future resourcing decisions; and may inform future decisions on the selection of staff developers and on the form of the staff development process. Evaluation can also serve what Nevo calls a socio-political function, which makes a case for more staff development, or is intended to gain support for particular programmes of staff development. (He reports a fourth function, which he calls administrative: to exercise authority. For most staff development activities this function is probably best considered within the summative function of evaluation.) It is worth stressing that these are not necessarily different types of evaluation; they do not necessarily require different methods of evaluation to be used. Rather they are different uses of evaluation, in some cases making different uses of the same data.

What are the main kinds of staff development objects to be evaluated? We suggest that there are four. A policy for staff development (whether national policy or policy within an institution); a staff development unit or service; a staff development programme; and a staff development event or activity.

Having identified the four broad classes of staff development objects we may wish to evaluate, the next step is to decide which aspects of these objects should be evaluated. Nevo (1986) suggests: the goals, the strategies and plans, the process of implementation, and the outcomes and impacts. For example, when a university staff development policy is being evaluated, information should be collected on the goals of the policy; the strategies and plans contained within or derived from the policy, which shade into the detailed process of implementation; and finally, the extent to which the policy's goals were in fact achieved. Additionally, information should always be sought on any unintended effects or consequences.

There are four broad sets of criteria against which any staff development object can be evaluated. First and most directly, the extent to which the immediate expressed needs or goals were met. Then, the contribution which the staff development policy or service or programme or event made to the achievement of broader institutional and even national goals. Easily overlooked in an evaluation, but very important, the extent to which agreed institutional standards and norms in areas such as equal opportunities are met. Finally, the effectiveness of the staff development method adopted compared to other possible methods of achieving the same goals. For example, might a learning package have been more cost-effective than the workshop which was actually run?

The evaluation should meet the needs of each of the stakeholders. Weiss characterizes stakeholders as:

> Members of groups that are palpably affected by the programme, and who therefore will conceivably be affected by evaluative conclusions about the programme, or the members of groups that make decisions about the future of the programme, such as decisions to continue or discontinue funding or to alter modes of programme operation.
>
> (Weiss 1986: 187)

Weiss, who is primarily concerned with the evaluation of large American educational programmes, characterizes four major classes of stakeholder: policymakers; those who manage the programmes to be evaluated; those who deliver the programmes to be evaluated; and the clients to whom the programmes are delivered. Translating to the higher education staff development context, a more-or-less standard list of possible stakeholders and their interests can be drawn up for most staff development units, programmes and events and other activities and services in an institution of higher education:

• *Policymakers* may variously be beyond the university, the profession or subject, the government and its various funding, quality and other agencies; and within the university, heads of department/schools, heads of faculty, specified members of senior management, and the university itself and its various committees and boards. Policymakers may want to know what changes should be made to a staff development programme as it operates, but generally only for large programmes. In most cases policymakers want to know if the programme achieved its goals, and whether the programme should be extended or repeated, or not. Policymakers are interested in summative assessments. They may also be interested in evaluations for socio-political purposes, i.e., to make a case to a further level of decision making to continue funding.

- *Programme managers* are the immediate managers of the staff development service or programme. They need to have the information on which to modify current programmes, to inform future decisions on the use of particular staff developers, and to persuade policymakers and resource managers of the need for continued funding. They need the results of formative, summative and socio-political evaluations.
- *The Practitioners* who facilitate and deliver the staff development need formative evaluations to guide their future practice.
- *The Clients* are immediately the staff who participate, whether they be lecturers, allied staff, course leaders, heads of department or senior management. However, the managers of the participants, and less immediately, but not to be forgotten, the students, are also clients. Participants and participants' managers use evaluations of staff development programmes to inform their future choices about participation. They also gain from the reflection on the staff development process which they undertake in providing feedback.

The main steps in undertaking an evaluation are: clarifying the purpose of the evaluation; planning the evaluation; collecting and analysing the data; and communicating the findings to the various stakeholders. Methods are described in more detail below. Evaluation should be carried out by people with the necessary technical skills for the method to be used – people who understand fully the context, can establish and maintain appropriate relationships and can adopt, adapt or develop a conceptual framework within which the evaluation will be conducted and reported.

The evaluation should be judged above all in terms of its usefulness to the stakeholders. Other criteria include its practicality, accuracy, feasibility (technical and economic) and propriety (with respect to legal and ethical standards).

A system for evaluating staff development

Building on the ideas described above and the survey referred to briefly in the introduction, this section develops a systematic nine-step approach to planning and carrying out the evaluation of staff development, and offers some instruments and some approaches to developing instruments. This process will ensure an appropriate evaluation of any staff development object from an individual workshop or consultation to a major national programme. The list may feel rather heavy for planning the evaluation of a single workshop. A worked example immediately below the list shows how the method works in practice. We suggest that staff development units and services could use this checklist to devise a set of standard procedures for evaluating each of the main staff development objects of their service, which, continuing to use our adaptation of Nevo's classification, are: policy for staff development, the unit or service, a staff development programme, and an individual activity or event. The nine steps are:

1. *Identify* the staff development *objects* to be evaluated from the four categories of policy, staff development unit or service, programme, and event or activity. These objects may be a policy, unit, programme or event or plans for any of these.
2. *Identify* the main *stakeholders* from within the four categories of policy makers, staff development managers, individual deliverers of staff development, and participants and their managers.
3. *Identify* the *questions or concerns* for each identified stakeholder with respect to four key groups of variable about each staff development object, namely the goals, strategies and plans, process of implementation, and outcomes.
4. Further *identify* the *criteria* for judging the answers to stakeholders' questions. These criteria should be developed from four bases: the extent to which the object meets the expressed needs of stakeholders, the extent to which broader institutional and even national goals are achieved, the extent to which agreed standards or norms are met, and the effectiveness of the chosen method compared to other actual or possible methods.
5. *Devise* and pilot evaluation *methods* and instruments.
6. *Carry out* the evaluation.
7. *Report* to the various stakeholders on their various concerns in an appropriate form.
8. *Make* such *changes* to current and future staff development practice as are within your area of responsibility.
9. Periodically *review* evaluation methods with respect to their effectiveness and efficiency.

A worked example

This worked example assumes a relatively conventional allocation of responsibilities between policy maker, service manager and facilitator. Different services with different structures and different management styles will, of course, make for different definitions of responsibility. For example, where the service manager is also the facilitator, responsibilities are combined. However, this chapter is not concerned to pursue issues relating to the management of staff development.

1. The staff development *object* is a workshop on learning contracts on a new staff course.

2.   The main *stakeholders* in this workshop are the staff development service manager, the facilitator, and the participants and their managers. The policymakers are interested in the new staff programme as a whole, but probably not in an individual workshop.

3/4. Before the workshop, the *staff development manager* wants to know if the goals of the workshop are consistent with the overall aims of the new staff programme and whether the intended process is consistent with the norms, standards and values of the staff development service. A prior decision will already have been taken in planning the new staff programme that the most effective and efficient way of achieving the overall goals of the programme is through a workshop series of which the current workshop is a part. After the event, the staff development manager wants to know if the goals of the event were achieved. From time to time they will also want to be sure that the norms, standards and values of the staff development service are embedded in individual workshop practice.

After the workshop, the *facilitator* also wants to know if the goals, and also the intended outcomes, of the event were achieved, and if the methods used were appropriate to the participants and to the norms, standards and values of the service.

The *participants* want to know whether they achieved the outcomes of the workshop. They want their views to be heard on whether the process was acceptable to them. They want to be able to judge whether the workshop was the best way in which their needs could have been met.

5.   A *questionnaire* format has previously been developed and tested by the service. A version is drawn up which includes the intended outcome of this workshop.

6.   At the end of the workshop, the questionnaire is completed by participants and collected before participants leave. The results are collated by the unit administrator.

7.   The *collated results* are copied to the staff development manager, the facilitator and participants. There is no need in this case to produce reports in different formats for different audiences.

8.   The *feedback* reveals a high level of attainment of goals and general satisfaction with the process. A wish is expressed for some selected reading matter to be given to participants a week or so before the workshop to allow more time in the workshop for working up practical ideas. This informs future practice on the new programme.

9.   At the end of the first semester of the programme, a few minutes are devoted to reviewing the continued appropriateness of the questionnaire method. Participants say that they want to explore different methods, in particular the use of 'rounds', partly for variety and partly to give experience of different methods which they can use in their own teaching. This is agreed, but the programme leader explains that the forms will also have to continue to be used to establish comparative data for the course from year to year for quality assurance purposes.

The University of Westsea
Staff Development Service
Workshop Planning and Evaluation Form

Course: Programme for new teaching staff
Event: Workshop on Learning Contracts

Intended outcome of the workshop:

Evaluation (circle or underline)
To what extent did you get each out of the workshop?

1 Participants will have started to develop an approach to using learning contracts in one of the units on which they teach.

1 Fully/Mostly/Partly/A bit/Not

Additionally, what do you want to get out of this workshop:
2
3
4
5

2 Fully/Mostly/Partly/A bit/Not
3 Fully/Mostly/Partly/A bit/Not
4 Fully/Mostly/Partly/A bit/Not
5 Fully/Mostly/Partly/A bit/Not

Evaluation

To what extent was the workshop:

6 Interesting?
7 Informative?
8 Enjoyable?
9 Conforming to published staff development service norms?

6 Fully/Mostly/Partly/A bit/Not
7 Fully/Mostly/Partly/A bit/Not
8 Fully/Mostly/Partly/A bit/Not
9 Fully/Mostly/Partly/A bit/Not

---

10 **Please make any further comments you wish on the workshop**

Planning future work
11 Would future workshops, consultancy, published information, whatever, on this topic be useful?
(If so, please suggest what form these might take)

Name and Department (optional)

Figure 13.1

Undertaking each step of the system

After the worked example, there now follows a more general account of each step of the system, with suggestions on how the system can be adapted to particular situations.

Identifying the staff development objects to be evaluated
The first step is simply to identify the major staff development objects for which you have some responsibility. It is useful to categorize these under appropriate headings chosen from policies, staff development unit or service, programme, and event or activity. It is important to consider as evaluation objects all the rich variety of services provided, including products (leaflets and newsletters), short informal consultations and use of a resource centre.

The second step is to decide on an overall evaluation strategy and time scale within which each of the objects identified will be evaluated. Some of these decisions will already have been made at institution level. For example, there is likely to be a policy on the frequency and conduct of the review of programmes and courses, and perhaps also on the review of units and departments. On the evaluation of policies there may be little or no clear guidance, and it may be up to the manager of a staff development service, for example, to decide on an appropriate frequency for reviewing the unit's policies and strategies. At the other end of the scale decisions will have to be made about the frequency with which individual events are evaluated. We suggest starting by evaluating everything and then reducing frequency if the costs, in terms of time and even 'evaluation fatigue', start to outweigh the value of the data generated. Like everything else, an evaluation strategy needs evaluating!

Identifying the main stakeholders
The grid below, and the subsequent commentary, is intended to help to identify the most likely stakeholders in each type of staff development object:

	Policy	Unit or Service	Programme	Event
Policymaker	1	2	3	4
Service manager	5	6	7	8
Facilitator	9	10	11	12
Participant	13	14	15	16

Policymakers will have a legitimate interest in the evaluation of policy (1), and in the evaluation of units or services which deliver that policy (2). They may also have some interest in overall programmes, for example, those designed to move an institution towards greater use of resource-based learning (3), but they will be less interested in the evaluation of the design and delivery of individual events (4).

As an implementer of some university policies, *the manager of a staff development service or unit* is normally interested in, and hopefully contributes to the evaluation of, university policy (5). They will be involved in the evaluation of the policies of the unit or service itself. However their main concern is in the evaluation of the unit or service (6) and of the programmes run by their service (7). Their interest in the evaluation of specific units or events may be confined to the issues of attainment of goals and adherence to standards rather than fine evaluation detail (8). However they are likely to have a management and a developmental role for the facilitator who delivers the activity or event.

The *facilitator* may be asked to contribute to the evaluation of policy at service or unit level (9) and to the evaluation of the unit or service of which they are a member or for which they have worked (10), but their main concern is with the evaluation of individual programmes (11) or events (12) for which they are responsible. *Participants* in events or programmes are not generally involved in the evaluation of policies (13). They may be asked to contribute to the evaluation of the service (14). They should have a major input into the evaluation of a programme (15) and individual events (16). They will also make evaluative judgements about the unit or service, programme or event, whether or not they are asked to do so!

Identify the questions or concerns, and the criteria for judging the answers, for each identified stakeholder
What follows are suggestions. The only safe way to identify stakeholders' questions and concerns is to ask them!

Stakeholder: Policymaker

	Policy	Unit or Service	Programme	Event
Goals	1	2	3	4
Strategies and plans	5	6	7	8
Process of implementation	9	10	11	12
Outcome	13	14	15	16

Policymakers are likely to be very interested in evaluations of the goals (1), strategies and plans (5), process of implementation (9) and outcomes (13) of policies. They will also be interested in the goals (2) and the outcomes (14) of units and services charged with implementing the policies. Being concerned with policy and the success of its implementation they will probably be little interested in details of unit strategies and plans (6) and processes of implementation (10), and, as previously established, interested much less or not at all in programmes and individual events.

Within this framework, policymakers' questions on the goals of the policy and the unit or service will be about their appropriateness to wider goals and policies. Their questions on strategies and plans will concern their feasibility. Their major concerns on processes of implementation will probably be on resourcing. They will be interested in the extent to which planned outcomes are achieved, and in any unexpected outcomes.

How will policymakers judge the answers to the evaluation questions in which they are interested? What criteria will they use? They will be interested in four things: the extent to which the policy, and the unit or service charged with delivering that policy, meets the university's needs; the extent to which the policy contributes to the university's mission and even to national goals; the extent to which the agreed standards or norms of the university are met by the staff development service; and the effectiveness of the policy and the staff development service compared to other possible policies or systems for delivering staff development.

Stakeholder: Staff development service manager

	Policy	*Unit or Service*	*Programme*	*Event*
Goals	1	2	3	4
Strategies and plans	5	6	7	8
Process of Implementation	9	10	11	12
Outcome	13	14	15	16

Service managers may be invited to make some contribution to evaluating the goals and outcomes of policies (1 and 13), but they will be more involved in the evaluation of strategies and plans for delivering those policies (5 and 9). They will be heavily involved in evaluating all aspects of their service (2, 6, 10 and 14). They will be interested in evaluating all aspects of programmes run by their service (3, 7, 11 and 15), and in the goals and outcomes of particular events (4 and 16), though to a lesser extent in detailed strategies and plans and processes of implementation (8 and 12).

What criteria will service managers use to judge the answers to the evaluation questions in which they are interested? Again they will be interested in four things: the extent to which the service and its activities responds to and meets the needs of the university and its members; the extent to which the service and its activities contribute to the university's mission; the extent to which the agreed standards or norms of the university are met by the staff development service and its programmes; and the effectiveness of the current programme of events compared to other possible methods of delivering staff development.

Stakeholder: Staff development event facilitator

	Policy	*Unit or Service*	*Programme*	*Event*
Goals	1	2	3	4
Strategies and plans	5	6	7	8
Process of implementation	9	10	11	12
Outcome	13	14	15	16

The facilitators of an individual staff development event are only concerned with the evaluation of their event, albeit they are concerned with all aspects of that event. Where the facilitator is responsible for a whole series or programme of events then their involvement in evaluation, of course, increases accordingly.

Again the facilitator will use four sets of criteria: the extent to which the event (or programme) meets the published goals of the programme (and, if these are sought at the start of the event or programme, the individual goals of the participants); contributions to any broader goals of the service and the university of which the facilitator has been made aware; as with the other stakeholders, the extent to which to the agreed standards and norms of the service and the programme are met within the event or programme; and, finally, the effectiveness of the current methods used within the event or programme compared to other methods which might have been adopted.

Stakeholder: Participants and their managers

	Policy	Unit or Service	Programme	Event
Goals	1	2	3	4
Strategies and plans	5	6	7	8
Process of implementation	9	10	11	12
Outcome	13	14	15	16

Participants and their managers are interested in the extent to which the stated goals of the events or programme, and any individual goals they have, are met and the desired outcomes are achieved. They are also interested in the appropriateness and efficiency of the strategies, plans, and methods adopted.

Devising, piloting and carrying out evaluation methods
The design and conduct of evaluations can be a complex business, and some thorough guides are available (see for example, Cronbach 1982; Morris 1990 and Tessmer 1993). What follows does not replace those. Rather it introduces some of the key issues involved in the practical evaluation of staff development.

If the purpose of the evaluation is formative, then the evaluation clearly needs to be conducted, analysed and considered in time for the results to influence the current operation of the event, programme, service or policy. Timing of evaluation will also depend on the outcomes being evaluated. For example, the attainment of outcomes concerned with changed behaviour back in the workplace cannot be evaluated during a workshop.

The question as to the appropriate sample size is normally answered on grounds of economics and feasibility. It is simple and useful to obtain the views of all six participants in a small workshop, still manageable and useful to gain feedback from all 36 participants in a programme, but certainly not feasible to conduct a detailed assessment of the views of 606 recipients of a newsletter. Within some overall goal, such as spending 5 per cent of the unit's time on evaluating its activities, detailed allocations of effort can be made and then reviewed in the light of the value of the data collected.

Ideally for summative evaluation, someone not directly involved in the delivery of the programme or the management of the service could usefully conduct the evaluation. However, formative feedback may most usefully be collected by the person carrying out the activity. This would be particularly true, for example, when collecting feedback at the end of the first day of a two-day workshop in a way which can influence the delivery of the second day.

Questionnaires can obtain participants' views on stakeholders' concerns and issues. Guidance on questionnaire design can be found in Oppenheim (1992) and many other sources. Open-ended questionnaires can gather rich data which can be slow and expensive to collate and analyse. The results of closed questionnaires are easy to collate and analyse. A range of intermediate methods is available. For example, a small sample of interviews can be used to generate statements which can then be used with multi-point agree–disagree rating scales in a questionnaire. An appropriate method for the evaluation of policy might be a questionnaire sent to every member of staff affected by the policy on its continued appropriateness, the methods being used for implementing it, and the outcomes of the policy as the respondents experience them. The questionnaire could be preceded or supplemented by a series of semi-structured interviews.

Oral feedback can be conducted through a round at the end of a workshop, or programme. Participants can be asked open questions, for example, 'What was the best thing for you about this workshop?'; 'In what one respect should the next workshop be different?' Oral feedback assumes that the participants are willing to be open with each other and with the facilitator.

If a service or policy is being evaluated, a series of semi-structured interviews may be a more appropriate tool, allowing as it does the evaluator's concerns to be addressed while allowing space for the interviewee to voice concerns which were not the subject of specific questions.

A staff development service can be evaluated with respect to its various goals, methods and outcomes by a combination of telephone or questionnaire enquiries to users of the service (and to people entitled to use the service who have not done so), and by the collation of the results of evaluations of its programmes and events. Again, interviews might also be undertaken, preferably by an independent evaluator.

Report to the stakeholders, make necessary changes to staff development practice and review evaluation methodologies
Evaluation results will need to be presented in such a way as to make them capable of being easily scrutinized by the various stakeholders. The main criteria used for judging them are likely to be the clarity with which summative evaluations demonstrate the success or otherwise of the objects, the

extent to which formative evaluations provide clear bases for appropriate action, and the efficiency of the evaluation process. It will generally be the case that summative evaluations are found more useful when they comprise mainly numerical data, while formative evaluations are more useful when expressed in words and provide guidelines for future action. On the basis of evaluation reports, actions can be determined to change the policy, service or practice being evaluated. The details of how to make these changes, how to use the results of the evaluation, take us outside the scope of this chapter.

Reflection

As we suggested in the introduction, all this, though clearly worthy and rigorous, may still feel a bit much. On reflection, it seems to us that to ask just one or two of Nevo's questions of the staff development currently being planned or undertaken is still useful, even if time and other pressures do not allow the full evaluation system to be used. Who are the main stakeholders and what do they want? What criteria should be used to judge the worth of the piece of staff development to be evaluated? Even in isolation, these are powerful questions.

It also seems to us that, like many activities, systematic evaluation becomes rapidly easier with a little practice. What looks initially daunting becomes, after the second or third round, routine, though hopefully still useful. Not all of the questions need to be asked all the time. For example, policies change slowly, and the stakeholders for each of six workshops may be the same.

The idea that all professionals are reflective practitioners is fast becoming a tired cliche. Reflection alone can slide into empty cogitation. Reflection needs evidence on which to reflect, data to process. The system described here provides that evidence and data on which individual staff developers can sharpen up their practice and on which staff development as a profession can grow and demonstrate its rigour and worth.

Acknowledgements

Graham Gibbs and James Wisdom gave us feedback on an earlier draft. We followed most of their advice, and the chapter is much better as a result. We thank them.

14

Meeting the Challenges

David Boud

As this volume has illustrated, staff development in higher education has gone through a period of rapid growth of a kind hard to imagine even as recently as five years ago. Not only has the overall magnitude of activity increased, but it has moved to centre stage in institutional priorities. It has become a vehicle for responding to some of the pressures which are presently impinging on university systems, for example, in the areas of accountability, appraisal and quality. Can we expect the present level of activity to continue, but more importantly, what challenges remain to be faced? This chapter explores some of the issues which staff development confronts now and which will need to be effectively addressed in the near future.

There are many ways to envisage the field of staff development all of which are related to the perspective of those who articulate them. The point of view I adopt is rooted in my experience and, rather than pretend that I am not partisan, I wish to start by briefly outlining the background I bring to the discussion. Since 1969 I have been an observer and sometimes active player in staff development in the UK and, since 1976, in Australia. At the end of the eighties, I was involved in establishing the Professional Development Centre at the University of New South Wales. This was a Centre which provided a new model for staff development in universities; a partnership between academic and allied staff and individual and organizational development. Too often staff development was identified with one or another group in the institution: teaching development for the academics, or short courses for allied staff. At UNSW we broke away from this with the intention of avoiding the unfortunate divisions, almost along class lines, which we see so often.

For the past three years at the University of Technology, Sydney, I have been away from the role of direct provider of staff development, but among my responsibilities has been the education of staff development personnel in a variety of industries and organizations. Within the School of Adult and Language Education we have a wide range of programmes in what is now called human resource development and a large number of undergraduate and postgraduate students, all of whom are concurrently practising in this area. As Head of a large school I had the staff development responsibilities which go with this position. I was able to observe, from the other side of the fence as it were, attempts to develop me as a manager and to see the operations of university staff development in an institution which maintains two separate operations in this area.

Over the years I have seen the position of staff development move from a marginal or non-existent position in most institutions to one which, if not central, cannot be ignored. Some of us who were pioneers of staff development during the years of famine may be rather uncomfortable with the success that institutionalization has brought. Along with the achievements are the obligations which go with it and the expectations about the delivery of programmes which are part of a mainstream function. Innovation is still important, but it now has to satisfy many more demanding agendas than those of the developer.

Current conceptions of staff development

Despite the variety of changes in the context of higher education which have already been identified, the current modes of operation of staff development are more limited than might be expected. My own experience has led me to the view that, in practice, there are two principal conceptions of the role. Different aspects of these have appeared in various chapters. There are a number of other conceptions, but in general, they are either variations on the two basic ones, or versions which have more limited currency, perhaps arising from particular local circumstances. These conceptions arise from recent institutional history, they are strongly defended and both have many advocates. Future developments will need to take account of the cultures they represent as it is in these environments that new ideas will either flourish or be inhibited.

- *Conception 1: The conscience of teaching and learning*
  Units which exemplify this conception are characterised by staff who jealously guard their academic status, who actively engage in research and publish in the key journals in the field. Their disciplinary background is quite diverse, but they have all become involved in either re-searching their own practice or working collaboratively with others in their investigations. Typically they have PhDs, increasingly in research on higher education, and are relatively unfamiliar with the world external to the university. Practitioners in this conception often appear uneasy with the descriptor staff development and prefer words such as educational development or teaching and learning in the titles of their unit. They are keen to distance themselves from anything which might be associated with a personnel or instrumental function. Their view of their work involves that of changing the conceptions of teaching staff towards views of teaching and learning which are consistent with the quality learning

practices which research has identified. While they are usually comfortable with the idea of conducting workshops for staff, they prefer to work with individuals or groups on projects which enable them to have a deeper engagement with the issues and problems faced in the world of teaching and learning. They recognize that allied staff have an important place in the university, but they would generally prefer that development issues for this group were dealt with by others. Academic management is also important in this conception, but its main role is to provide the environment in which desirable teaching and learning practices and research can flourish.

- *Conception 2: A key institutional and personnel function*
Units exemplifying this conception are characterized by staff who see themselves as professionals who go to great lengths to maintain their currency as staff developers and who make use of useful practices wherever they find them, whether inside universities or elsewhere. Their background is quite diverse, but they are likely to have held at one time or another some management or supervisory responsibility and may have engaged in formal study of management, personnel or a related area. Typically they do not have research degrees and have not engaged in any substantial research study, although they would have undertaken significant projects which they (but probably not professional researchers) would claim as research. They tend to be more aware than their educational development colleagues of the wider field of staff development wherever it occurs and of educational administration in higher education. Newer members of such units might have relatively little experience of working in universities: they would not see this as a significant disadvantage in their work, however. In this conception staff development is viewed as intimately linked with personnel and performance management and staff are not self-conscious about using current management language. The substantial division of staff between academic and allied is one with which staff within this conception are uncomfortable. They believe that in terms of the provision of resources for development, allied staff have been relatively neglected. Management of all kinds is very important to this conception which places particular emphasis on the development needs of managers as they are seen as the key to all other changes in the institution. The development of policy to formally guide staff development is often a high priority.

These conceptions have evolved in response to both staffing decisions made about the staff development function and related activities within an institution and the inclinations of staff who have had responsibilities in these areas. There has rarely been a considered decision at institutional level to pursue one path rather than another.

As can be inferred from the above descriptions, each conception has its own substantial strengths and clear weaknesses. Units following the first conception are very strong on the impact they have on teaching and learning and, in the case of some newly designated universities, they are also having an impact on research. They are not good at responding to the needs of allied staff or to administrative matters whether or not these are conducted by academics. Staff development following the second conception is very good at responding to institutional and management priorities and in meeting the needs of non-teaching staff. It is poor at dealing with matters related to teaching and learning.

One obvious strategy is to bring together the strengths of both conceptions, but this is easier said than done as there are stronger traditions underpinning each conception than may be obvious at first sight. Nevertheless, such an initiative was taken when the Professional Development Centre at the University of New South Wales was established. The new Centre was created from the ashes of the Tertiary Education Research Centre (Conception 1) and the Staff Development Unit (Conception 2) and it attempted to take the best from both worlds. It was mainly staffed with experienced development personnel of academic status and a director was appointed at professorial level. New staff were recruited who subscribed to the concept of a combined unit that was to respond effectively to the needs of academic and allied staff and managers – not systematically favouring one group. Applied research on the practice of staff and educational development and directly related areas was supported. Care was taken to gain the support of representatives of all categories of staff, through the relevant unions, to reassure them that the Centre would be meeting staff needs in all that it did.

This is not a recipe for all institutions though. It worked because the core staff, who had come from the first of the predecessor units, had a deep commitment to this approach and to making it work. They had a good practical understanding of the internal politics of the university. There were sufficient numbers of staff and there was the opportunity to make new appointments (from vacancies left in the two earlier units) with a careful eye on the ways in which the new staff would further the combined conception. The permanent heads of the two predecessor units had recently retired and there was no one in post who held strongly to either of the earlier conceptions. The latter is probably one of the key features that made the new enterprise work effectively. It was a challenge to bring it together, but I think the general consensus within the Centre and in the University was that it worked. It enabled some of the successful action research strategies that worked well with academic departments to be used with administrative units, it provided unitary programmes for senior management which take account of both academic and allied staff perspectives, and it gained the confidence of those at the highest levels without staff feeling that their needs had been subordinated to those of management. There were minor losses, although not all parties would agree that they were losses at all. The staff of the Centre were not able to pursue their own research agendas in such a ruthlessly individualistic way as their colleagues elsewhere and the publication output took a more applied slant.

The reason for including this discussion here is not to provide *the* model for future staff development practice, but to illustrate some of the considerations which must be taken into account in introducing change in this area. Staff development is intimately linked with changing conceptions of the university. It must respond to the conceptions that the institution it serves has of itself, or be dismissed as irrelevant. As those conceptions change and grow so must staff development lead, and respond to, change.

Responding to tensions and dilemmas

Whatever the organizational arrangements for staff development, there will always be tensions to be addressed and dilemmas to be faced – staff development is contested territory. In coming in from the margins it has become a part of the core of what constitutes a modern university and is therefore no longer in the hands of isolated idealists; it may be led by management into new instrumental realms, such as responding to the latest corporate inititive. Will the notion of the learning organization, which has been stressed by a number of contributors, take root and become a model to give direction to future developments? Indecd to what extent will the universities of the near future retain a collegial ethos or become more highly managed institutions? The future of staff development lies centrally with the future of the university. All that is clear is that although what lies ahead will be unlike that which has preceded it, it will be grounded in our present traditions and conceptions.

One of the key tensions is that between forging a university view versus importing ideas from business and the public service. As we have seen in Part 2, there are many useful ideas to be drawn from staff development practices elsewhere. However, it is naïve to think that these practices can be imported into the university, or indeed any other different type of organization, without considerable thought being given to their applicability and appropriateness in the unique context of the organization. For example, a lot of ideas from corporate management, such as notions of performance management, have been introduced with little attention being given to ways in which they might subtly act to change the ethos of the institution. It may be that universities will race along the route to becoming corporations, but to what extent will they remain universities committed to the values which we still cherish today? Staff development is not the only conduit for these ideas, but it is often enlisted by senior management to pursue their own short-term agenda.

Human resource development is the field from which many of the new staff development ideas in higher education are being drawn. However, in many ways it is not as highly developed as teaching and learning in higher education. At times it is unduly susceptible to the influences of the latest management gurus (Huczynski 1993). This is not to suggest that there are not sophisticated and expert practitioners who have much to offer, and that a research and conceptual base is not becoming established (Anderson and Gonczi 1992), but that the process of critical scrutiny of ideas and consideration of their translation to different contexts must be given more emphasis than might at first sight appear to be the case. Hopefully, the human capital theory on which much of human resource development and university management is now based (Margison 1993) will not so comprehensively dominate the external culture in the future.

Not long ago we assiduously avoided the term staff development in my own centre when referring to activities for academics as we felt that they would regard the use of such a term to describe the staff development programme we were offering as demeaning and off-putting. There is much less sensitivity now to this matter. However, the term staff development is a product of a particular historical context and is now perhaps becoming too limiting. While it has been useful in pointing to activities to which universities had not given sufficient attention, it may be becoming progressively restrictive as conceptions of staff development change and merge with organizational development and workplace learning. I suspect that in ten years those who currently identify with the term staff development might be as embarrassed about being called staff developers as staff developers are now about being referred to as trainers.

What considerations will influence staff development in the future?

It would be a brave person who predicted the precise direction that staff development will take. However, on the basis of what we know now we can be confident of the general tendencies. Some of these have been signalled earlier. They have been brought together to represent an agenda for discussion of future developments.

Staff development will take account of what is known about learning
Useful information and ideas which have arisen from research on student learning, learning from experience, adult learning and, increasingly, learning in the workplace will inform staff development. The fact that much of the work on student learning has been undertaken by researchers who also have a staff development role has meant that there has been a rapid dissemination of these ideas into staff development programmes about teaching and learning. As units undertake research on staff learning there should be an increasing impact from that side also. Table 14.1 indicates some of the ideas about learning which are likely to continue to inform staff development practice. These are discussed further in a number of sources including Boud (1993); Boud and Feletti (1991); Marsick and Watkins (1990); and Ramsden (1988).

Table 14.1 Developments in learning theory and implications for staff development

Learning occurs whether or not there is formal instruction.	There is a need to recognize that most of the learning which occurs in any organization is informal and incidental. Staff development needs to build upon rather than ignore this.
Learning is relational.	What people learn is not just a function of what is taught, but of the complex interrelationship between what is being learned and the person's perceptions of the contingencies in the environment in which they are operating. An understanding of these perceptions is vital for any effective development.
Learning which occurs away from the workplace may be necessary, but it is intrinsically limited.	Learning through courses requires special effort to link it to the world of practice; transferability of learning is problematic. Individual learning requires particular effort to integrate it with the workgroup. Working with workgroups is likely to be an increasing mode of operation.
Learning in organizations is typically problem-oriented.	One of the earliest findings of staff development practitioners, which is no less important now, is that staff are interested in learning that which enables them to address the problems they have met in their practice. Learning to this end is normally problem-based, drawing on appropriate theory and concepts rather than organized around academic fields.
Learning in the workplace is a social activity which is influenced by the norms and values of the workplace.	The greatest constraints on learning and the greatest opportunities are provided by peers. Developing the culture of the workplace to legitimize learning from and with each other is often a prerequisite to any other effective learning. Gaining the commitment of work teams is vital to the newer collaborative, work-based forms of staff development.
Learner's expectations are a function of their prior experience.	The most important consideration in what and how a person will learn is their prior experience and the expectations which arise from that experience. Part of the difficulties in the early days of staff development was that staff had no expectation of what staff development had to offer to them. Now it is necessary to organize such activities so that they do take account of expectations and experience.
Learning from experience requires attention to reflection and processing of experience.	Too little attention is often given to the dynamics of learning and the importance of critical reflection on one's own practice. Opportunities for learning to be processed and made one's own need to be emphasized and to form part of programme designs.

*Staff development will take account of the contextualized nature of
learning in organizations*
Staff development is highly context-related and context-influenced. The
context in which a person operates often defines what is and is not legitimate learning for them and the context of the institution will tend to
define what is legitimate in staff development. There are many examples in
the past of innovative and effective interventions in staff development which
have foundered on a lack of acceptance either by senior management or by
other parties. Resources of the organization will ultimately only be expended
on what the institution, and its constituent parts, values. Staff developers
have a role in shaping the perceptions of decision-makers about the policies and kinds of activities in which they should be engaged and in being
sensitive to shifts of priorities in times of great change.

*Staff development will take account of differences among staff and within
the units in which they operate*
Recognition of the gendered and class-influenced nature of employment
within institutions will mean that related issues will increasingly have to be
acknowledged in the provision of programmes, in the support given to
individual staff members and in policies for staff development. Barriers
which inhibit the full development of staff will need to be addressed, not
only through more effective and sophisticated equal opportunity provisions
generally, but specifically through the ways in which staff development units
conduct their business in relation to the targeting of staff for participation,
the structure and dynamics of programmes and the assumptions on which
education and learning is manifest within the institution. Interventions will
need to take account of the lived experiences of staff within and outside the
institution. Difference will be respected and celebrated rather than acting
as a prompt for oppressive behaviour (Pettman 1991).

*Staff development will take account of institutional priorities, but will not
be totally subservient to them*
There will always be a role for staff development personnel in providing
assistance to senior management in achieving the overall mission of the
university as well as responding to staff initiatives. A broad-based service is
necessary to gain the confidence of staff. If they see staff development only
acting in response to management demands they will gain the impression
that it is primarily a tool of management and not really concerned with
their needs. A degree of independence is required and it will be essential
that those in positions of leadership in staff development are able to pursue
such independence responsibly without compromising institutional priorities
or their own professional integrity. The role of units as critics of policies
and practices is as vital as it is difficult to perform without alienating significant, and sometimes senior, members of the university community.
  Staff development in any organization is only valued if it is in accord with
the central mission of that organization. Universities are crucially about

learning no matter how they might dress it up in the language of the day. Staff development too must be about learning, for individuals, for groups and for the organization, but it must be pursued in full awareness of the pressures and trends which higher education is currently facing.

Staff developers will inevitably face demands from senior managers to assist them in responding to the requirements which impinge on the institution, and there will always be a risk that more fundamental and long-term strategies will be threatened by the anxieties of the day. The move towards strategic planning and the establishment of goals for the institution, once the initial start-up errors have been overcome, has the potential to help in avoiding the worst excesses of opportunism so long as it is done well and genuinely involves those who will be affected. However, within this context there will be a need for staff developers to create their own secure base in promoting learning for staff which is not subject to the fashions of the latest five-year plan. They will need to embed their work in the most fundamental way so that it is regarded as normal for staff to be engaged in staff development as it is now for students to be enrolled in courses. Funding for this activity will not be in the margins of the budget. It will be a core item in the recurrent budget as unthinkable to remove as it would be to get rid of car parking or the Faculty of Medicine.

Staff development will recognize the aspirations of staff for development and enhancement and will support them to the extent that these take forms which are valued by the institution
We should note here that non-academic enterprises such as Ford and Rover have put considerable funds into non-vocational education for employees. If universities value learning for its own sake they should similarly contribute to the achievement of the learning goals of their staff. As criteria for advancement and appointment become more explicit, and as career structures for allied staff become established, it is necessary to ensure that there is an increasing correspondence between these and the opportunities provided by staff development. This is inextricably linked with the next point.

Staff development will more actively consider the accreditation of courses and training which are offered in-house
The society-wide moves towards the formal recognition of training and the documentation of learning outcomes will not by-pass higher education. Staff will wish to have their achievements recognized so that they can be used for promotion and career advancement, and they will seek additional opportunities to develop their professional and other skills. While this at first sight might appear to relate more to allied than academic staff, as we have seen, we are increasingly observing postgraduate courses in teaching and learning in higher education undertaken by lecturing staff who wish to see their documented achievements in these courses recognized at least for tenure, probation decisions and promotion. Such initiatives provide the first clear sign that staff development is getting embedded in ways which

make it very difficult for it to be ignored. When staff development is career-linked and there are direct employment-related consequences for individuals, then it is in the interests of all staff to ensure that it gets done and gets done well.

Staff development will recognize the groupings in which staff work as the normal unit of development
While there will always be some individualistic focus related to specific skills and career development, increasingly there will be a focus on learning occurring in natural work-groupings, whether these be departments, research teams or offices. The use of development to affect change in institutions is impossible when the focus is primarily on the individual. No matter what new ideas and ways of operating have been developed outside the immediate working environment, it is only there that they will be practised and supported (or not) by peers and managers. The workgroup will increasingly become the focus of development activities and the notion of the course or the separate training room will be less and less central to normal practice. Developing reflective practice within the context of the normal working environment will increasingly become central to any staff development activity. A number of illustrations in earlier chapters have highlighted the importance of this and shown ways in which it can be done.

Staff development will be research-based and reflexive
Whether or not any particular staff development practitioner is actively involved in research, and I believe that all professionals should be involved in some form of reflective practice which is building at least a local body of knowledge, staff development will draw increasingly on the work mentioned elsewhere in this book and there will be a substantial number of practitioners who will be actively contributing to the literature. This is particularly important as it is only through public dialogue that trends in staff development practice can be examined critically and staff development move beyond a body of folk knowledge into an era in which it is genuinely open to scrutiny of a kind which will move it forward. A sufficient number of staff development operations will need to engage in more substantial forms of research, particularly in the area of staff and student learning to provide the academic base.

Staff development will become an increasingly devolved and diverse notion
Everyone in the institution will accept themselves in a development role *vis-à-vis* their own learning and that of others, be they peers or staff for whom they have supervisory responsibility. Special responsibility accrues to academic heads, managers and supervisors and they will need appropriate forms of support to assist them in the discharge of these responsibilities. In heading a school I have been struck by the extent to which considerations of staff development permeate just about every decision about staffing, administration and academic matters. Staff development takes on a broader

conception – one in which it is hard to distinguish where its boundaries end and all the rest of the normal functioning of the university begins. Any unit established for staff development has a responsibility for responding to this diversity but it also needs to act strategically when a central initiative is required for maximum effectiveness.

Conclusion

It is a wonderful irony that, until now, institutions which are so profession-ally committed to education at the highest level and to the importance of learning, have in the past been so lacking in their ability to organize them-selves to prompt learning for their own employees for the benefit of their own organization. Teaching is about learning; research is about learning; all work requires learning; staff development is about learning. We need to be able to utilize these connections in the developments of the future. In the same way that we have realized that it is not sufficient to think about teaching students, we have to think about how they are learning, we need to think not only about managing staff but how they can learn as part of their normal work.

The challenge to staff development is how it can further conceptualize its work and organize its practices to meet the changes which will inevitably confront higher education institutions. It has come a long way in a short period of time, but the task has only just begun. Staff development must be at the heart of the creative and responsive institutions which we need, in order to ensure the health and vitality of higher education.

References

Academic Audit Unit (1991) *Notes for the Guidance of Auditors*. London, Committee of Vice-Chancellors and Principals, Academic Audit Unit.

Academic Audit Unit (1992) *Annual Report of the Director 1990/91*. London, Committee of Vice-Chancellors and Principals Academic Audit Unit.

Adelman, C. and Silver, H. (1990) *Accreditation: The American Experience*. London, Council for National Academic Awards.

Anderson, G. and Gonczi, A. (eds) (1992) Human resource development for the global economy. Special issue of *Studies in Continuing Education*, **14**, 2.

Andresen, L. (1991) Handout presented at the Developers' Day of the Higher Education Research and Development Society of Australasia (HERDSA) Conference 29 August–1 September. Victoria University, Wellington, N.Z.

Angelo, T.A. and Cross, K.P. (1993) *Classroom Assessment Techniques: A Handbook for College Teachers*. San Francisco, CA, Jossey-Bass.

Argyris, C. and Schön, D. (1978) *Organizational Learning: A Theory-of-Action Perspective*. Reading, MA, Addison-Wesley.

Arnstein, G. (1979) *Two Cheers for Accreditation*. Association of Governing Bodies Reports, 36–9.

AVCC (Australian Vice Chancellors Committee) (1981) *Report of the AVCC Working Party on Staff Development*. Canberra ACT, AVCC.

Badaracco, J.L., Jr. and Ellsworth, R.R. (1989) *Leadership and the Quest for Integrity*. Boston, MA, Harvard Business School Press.

Ball, C. (1990) *More Means Different: Widening Access to Higher Education*. London, Royal Society of Arts, Industry Matters.

Bandura, A. and Walters, R.H. (1963) *Social Learning and Personality Development*. New York, Holt, Rinehart & Winston.

Barlow, J.D. (1985) *Guidelines on Evaluation in Release Projects*. Brighton, Learning Resources, Brighton Polytechnic.

Barlow, J.D. (1987) The Brighton Polytechnic scheme. In Jaques, D. (ed.) *Staff Release Schemes*. Birmingham, Standing Conference on Educational Development (SCED) Paper No. 25.

Barlow, J.D. (1991) *Guidelines on the Educational Development Release Scheme*, Revised Edition. Brighton, Learning Resources, Brighton Polytechnic.

Barrows, H.S. and Tamblyn, R. (1980) *Problem-Based Learning: An Approach to Medical Education.* New York, Springer.

Bateson, G. (1972) *Steps to an Ecology of Mind.* New York, Ballantyne.

Baume, C. (ed.) (1992) *SCED Teacher Accreditation Year Book.* 1, Birmingham, Standing Conference on Educational Development.

Beaty, E., Dall'Alba, G. and Marton, F. (1992) Conceptions of learning, *International Journal of Educational Research,* 19, 277–300.

Becher, A. (1988) A sense of discipline: Second order training and the differences between academic fields, *Higher Education Management,* 1 (2), 145–53.

Becker, H.S. (1970) The nature of a profession. In Becker, H.S., *Sociological Work: Method and Substance.* London, Allen Lane.

Bennett, J. (1983) *Managing the Academic Department.* New York, American Council on Education/Macmillan Series on Higher Education.

Bennis, W. (1989) *On Becoming a Leader.* London, Hutchinson.

Bensimon, E., Neumann, A. and Birnbaum, R. (1989) *Making Sense of Administrative Leadership: The 'L' Word in Higher Education,* Washington, DC, ASHE/ERIC Higher Education Reports, No. 1.

Billing, D. (1982) The role of staff development. *Standing Conference on Educational Development Services in Polytechnics (SCEDSIP) Occasional Paper 6.* Birmingham.

Birnbaum, R. (1989) Responsibility without authority: The impossible job of the college president. In Smart, J. (ed.) *Higher Education Handbook of Theory and Research,* Vol. V, New York, Agathon Press.

Blackmore, M.A. and Harries-Jenkins, E. (1994) Open learning: The route to improved learning? In Gibbs, G. (ed.) *Improving Student Learning: Theory and Practice.* Oxford, Oxford Centre for Staff Development, Oxford Brookes University.

Boud, D. (1993) Experience as the base for learning, *Higher Education Research and Development,* 12 (1), 33–44.

Boud, D. and Feletti, G.F. (eds) (1991) *The Challenge of Problem-based Learning.* London, Kogan Page.

Boud, D. and McDonald, R. (1981) *Educational Development through Consultancy.* Guildford, Society for Research into Higher Education.

Boud, D., Keogh, R. and Walker, R. (1988) What is reflection in learning? In Boud, D., Keogh, R. and Walker, R. (eds) *Reflection: Turning Experience into Learning.* London, Kogan Page, 7–17.

Bowden, J. (1988) Achieving change in teaching practices. In Ramsden, P. (ed.) *Improving Learning: New Perspectives.* London, Kogan Page, 255–67.

Boyer, E.L. (1990) *Scholarship Reconsidered: Priorities of the Professoriate.* The Carnegie Foundation for the Advancement of Teaching, Princeton, NJ, Princeton University Press.

Brew, A. and Wright, T. (1990) Changing teaching styles, *Distance Education,* 11 (2), 183–211.

Brookfield, S.D. (1986) *Understanding and Facilitating Adult Learning.* San Francisco, CA, Jossey-Bass.

Brookfield, S.D. (1990) *The Skilfull Teacher.* San Francisco, CA, Jossey-Bass.

Burgoyne, J. (1988) Management development for the individual and the organization, *Personnel Management,* June, 40–4.

Butterworth, P. and Goldfarb, P. (1993) Advancing the University's research base, *Surrey Matters,* 28, 6.

Cadbury, Sir A. (1992) Ethical managers make their own rules. In Mercer, D. (ed.) *Managing the External Environment.* London, Sage.

Candy, P. (1991) Priorities for academic staff development in the nineties: A personal view. Paper presented at Higher Education Research and Development Society of Australasia (HERDSA) Conference 29 August–1 September. Victoria University, Wellington, N.Z.

Capra, F. (1983) *The Turning Point,* (2nd edn). London, Fontana, Flamingo.

Carr, W. and Kemmis, D. (1986) *Becoming Critical: Education, Knowledge and Action Research.* London, Falmer Press.

Centre for Higher Education Studies (1994) *Assessment of the Quality of Higher Education: A Review and an Evaluation,* Report for the Higher Education Funding Councils of England and Wales. London, Institute of Education, University of London.

Clark, B. (1987a) *The Academic Profession.* Berkeley, Ca. University of California Press.

Clark, B. (1987b) *The Academic Life.* Berkeley, Ca. Carnegie Foundation for the Advancement of Teaching.

CNAA (1990) *Briefing Paper No. 24.* London, Council for National Academic Awards.

CNAA (1992) *Evaluating the Quality of the Student Experience.* London, Council for National Academic Awards.

Cohen, M.D. and March, J.G. (1986) *Leadership and Ambiguity: The American College President,* 2nd edn. Boston, MA, Harvard Business School Press.

Constable, J. and McCormick, R. (1987) *The Making of British Managers.* London, British Institute of Managers and the Council for British Industry.

Coomber, R. and Harrison, W.C. (1992) *Course Evaluation and Monitoring: Report on an EHE Pilot Project.* London, University of Greenwich.

Crawford, F. (1991) *Total Quality Management.* A Committee of Vice-Chancellors and Principals Occasional Paper. London, Committee of Vice-Chancellors and Principals.

Cronbach, L.J. (1982) *Designing Evaluations of Educational and Social Programs.* San Francisco, CA, Jossey-Bass.

Cryer, P. (ed.) (1992) *Effective Learning and Teaching in Higher Education.* Sheffield, Committee of Vice-Chancellors and Principals, Universities' Staff Development and Training Unit.

Cryer, P. (1993) *Preparing for Quality Assessment and Audit.* Sheffield, Universities' Staff Development and Training Unit.

Cryer, P. and Elton, L. (1993a) A distance programme for resource-based training of academic staff, *Symposium on Improving Student Learning: Theory and Practice.* Oxford, Oxford Brookes University.

Cryer, P. and Elton, L. (1993b) Active learning in large classes and with increasing student numbers. In Cryer, P. (ed.) *Effective Learning and Teaching in Higher Education.* Sheffield, Universities' Staff Development and Training Unit, Module 4, 2nd edn.

Cunningham, J., Doidge, J. and Vidgeon, C. (1994) Quality through people, *Accounting Technician,* February, 18–19.

Davies, G. and Samways, B. (eds) (1993) *Teleteaching: IFIP Transactions A-29.* Amsterdam, North Holland Publishers.

Davies, J.L. (1980) The politics of institutional evaluation, paper delivered on IMHE Travelling Seminars in Australia and New Zealand.

Davies, J.L. (1987) The entrepreneurial and adaptive university: Report of the second US study visit, *International Journal of Institutional Management in Higher Education,* OECD, 11 (1), 12–104.

Davies, J.K. (1992) On being an auditor. Paper presented at European Association for Institutional Research Forum, Brussels.

References 217

Deming, W.E. (1982) *Out of the Crisis.* Cambridge, MA, Productivity Press.
Department of Education and Science (DES) (1991) *Higher Education: A New Framework,* Cmd. 1541, London, HMSO.
Doidge, J. and Whitchurch, C. (1993) *Total Quality Matters.* Conference of University Administrators, Good Practice, Series 13.
Doidge, J., Cunningham, J. and Vidgeon, C. (1994) Quality through people, *Accounting Technician,* February, 18–19.
Elton, L. (1986) Research and teaching: Symbiosis or conflict. *Higher Education,* 15, 299–304.
Elton, L. (1987a) University Grants Committee resource allocation and the assessment of teaching quality. *Higher Education Review,* 19, 9–17.
Elton, L. (1987b) *Teaching in Higher Education: Appraisal and Training.* London, Kogan Page.
Elton, L. (1991) Enterprise in higher education: Work in progress. *Education and Training,* 33 (2), 6–9.
Elton, L. (1992a) Research, teaching and scholarship in an expanding higher education system, *Higher Education Quarterly,* 46, 252–68.
Elton, L. (1992b) Quality enhancement and academic professionalism. *The New Academic,* 1 (2), 3–5.
Elton, L. (1994a) Enterprise in higher education: An agent for change. In Knight, P. (ed.) *Staff Development and Institutional Change.* Staff and Educational Development Association, Paper 83. Birmingham, SEDA.
Elton, L. (1994b) Managing universities. Paper presented at the CVCP/SRHE seminar, March.
Elton, L. (ed.) (1994) *Staff Development in Relation to Research, Occasional Green Paper,* No. 6. Sheffield, Universities' Staff Development Unit.
Elton, L. and Gilbert, J. (1980) The Institute for Educational Technology at the University of Surrey, *European Journal of Science Education,* 2, 333–7.
Elton, L., Gray, H. and Marshall, L. (1990) Employers and the higher education curriculum: The Enterprise in Higher Education Initiative, Guildford, Annual Conference of the Society for Research into Higher Education.
Elton, L. and Partington, P. (1991) Teaching standards and excellence in higher education: Developing a culture for quality, *Occasional Green Paper, No. 1,* London, Committee of Vice-Chancellors and Principals, Universities Staff Development Unit.
Employment Department (1990) *Investors in People: An Initial Briefing Pack for TECs.* Briefing Document, 2, 3.
Entwistle, N.J. and Ramsden, P. (1983) *Understanding Student Learning.* Chichester, Wiley.
Entwistle, N.J. and Tait, H. (1990) Approaches to learning, evaluations of teaching and preferences for contrasting academic environments, *Higher Education,* 19, 169–94.
Evans, T. and King, B. (1991) *Beyond the Text: Contemporary Writing on Distance Education.* Geelong, Australia, Deakin University Press.
Fender, B. (1987) *Investing in People.* Report prepared for Universities' Committee for Non-teaching Staff. London, Centurian Press.
Fender, B. (1993) *Promoting People.* London, Committee of Vice-Chancellors and Principals.
Fleming, N. (1992) Academic staff development: A comparative perspective, *Higher Education Research and Development Society of Australasia, (HERDSA) News,* 14 (1), 3–5.

Flood Page, C. (1974) *Student Evaluation of Teaching: The American Experience.* Guildford, Society for Research into Higher Education.

Fox, D. (1983) Personal theories of teaching, *Studies in Higher Education,* **8**, 151–63.

Fredericks, M., Westerheijden, D. and Weusthof, P. (1993) Self-evaluations and visiting committees. Paper presented at European Association for Institutional Research Forum, Turku, Finland.

Garratt, R. (1987) *The Learning Organization,* London, Fontana.

Gibbs, G. (1981) *Teaching Students to Learn.* Milton Keynes, Open University Press.

Gibbs, G. (1983) Changing students' approaches to study through classroom exercises. In Smith, R.M. (ed.) *Helping Adults Learn How to Learn: New Directions for Continuing Education.* **19**, San Francisco, CA, Jossey-Bass, 83–95.

Gibbs, G. (1992) *Improving the Quality of Student Learning.* Bristol, Technical and Educational Services.

Gibbs, G. (1994) *Improving Student Learning: Theory and Practice.* Oxford, Oxford Brookes University, Oxford Centre for Staff Development.

Gibbs, G., Habeshaw, S. and Habeshaw, T. (1984) *53 Interesting Things to Do in your Lectures.* Bristol, Technical and Educational Services.

Gibbs, G., Habeshaw, T. and Habeshaw, S. (1989) *53 Interesting Ways to Appraise your Teaching,* Bristol, Technical and Educational Services.

Gibbs, G., Morgan, A. and Taylor, E. (1984) The world of the learner. In Marton, F., Hounsell, D. and Entwistle, N.J. (eds) *The Experience of Learning.* Edinburgh, Scottish Academic Press.

Glaser, B. and Strauss, A. (1967) *The Discovery of Grounded Theory.* Chicago, IL, Aldine.

Glover, D. (1990) Enterprise in Higher Education: A briefing for employers, Cambridge, Careers Research and Advisory Centre (CRAC).

Gordon, G. (1988) The Strathclyde University Programme for Heads of Departments, *Higher Education Management,* **1** (2), 154–61.

Gordon, G. and Partington, P. (1993) Quality in higher education: Overview and update, *Universities Staff Development Unit Briefing Paper Three,* November. Sheffield, Universities' Staff Development Unit.

Green, M.F. and McDade, S.A. (1991) *Investing in Higher Education: A Handbook of Leadership Development.* New York, American Council on Education.

Guildford, P. (1990) *Staff Development Provision in Universities of the United Kingdom.* Sheffield, Committee of Vice-Chancellors and Principals, Universities' Staff Development and Training Unit.

Guildford, P. (1992) *Continuing Professional Development for Administrators (CPDA).* Sheffield, Universities' Staff Development Unit.

Hampden Turner, C. (1990) *Charting the Corporate Mind: From Dilemma to Strategy.* Oxford, Blackwell.

Harding, A.G., Kaewsonthi, S., Roe, E. and Stevens, J.R. (1981) *Professional Development in Higher Education: State of the Art and Artists.* Bradford, University of Bradford.

Hardwick, B. and Greenwood, D. (1993) Managing the Introduction of Appraisal for Allied/Support Staff, *Occasional Green Paper,* No. 4. Sheffield, Committee of Vice-Chancellors and Principals and the Universities' Staff Development Unit.

Heycock, M.C. (1991) Managing change in a large institution: A case study of the EHE project, *Education and Training,* **33** (2), 19–21.

Hewton, E. (1982) *Rethinking Educational Change,* Guildford, Society for Research into Higher Education.

Higher Education Funding Council England (1993a) *Assessment of the Quality of Education*, Circular 3/93. Bristol, HEFCE.

Higher Education Funding Council England (1993b) Draft assessor handbook. Reproduced in *Loughborough University ST & D Newsletter*, **46**, Summer.

Higher Education Funding Council Wales (1993a) *Arrangements and Future Plans for Assessing the Quality of Education in the HEFC Sector in Wales*. Cardiff, HEFCW.

Higher Education Funding Council Wales (1993b) *Partnership in Assessment Consultation Document*. Cardiff, HEFCW.

Higher Education Quality Council (1993a) *The University of Brighton: Quality Audit Report*. London, Higher Education Quality Council Division of Quality Audit.

Higher Education Quality Council (1993b) *Request for Briefing Documentation*. London, Higher Education Quality Council, Division of Quality Audit.

Hodgson, V., Mann, S.J. and Snell, R. (1987) *Beyond Distance Teaching – Towards Open Learning*. Milton Keynes, Society for Research into Higher Education and the Open University Press.

Huczyncski, A. (1993) *Management Gurus*. London, Routledge.

Hunt, J. (1992) *Leadership: A New Synthesis*. London, Sage.

Hurley, J. (1988) The development of heads of academic departments in universities. Paper presented in IMHE Special Topic Workshop. Training Heads of Academic Departments: Design and Implementation of Programmes, Paris, May.

Jaques, D. (ed.) (1987) *Staff Release Schemes*. Birmingham, Standing Conference on Educational Development, Paper No. 25.

Jalling, H. (1988) Training departmental heads in Sweden: Status and approaches, *Higher Education Management*, **1** (2), 127–33.

Jarrett, Sir A. (1985) *Management in Universities*. Report of the Steering Committee for Efficiency Studies of the Committee of Vice-Chancellors and Principals. London, CVCP.

Jowitt, T. (1993) Lifelong Learning – Holy Grail or Poisoned Chalice? Paper presented at the Seventh National PICKUP Conference.

Kelly, M.E. (1987) Course teams and instructional design, *Distance Education*, **8** (1), 106–120.

Kells, H.R. (1988) *Self-Study Processes*. London, Macmillan.

Kember, D. and Gow, L. (1992) Action research as a form of staff development in higher education, *Higher Education*, **23** (3), 297–310.

Kember, D. and Kelly, M. (1993) Improving teaching through action research, *Higher Education Research and Development Society of Australasia, Green Guide*, 14. Sydney, HERDSA.

Kemmis, S. and McTaggart, R. (eds) (1988) *The Action Research Planner*. Geelong, Australia, Deakin University Press.

Knight, P. (Ed.) (1993) *The Audit and Assessment of Teaching Quality*, Birmingham, Standing Conference on Educational Development and the Staff Development Group of the Society for Research into Higher Education.

Knudsen, L. (1988) Training programmes for heads of departments at the University of Oslo, *Higher Education Management*, **1** (2), 162–9.

Kotter, J.P. (1990a) *A Force for Change: How Leadership Differs from Management*. New York, Free Press.

Kotter, J.P. (1990b) What leaders really do, *Harvard Business Review*, **68**, 103–11.

Kouzes, J.M. and Posner, B.Z. (1987) *The Leadership Challenge*, San Francisco, CA, Jossey-Bass.

Lewis, B.N. (1974) Course production at the OU. In Tunstall, J. *The Open University Opens*. London, Routledge & Kegan Paul.

Loder, C. (1993) Identifying and developing a quality ethos for teaching in higher education, *Centre for Higher Education Studies, Newsletter 3*. London, University of London Institute of Education.

Lonsdale, A. (1990) Achieving institutional excellence through empowering staff: An approach to performance measurement in higher education. In Moses, E. (ed.) *Higher Education in the Late Twentieth Century: Reflections on a Changing System. A Festschrift for Ernest Roe*. Queensland, Australia, Higher Education Research and Development Society of Australasia.

McCall, M.W., Lombardo, M.M. and Morrison, A.M. (1988) *The Lessons of Experience*. Lexington, MA, Lexington Books.

McDonald, R. (1989) Training heads of academic departments in Australia: Some recent developments, *Higher Education Management*, 1 (2), 117–26.

McDowell, L. (ed.) (1991a) *Putting Students First: Listening to Students and Responding to Their Needs*, SCED Paper 64, Birmingham, Standing Conference on Educational Development.

McDowell, L. (ed.) (1991b) *Course Evaluation: Using Students' Experiences of Learning and Teaching*, Educational Development Service at Newcastle Polytechnic and the CNAA.

MacFarlane, A. (1992) Teaching and learning in an expanding higher education system, Edinburgh, SCFC.

McGill, I. and Beaty, E. (1992) *Action Learning: A Practitioner's Guide*. London, Kogan Page.

McKernan, J. (1991) *Curriculum Action Research*. London, Kogan Page.

Main, A. (1985) *Educational Staff Development*. London, Croom Helm.

Margison, S. (1993) *Education and Public Policy in Australia*. Melbourne, Cambridge University Press.

Marsick, V.J. and Watkins, K.E. (1990) *Informal and Incidental Learning in the Workplace*. London, Routledge.

Marton, F., Hounsell, D. and Entwistle, N. (eds) (1984) *The Experience of Learning*. Edinburgh, Scottish Academic Press.

Matheson, C. (1981) *Staff Development Matters*, London, Coordinating Committee for the Training of University Teachers.

Mellows, S. and Roy, S. (1992) Marking the markers. Paper presented at European Association for Institutional Research Forum, Brussels.

Mezirow, J. and Associates (eds) (1990) *Fostering Critical Reflection in Adulthood*. San Francisco, CA, Jossey-Bass.

Middlehurst, R. (1988) Evaluation and development of a leadership course for heads of departments in the United Kingdom, *Higher Education Management*, 1 (2), 17–82.

Middlehurst, R. (1989) *Leadership Development in Universities, 1986–1988*, Final Report to the Department of Education and Science, University of Surrey (also published in *CORE*, 16 (1), 1992, Fiche 3 BO1).

Middlehurst, R. (1993) *Leading Academics*. Buckingham, Society for Research into Higher Education and the Open University Press.

Middlehurst, R. and Elton, L. (1992) Leadership and management in higher education, *Studies in Higher Education*, 17, 251–264.

Middlehurst, R., Pope, M. and Wray, M. (1992) The Changing Roles of University Leaders and Managers, *CORE*, 16 (1), Fiche5 E11.

Mintzberg, H. (1973) *The Nature of Managerial Work.* New York, Harper and Row.
Morris, N. (1990) *Understanding Educational Evaluation.* London, Kogan Page.
Moses, I. (1987) Educational development units: A cross-cultural perspective. *Higher Education*, **16**, 449–79.
Mumford, A., Robinson, G. and Stradling, D. (1987) *Developing Directors: The Learning Processes.* Sheffield, Manpower Services Commission.
Myers, I.B. and McCaulley, M.H. (1985) *Manual: A Guide to the Development and Use of the Myers-Briggs Type Indicator.* Palo Alto, CA, Consulting Psychologists Press.
Nevo, D. (1986) The conceptualization of educational evaluation: An analytic review of the literature. In House, E.R. (ed.) *New Directions in Educational Evaluation.* Lewes, Falmer Press, 15–29.
Northedge, A. (1976) Examining our implicit analogies for learning processes, *Programmed Learning and Educational Technology*, **13** (4), 67–78.
O'Neil, M. and Pennington, G. (eds) (1992) *Evaluating Teaching and Courses from an Active Learning Perspective*, in Cryer, P. (Series ed.) *Effective Learning and Teaching in Higher Education*, Module 12. Sheffield, Committee of Vice-Chancellors and Principals, Universities' Staff Development and Training Unit.
O'Neil, C. and Wright, A. (1992) *Recording Teaching Accomplishment.* Halifax, Nova Scotia, Office of Institutional Development and Technology, Dalhousie University.
O'Neil, M. and Pennington, G. (eds) (1992) Evaluating Teaching and Courses from an Active Learning Perspective, in Cryer, P. (ed.) *Effective Learning and Teaching in Higher Education.* Sheffield, Committee of Vice-Chancellors and Principals Universities' Staff Development and Training Unit.
Oppenheim, A.N. (1992) *Questionnaire Design, Interviewing and Attitude Measurement.* London, Pinter.
Oxford Centre for Staff Development (1989) *Certificate in Higher Education by Open Learning.* Oxford, Oxford Polytechnic.
Padley, J. and Porter, D. (1982) (eds) *The Training of University Administrators in Europe.* Aldershot, Gower Press.
Partington, P. (ed.) (1993) *Student Feedback – Context, Issues and Practice*, Sheffield, Committee of Vice-Chancellors and Principals, Universities' Staff Development and Training Unit.
Partington, J., Brown, G. and Gordon, G. (1993) *Handbook for External Examiners in Higher Education.* Committee of Vice-Chancellors and Principals, Universities Staff Development Unit.
Pavett, C.M. and Lau, A.W. (1983) Managerial work: the influence of hierarchical level and functional speciality, *Academy of Management Proceedings*, 95–9.
Pedler, M., Burgoyne, J. and Boydell, T. (1991) *The Learning Company: A Strategy for Sustainable Development.* London, McGraw-Hill.
Perry, W.G. (1970) *Forms of Intellectual and Ethical Development in the College Years: A Scheme.* New York, Holt, Rinehart and Winston.
Pettman, J.J. (1991) Towards a (personal) politics of location, *Studies in Continuing Education*, **13** (2), 153–66.
Quality Support Unit (1993) *A Guide to Changes in Higher Education.* London, The Open University, Quality Support Unit.
Raggatt, P. (1993) Post-Fordism and distance education – a flexible strategy for change, *Open Learning*, **8** (1), 21.
Ramsden, P. (ed.) (1988) *Improving Learning: New Perspectives.* London, Kogan Page.

Ramsden, P. (1992) *Learning to Teach in Higher Education.* London, Routledge.
Ramsden, P., Beswick, D. and Bowden, J. (1986) Effects of learning skills interventions on first-year university students' learning, *Human Learning*, **5**, 151–64.
Rogers, C. (1969) *Freedom to Learn*, Columbus, OH, Merrill.
Ross, B. (1988) *Squaring the Circle: Structuring Student Autonomy*, Congress Papers, OSLO, International Congress for Distance Education.
Rutherford, D. (1982) Developing university teaching: A strategy for revitalisation, *Higher Education* **1**, 177–91.
Säljö, R. (1979) Learning about learning, *Higher Education*, **8** (4), 443–51.
Schön, D.A. (1983) *The Reflective Practitioner: How Professionals Think in Action.* London, Temple Smith.
Schön, D.A. (1987) *Educating the Reflective Practitioner: Toward a New Design for Teaching and Learning in the Professions.* San Francisco, Jossey-Bass.
Scottish Higher Education Funding Council (1992a) *Quality assessment: The SHEFC approach, Circular: QA/1.* Edinburgh.
Scottish Higher Education Funding Council (1992b) *Quality framework*, Circular: QA/2. Edinburgh.
Scottish Higher Education Funding Council (1992c) *Guidance notes on institutional self-assement*, Circular QA/3. Edinburgh.
Seldin, P. (1991) *The Teaching Portfolio.* Bolton, MA, Ankara.
Silver, H. (1993) *Student Feedback: Issues and Experience*, Council for National Academic Awards Project Report No. 39.
Sizer, J. (1987) Institutional responses to financial reduction in the university sector. Report in three parts. London, DES.
Smith, B. and Smith, D.C. (1993) *The Smith Guide to the Staff Development Jungle.* Brighton, University of Sussex, Chatfield Publications.
Smith, G. (1992) A categorisation of models of staff development in higher education, *British Journal of Educational Technology*, **23**, 39–47.
Sommerlad, E. (ed.) (1993) *A Guide to Local Evaluation* and *Evaluation Practice in the Enterprise for Higher Education Initiative*, Development and Review Report prepared by the Tavistock Institute of Human Relations for the Training, Enterprise and Education Directorate of the Department of Employment.
Sternberg, R.J. (1990) Intellectual styles. In Clark, K.E. and Clark, M.B. (eds) *Measures of Leadership.* West Orange, NJ, Leadership Library of America, 481–92.
Streufert, S. and Nogami, G. (1989) Cognitive style and complexity: Implications for I/O psychology. In Cooper, C.L. and Robertson, I. (eds) *International Review of Industrial and Organizational Psychology.* Chichester, Wiley, 93–143.
Tannock, J. and Burge, S. (1992) A new approach to quality assurance in higher education, *Higher Education Quarterly*, **46** (1), 108–22.
Tavistock Institute of Human Relations (1991) *The First Year of Enterprise in Higher Education*, Sheffield, Employment Department.
Taylor, W. (1987) *Universities Under Scrutiny.* Paris, OECD.
Tessmer, M. (1993) *Planning and Conducting Formative Evaluations.* London, Kogan Page.
Tipton, B.F.A. (1981) Staff development, solidarity and social change. *Journal of Further and Higher Education*, **5** (2), 76–83.
Tobin, K. and Fraser, B.J. (1988) Investigations of exemplary practice in high school science and mathematics, *Australian Journal of Education*, **32**, 75–94.
Trigwell, K., Prosser, M. and Taylor, P. (1993) Qualitative differences in approaches to teaching first year introductory science, Higher Education Research and Development Society of Australasia Annual Conference.

Trow, M. (1992) Thoughts on the white paper of 1991, *Higher Education Quarterly*, **46** (3), 213–26.

Tucker, A. (1984) *Chairing the Academic Department*. New York, American Council on Education/Macmillan Series on Higher Education.

Tucker, A. (1988) Leadership training programmes for academic department chairpersons and heads in American colleges and universities. Paper presented at the IMHE Special Topic Workshop of Training Heads of Academic Departments: Design and Implementation of Programmes. Paris, May.

Universities' Staff Development Unit (1993) An overview of UK approaches to management and leadership development (unpublished paper), Sheffield, USDU.

University of Portsmouth (1994) *Enterprise in Higher Education National Project Directory* (2nd edn) Portsmouth, University of Portsmouth and the Employment Department.

Van Rossum, E.J. and Schenk, S.M. (1984) The relationship between learning conception, study strategy and learning outcome, *British Journal of Educational Psychology*, **54**, 73–83.

Van Rossum, E.J. and Taylor, I.P. (1987) The relationship between conceptions of learning and good teaching: A scheme for cognitive development, Paper presented to the American Educational Research Association Annual Meeting, Washington, DC.

Wagemans, L. and Dochy, F. (1991) Principles in the use of experiential learning as a source of prior knowledge, *Distance Education*, **12** (1), 85–108.

Walker, D. (1988) Writing and reflection. In Boud, D., Keogh, R. and Walker, D. (eds) *Reflection: Turning Experience into Learning*. London, Kogan Page, 52–68.

Warren Piper, D. (1992) Are professors professional? *Higher Education Quarterly*, **46** (2), 145–56.

Weeks, P. and Scott, D. (eds) (1992) *Exploring Tertiary Teaching*. Brisbane, Australia, University of Queensland.

Weiss, C.H. (1986) Toward the future of stakeholder approaches in evaluation. In House, E.R. (ed.) *New Directions in Educational Evaluation*. Lewes, Falmer Press. 186–98.

Wille, E. (1990) Should management development just be for managers?, *Personnel Management*. August, 34–7.

Willerman, M., McNeely, S. and Koffman, E. (1991) *Teachers Helping Teachers: Peer Observation and Assistance*. New York, Praeger.

Williams, B.R. (1979) *Education, Training and Employment: Report of the Committee of Inquiry*. Canberra, Australian Government Publishing Service.

Yorke, M. (1977) Staff development in further and higher education: A review. *British Journal of Teacher Education*, **3** (2), 161–7.

Zaleznik, A. (1977) Managers and leaders: Are they different?, *Harvard Business Review*, **55**, 67–78.

Zuber-Skerritt, O. (1991) *Action Research for Change and Development*. Aldershot, Avebury.

Zuber-Skerritt, O. (1992) *Action Research in Higher Education: Examples and Reflections*. London, Kogan Page.

Zuber-Skerritt, O. (1993) Departmental Excellence in University Education (DEUE) Programme 1992, Final Report. Brisbane, Australia, University of Queensland.

Index

The Society for Research into Higher Education

The Society for Research into Higher Education exists to stimulate and co-ordinate research into all aspects of higher education. It aims to improve the quality of higher education through the encouragement of debate and publication on issues of policy, on the organization and management of higher education institutions, and on the curriculum and teaching methods.

The Society's income is derived from subscriptions, sales of its books and journals, conference fees and grants. It receives no subsidies, and is wholly independent. Its individual members include teachers, researchers, managers and students. Its corporate members are institutions of higher education, research institutes, professional, industrial and governmental bodies. Members are not only from the UK, but from elsewhere in Europe, from America, Canada and Australasia, and it regards its international work as amongst its most important activities.

Under the imprint *SRHE & Open University Press*, the Society is a specialist publisher of research, having some 45 titles in print. The Editorial Board of the Society's Imprint seeks authoritative research or study in the above fields. It offers competitive royalties, a highly recognizable format in both hardback and paperback and the world-wide reputation of the Open University Press.

The Society also publishes *Studies in Higher Education* (three times a year), which is mainly concerned with academic issues, *Higher Education Quarterly* (formerly *Universities Quarterly*), mainly concerned with policy issues, *Research into Higher Education Abstracts* (three times a year), and *SRHE News* (four times a year).

The Society holds a major annual conference in December, jointly with an institution of higher education. In 1992, the topic was 'Learning to Effect', with Nottingham Trent University. In 1993, it was 'Governments and the Higher Education Curriculum: Evolving Partnerships' at the University of Sussex in Brighton, and in 1994, 'The Student Experience' at the University of York. Future conferences include in 1995, 'The Changing University' at Heriot-Watt University in Edinburgh.

The Society's committees, study groups and branches are run by the members. The groups at present include:

Teacher Education Study Group
Continuing Education Group
Staff Development Group
Excellence in Teaching and Learning

Benefits to members
Individual

Individual members receive:

- *SRHE News*, the Society's publications list, conference details and other material included in mailings.
- Greatly reduced rates for *Studies in Higher Education* and *Higher Education Quarterly*.
- A 35% discount on all Open University Press & SRHE publications.
- Free copies of the Precedings – commissioned papers on the theme of the Annual Conference.
- Free copies of *Research into Higher Education Abstracts*.
- Reduced rates for conferences.
- Extensive contacts and scope for facilitating initiatives.
- Reduced reciprocal memberships.

Corporate

Corporate members receive.

- All benefits of individual members, plus
- Free copies of *Studies in Higher Education*.
- Unlimited copies of the Society's publications at reduced rates.
- Special rates for its members, e.g. to the Annual Conference.

Membership details: SRHE, 344–354 Gray's Inn Road, London, WC1X 8BP, UK. Tel: 071 837 7880
Catalogue: SRHE & Open University Press, Celtic Court, 22 Ballmoor, Buckingham MK18 1XW. Tel: (0280) 823388

HOW TO GET A PHD (2nd edition)
A HANDBOOK FOR STUDENTS AND THEIR SUPERVISORS

Estelle M. Phillips and D. S. Pugh

This is a handbook and survival manual for PhD students, providing a practical, realistic understanding of the processes of doing research for a doctorate. It discusses many important issues often left unconsidered, such as the importance of time management and how to achieve it, and how to overcome the difficulties of communicating with supervisors. Consideration is given to the particular problems of groups such as women, part-time and overseas students.

The book also provides practical insights for supervisors, focusing on how to monitor and, if necessary, improve supervisory practice. It assists senior academic administrators by examining the responsibilities that universities have for providing an adequate service for research students. This is a revised and updated second editions; it will be as warmly welcomed as the first edition:

> One way of providing a more supportive environment for PhD students is for supervisors to recommend this book.
>
> *(Teaching News)*

> Warmly recommended as a bedside companion, both to those hoping to get a PhD and to those who have the responsibility of guiding them, often with very little support themselves.
>
> *(Higher Education Review)*

> This is an excellent book. Its style is racy and clear . . . an impressive array of information, useful advice and comment gleaned from the authors' systematic study and experience over many years . . . should be required reading not only for those contemplating doctoral study but also for all supervisors, new and experienced.
>
> *(Higher Education)*

Contents
Preface – Becoming a postgraduate – Getting into the system – The nature of the PhD qualification – How not to get a PhD – How to do research – The form of a PhD thesis – The PhD process – How to manage your supervisor – How to survive in a predominantly British, white, male full-time academic environment – The formal procedures – How to supervise – Institutional responsibilities – References – Index.

224pp   0 335 19214 9 (Paperback)